Ergonomics in action
A practical guide for the workplace

Dr Céline McKeown

First published as *Workplace ergonomics: a practical guide* 2001
Second edition 2004
Third edition 2011
IOSH Services Limited

Published 2015 by Routledge
2 Park Square, Milton Park, Abingdon, Oxon OX14 4RN
711 Third Avenue, New York, NY, 10017, USA

Routledge is an imprint of the Taylor & Francis Group, an informa business

© Dr Céline McKeown 2011

All rights reserved. No part of this publication may be reproduced in any material form (including photocopying or storing it in any medium by electronic or photographic means and whether or not transiently or incidentally to some other use of this publication) without written permission of the copyright owner.

IOSH and IOSH Services Limited assume no responsibility for the contents of this book, in whole or in part, nor for the interpretation or concepts advanced by the author. The views expressed in this book are the author's own, and do not necessarily reflect those of any employing or other organisation. All web addresses are current at the time of going to press. The publisher takes no responsibility for subsequent changes.

Warning: The doing of an unauthorised act in relation to a copyright work may result in both a civil claim for damages and criminal prosecution.

Céline McKeown has asserted her right under the Copyright, Designs and Patents Act 1988 to be identified as the author of this work.

ISBN-13: 978-1-138-90422-4 (pbk)

Contents

About the author	4
1 Introduction to ergonomics	5
2 Anthropometrics	9
3 The design process	29
4 Hand tool design and use	61
5 Job design and work organisation	79
6 Manual handling	99
7 Display screen equipment work	145
8 Upper limb disorders	181
9 Risk assessment	203
10 Case studies	233
Index	249

About the author

Dr Céline McKeown BA (Hons) MSc PhD FIEHF MIES AFBPsS CMIOSH CPsychol

Dr Céline McKeown is the senior consultant with and director of Link Ergonomics. She specialises in work-related injury, particularly upper limb disorders and manual handling injuries. She works in heavy and light industry and in commercial organisations. Although she offers advice on dealing with working conditions that are already functioning, she also works alongside designers, engineers and architects who are starting with a blank slate and assists them in generating workplaces that suit the people who are employed there. She also runs training courses for engineers and health and safety professionals on ergonomics, manual handling, upper limb disorders and disability. She is a regular writer and speaker on ergonomics in the workplace and is a reviewer of academic ergonomics textbooks. She also acts as an expert witness in cases of work-related injury throughout the UK and Ireland.

1 Introduction to ergonomics

Ergonomics is the discipline that focuses on people and their environment. Within that environment, ergonomics looks at the work that people perform, the equipment and tools they use, the conditions in which they work and the psychosocial aspects of their workplace. The aim of ergonomics is to improve the 'fit' between people and the environment in which they work. Humans have a number of requirements if they are to work comfortably: the equipment they are given should be functional and safe to use, the tasks they are required to perform should meet their expectations, limitations and skill base, the environmental features should be compatible with basic human physiological needs and appropriate for the task being completed, and the tasks should take account of the workers' social and economic needs.

The term 'ergonomics' is derived from the Greek words ergos, meaning work, and nomos, meaning the natural law. It came into being after the Second World War as a consequence of researchers realising that the information that had been collated during wartime about improving the efficiency of soldiers and their equipment could be applied after the war just as effectively in the working environment.

Ergonomics calls upon the disciplines of biomechanics, anatomy, physiology, engineering and psychology to provide a workplace that is compatible with the capabilities and characteristics of people. Incompatibility is often shown up in situations where poor system functioning, 'human error' or injury occur. Making sure that the workplace is compatible with the needs of the individual who works in it dictates that the design should be user-centred. For that reason, the design must rely on available information relating to the physical characteristics of the user as well as what is known about their likely behaviours and previous experiences. Once the design has evolved, it should be tested to establish that it really is compatible with the needs of the individual. This process needs the involvement of the end user, who can provide insight into what is needed and feedback about the suitability of a design after using it under representative conditions. This approach aims to accommodate 'real' people as opposed to designing to suit idealised or 'average' people.

User-centred design takes account of the fact that all people cannot be accommodated in a one-size-fits-all approach. There is such diversity within the human race that designs should be capable of meeting the needs of a wide range of people simultaneously and be able to meet the demands of the range of tasks they are likely to perform. However, user-centred design recognises that there are limits to what can be achieved and it aims to provide the best possible solution within the constraints imposed by any particular environment.

In general, when ergonomics is being used as an effective tool in the working environment, it breaks that environment up into chunks and tries to mould them so that they fit neatly together and are suitable for the needs of the individual. To that end, the ergonomist will focus on workstation design, work equipment, task demands, organisational factors, environmental issues and the people themselves. When assessing the workstation design, the ergonomist will consider whether the design and layout are suitable for the person and the task they perform and, just as importantly, will question whether that workstation is being used correctly. Workers often experience symptoms that might suggest their workstation is faulty in some way but really the problems stem from the fact that they are not using their equipment correctly. For instance, it is not uncommon for office workers to complain about backache and identify their chair as the source of their problem. Often a simple change in chair height or backrest position is enough to eradicate the discomfort.

When considering work equipment, ergonomics focuses on the design of the interface between the worker and the equipment. In the case of tool design, the focus will be on the length, diameter and styling of the handle, the weight of the tool, the frequency of use, how it is stored and so on. All of these considerations will be matched against what is known about the characteristics of the user to establish whether there is a mismatch between them and their equipment.

Task demands are major determining factors in whether a person will make it through the working day without feeling discomfort or extreme fatigue. Ergonomics is the subject that will review the pace at which an individual works, how repetitive their task might be, whether there is any manual handling involved, whether their task has a high or low 'thinking' component, whether they have any control over how the job is done or whether they are driven by the system in place.

Organisational factors are sometimes the aspects of the workplace that can be used to exert control over the undesirable elements of a task, if that task cannot be changed in the short term. Organisational factors can be used effectively to limit exposure time to the stressful features in a task through job rotation and regular breaks. It can also be used to ensure that workers have appropriate training and supervision and that selection procedures take account of workers' suitability to do a task if they have a history of illness, injury or disability.

Environmental issues, such as lighting, temperature, noise and vibration, have a great influence over workers' wellbeing and sometimes this element does not attract the attention it should. For instance, it is widely accepted that exposure to cold conditions increases the likelihood of an operator experiencing an upper limb disorder if working in an already hazardous environment. Vibration is receiving much more attention than it did previously but there is still much room for improvement in terms of protecting the workforce from the negative effects of exposure to vibration over long periods or on repeated occasions. Even something as seemingly simple as lighting is significant because, for example, it can often influence posture: an operator may hunch over a subassembly because they cannot see what they are doing clearly enough if they sit more comfortably.

Finally, ergonomics never loses sight of the fact that people are individuals and each of them brings to the workplace a range of characteristics that could potentially make their working life easier or more difficult. Ergonomics sets out to rework their environment so that it suits their needs, as well as those of other people working alongside them.

A good view to have of ergonomics is that it is not usually considered a goal in itself within a working environment. It is one of the means by which a satisfactory, safe and efficient environment is achieved.

2 Anthropometrics

Anthropometrics is concerned with the subject of body measurements. It deals mainly with measurements relating to body size, shape and strength and is especially useful when it comes to designing for humans because they are so different in terms of weight, shape, bulk, size and proportion. Anthropometrics allows designers to take account of the huge variability in the population and puts them in a position of being able to fit the environment to the worker rather than the other way around. The designer's aim should be to match the physical form of the workspace and equipment to the characteristics and capabilities of the workforce.

When considering the issue of anthropometrics, one of the myths that needs to be dispelled from the outset is that designs should suit the 'average man'. The average person is someone who falls centrally in a range, which implies that there will always be people who will be bigger than the average person and there will always be people who are smaller. If designs are intended to suit the average person, a lot of other people will therefore be disadvantaged. Imagine, for example, designing the overwing exit of an aircraft so that an average-sized person could fit through it. This could potentially result in about 50 per cent of the passengers being unable to fit through the exit in the event of an emergency because they are larger than average. Anthropometrics can be used very successfully to produce designs that suit about 90 per cent of the population.

Before getting into a discussion about how anthropometrics can be used, an explanation of a few terms is necessary, as they clear the way for a greater understanding of its uses. Frequency distribution offers an indication of the range of dimensions within a population for a particular feature, such as stature. If a group of people were measured for height and their heights were plotted on a graph such as that shown in the figure opposite, so that height was recorded horizontally and the number of people with that height was recorded vertically, a smooth symmetrical curve would be displayed. This represents frequency distribution and illustrates that we are likely to meet more people around 'average' height from day to day and fewer people on the extremes. Given that the bell-shaped curve is symmetrical it is easy to see that 50 per cent of people are larger than average and 50 per cent are smaller, bearing in mind that the 'average' person falls centrally within the population for a particular characteristic. Those individuals who fall centrally on the curve are referred to as the 50th percentile. On the far left side of the curve is a point at which people are referred to as the 5th percentile – ie 95 per cent

The normal distribution

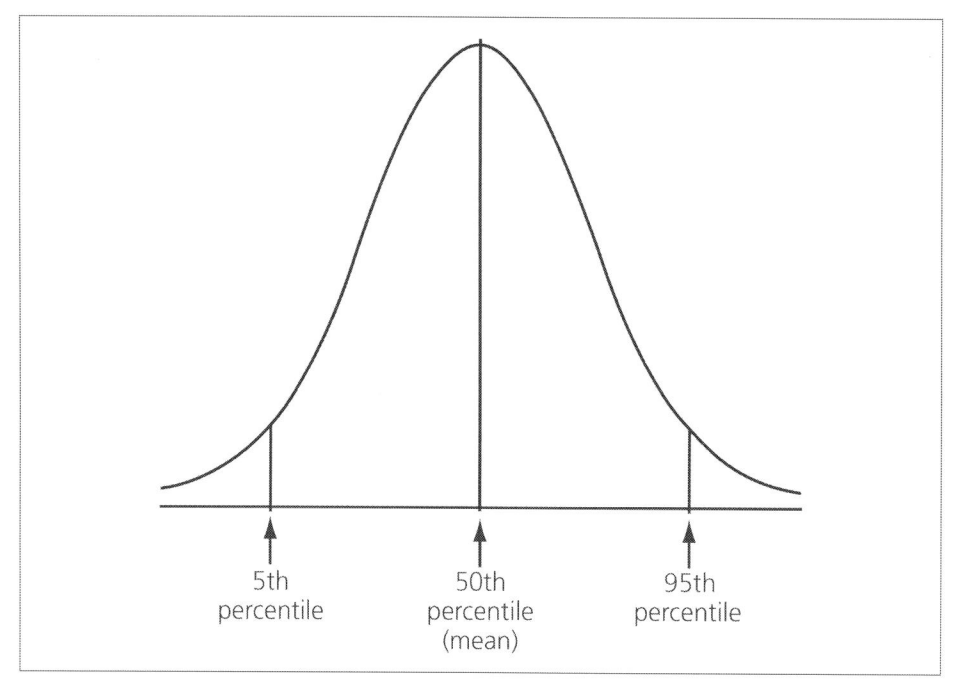

```
       5th            50th           95th
    percentile     percentile     percentile
                     (mean)
```

of the population are taller than them. On the far right side of the curve there is a point at which people are referred to as the 95th percentile – ie 95 per cent of the population are smaller than them.

When the term standard deviation (SD) is used, it denotes the extent of the variability in a population for a given characteristic. Depending on the population being examined, the standard deviation may be quite small or quite large. For instance, if the stature of the general population was compared with the stature of a group of basketball players, it would be clear that the standard deviation would be smaller among the basketball players. In other words, there is less variability for that characteristic within their group.

Before deciding what range of dimensions they will use, designers need to know who their target population is. Every population has its own characteristics and sometimes these characteristics impose constraints on the range of choices available to designers. Designers need to recognise that constraints will have an impact on their design criteria – ie the goals they wish to achieve. For example, in a food manufacturing facility one criterion may be to introduce a conveyor belt that is as wide as possible so that the maximum volume of food can be produced and processed in a given period of time. However, the constraint will be the length of the operator's arm. There is no point in investing in a conveyor that cannot be used fully because the operators cannot reach the far side of the line when dealing with the products.

This is where anthropometrics comes into its own. Anthropometric tables provide lists of data relating to the dimensions of humans such as arm length, shoulder width, leg length and so on. It is quite a straightforward process for a designer to use such data to make decisions about what dimensional aspects of a machine or workstation are critical in allowing the individual to work comfortably, safely and efficiently. What the designer has to decide when looking at the long list of figures on these tables is exactly who is their limiting user. The limiting user is an individual whose size the designer has to take account of when making decisions, in the knowledge that if they accommodate that particular size of individual, most of the workforce will be able to work with their design. For instance, if machinery was being installed in a factory and the engineers had to ensure that operators could walk between each machine during maintenance procedures, their limiting user would be the bulkiest person likely to work in the factory. If they provide sufficient space between the machines for the bulkiest person to walk through unhindered, they know that everyone else in the factory will also be able to do so.

Anthropometrics is typically applied in areas where there are four specific types of constraints: posture, reach, clearance and strength. Generally speaking, the posture adopted by a person at work is dictated by the design and dimensions of their workstation. Once an operator is presented with a workspace, they mould themselves to suit the layout of that environment. For instance, irrespective of the height of a bench or conveyor, the operator will raise their shoulders, arms and hands to a point that allows them to complete the work they have been employed to do. Alternatively, if their work surface is set at a low level, they will lean forwards at the waist to lower their hands to a point where they can carry out their task.

It is evident that the posture adopted by someone while they are at work has a significant impact on their feelings of wellbeing. For that reason, it is important that suitable workstation arrangements are put in place because they have a direct influence on posture. The difficulty when determining the layout of workstations is that both ends of the body size spectrum are important and, very obviously, large, tall people have different needs to petite operators. In this case there are two limiting users: the 5th and the 95th percentile user. The designer has to try to ensure that operators can work in an upright position, with their shoulders hanging naturally, with their arms close to the body and where they are able to maintain a symmetrical, balanced posture.

Being able to reach towards and grip an object, control or tool is an essential part of any working environment. The designer needs to ensure that everyone can grip their target without having to overextend their arm or lean forwards. This will be achieved if the 5th percentile person is identified as the limiting user.

Clearance ranges from having sufficient space for the whole body to pass through an area unhindered to simply having enough space to insert the fingers in a gap. Typical considerations include overhead clearance, which has an impact on whole body posture; leg clearance under a work surface; access around an area, which may need to allow for two people to pass each other or for the movement of wheelchairs; and hand or arm clearance, such as when an operator has to remove an object from within the confines of a machine. Generally, the limiting user is the 95th percentile because by accommodating the largest person, everyone else should be able to work without difficulty.

Sometimes clearance is set with a view to hindering the path of the individual, such as when the rails across an elevated walkway are set at such a distance apart that no adult would be able to fit between the rails and fall to the ground. In such a safety-critical circumstance, the limiting user would be less than the 5th percentile operator.

In some working environments, operators have to exert force in the execution of their jobs. For instance, they may need to open a sliding door, pull on a lever or press a trigger. In the main, it would make sense to select the 5th percentile person as the limiting user, because by accommodating the 'weakest' individual, everyone should have sufficient strength to complete a task. However, there will be some situations where selecting the 5th percentile person's level of strength may not be appropriate. In a safety-critical environment, or one where accidental activation of a control may cause serious problems, it may be appropriate to require higher levels of force so that a heavy-handed operator does not turn on a dangerous piece of equipment by accident.

Alongside the data relating to body size, the designer needs to look at the task being carried out, as this may require an adjustment to the figures being used. For instance, it is generally recommended that operators should be presented with a work surface height which is at or slightly below elbow height. This allows them to sit or stand upright when working, thereby avoiding lower backache, and they will be able to work with their shoulders and arms in a natural position, thereby avoiding upper limb discomfort. However, if the operator is assembling a large bulky object which sits on the work surface, this will present an actual working height above elbow height. The consequence of this is that the operator will have to raise their shoulders and arms to complete their work. The situation is compounded if they have to use tools which will cause them to raise their hands to a point above the assembly unit that allows them to tighten a screw or drill a hole. In this situation, the designer needs to recognise that in order to provide a working height of around or slightly below elbow height, they may need to set the bench well below elbow height given the bulk of the assembly unit.

Once the design has been established, no matter how simple the concept, it is always recommended to trial it before it is introduced into the working environment permanently. It is only by trialling a design under near normal conditions that it can be established whether it suits the operators and the task they have to perform, or whether some modifications are required.

Using anthropometric data

There are numerous tables of anthropometric data to be found in a range of academic textbooks. However, selecting the correct set of dimensions needs to be done with care and with an understanding of who the user population will be in any working environment. Most people recognise that men tend to be taller, bulkier and heavier than women; therefore the designer needs to consider whether they are simply designing for male users or a combination of male and female users. There are still many environments in which women do not actively choose to work, such as heavy industry. In such an environment the designer may choose to focus only on data relating to the male workforce.

It is not always clear from anthropometric tables where and when the data were originally collected. Caution is needed, as a lot of anthropometric data relate to specific nationalities – obviously, relying on data relating to the Japanese male population is not going to be particularly helpful in a factory being built in the United States. Some of the data currently being used were collected 50 years ago or more and as such may not reflect the body size and shape of people today, given that our diets have changed so considerably over this period. Some of the data that have been collated relate to specific groups of individuals who may not be considered representative of the whole population. For instance, it was common practice for body size information to be collected from the armed forces. However, these organisations often have a minimum height criterion, which results in the range of recorded statures or other physical characteristics not being truly representative of the country in which they operate. To ensure that they are reviewing the correct set of data, the designer needs to establish the sex, age, nationality and occupation of the target group. All of these factors influence the body size of the individual.

It also needs to be understood by those using anthropometric data that the measurements were taken of individuals who were not wearing any clothing or footwear and who were unlikely to have been slouching as they were measured. Again, adjustments need to be made to the data to provide more accurate dimensional guidance.

When making allowance for clothing, a distinction has to be made between light clothing, such as would be worn in an office, and heavy clothing, such as may be worn as protection in hot or cold environments. Designers must also consider whether the individual will be wearing a hat, such as a hard hat, and what type of footwear. As a general rule, an adjustment of 25 mm is added in situations involving stature or leg length data to accommodate the difference created by the heels on shoes. However, this really only covers the heels on men's footwear and standard workwear within a factory environment. Women often wear higher heels in office environments.

Body dimensions

The remainder of this chapter covers data relating to various body dimensions, which can be used when creating or re-developing a working environment. The data are presented for males and females and relate to the 5th, 50th and 95th percentiles in each case. The data are reproduced from Table 10.1 on page 244 of *Bodyspace – anthropometry, ergonomics and the design of work* by Pheasant & Haslegrave (2006, third edition) and cover the age range of 19 to 65. Under each set of data, guidance is provided on how it may be used and what corrections need to be made to make allowance for certain considerations. All measurements are in millimetres.

2 Anthropometrics

Stature	Men			Women		
	Percentile			Percentile		
	5th	50th	95th	5th	50th	95th
	1625	1740	1855	1505	1610	1710
	SD: 70			SD: 62		

Measurement: from crown of head to floor
Application: overhead clearance and as an indicator of the range of body sizes within a population

Corrections: shoes (25 mm), hat (25 mm), hard hat (35 mm)
Note: If the enquiry relates to individuals lying down, the body can lengthen by 15 mm

Standing eye height	Men			Women		
	Percentile			Percentile		
	5th	50th	95th	5th	50th	95th
	1515	1630	1745	1405	1505	1610
	SD: 69			SD: 61		

Measurement: from corner of eye to floor
Application: setting maximum viewing height for displays and defining maximum height for visual obstructions

Correction: shoes (25 mm)
Note: Eye height will be reduced if the operator does not keep their head upright

Standing shoulder height	Men			Women		
	Percentile			Percentile		
	5th	50th	95th	5th	50th	95th
	1315	1425	1535	1215	1310	1405
	SD: 66			SD: 58		

Measurement: from bony tip on top of shoulder to floor
Application: determining position of controls

Correction: shoes (25 mm)
Note: Controls used regularly should not be presented above this point. Manual handling above this point results in significant increase in risk

Standing elbow height	Men				Women			
	Percentile			SD	Percentile			SD
	5th	50th	95th		5th	50th	95th	
	735	790	845	35	685	740	795	33

Measurement: from point at back of elbow to floor
Application: establishing suitable working height

Correction: shoes (25 mm)
Note: Although ideal working height is around or slightly below elbow height, the work surface height may not be the same as elbow height as it is determined by the task and the components and tools being used

Hip height	Men				Women			
	Percentile			SD	Percentile			SD
	5th	50th	95th		5th	50th	95th	
	840	920	1000	50	740	810	885	43

Measurement: from bony protrusion of hip to floor
Application: establishing where workplace working heights may fall relative to the operator

Correction: shoes (25 mm)

Knuckle height	Men				Women			
	Percentile			SD	Percentile			SD
	5th	50th	95th		5th	50th	95th	
	690	755	825	41	660	720	780	36

Measurement: from knuckle of middle finger, when hand is closed in a fist, to floor
Application: defining lowest acceptable working height and lowest acceptable level for hand-operated controls

Correction: shoes (25 mm)
Note: Knuckle height is the lowest preferred height at which manual handling should occur

2 Anthropometrics

Fingertip height	Men				Women			
	\multicolumn{3}{c	}{Percentile}	SD	\multicolumn{3}{c	}{Percentile}	SD
	5th	50th	95th		5th	50th	95th	
	590	655	720	38	560	625	685	38

Measurement: from tip of middle finger, with fingers extended, to floor
Application: defining lowest acceptable level for finger-operated controls
Correction: shoes (25 mm)

Sitting height	Men				Women			
	\multicolumn{3}{c	}{Percentile}	SD	\multicolumn{3}{c	}{Percentile}	SD
	5th	50th	95th		5th	50th	95th	
	850	910	965	36	795	850	910	35

Measurement: from crown of head to point of contact between buttocks and seat surface
Application: determining overhead clearance when seated
Corrections: heavy outdoor clothing under buttocks (10 mm); hat (25 mm); hard hat (35 mm)

Sitting eye height	Men				Women			
	\multicolumn{3}{c	}{Percentile}	SD	\multicolumn{3}{c	}{Percentile}	SD
	5th	50th	95th		5th	50th	95th	
	735	790	845	35	685	740	795	33

Measurement: from corner of eye to point of contact between buttocks and seat surface
Application: setting maximum viewing height for displays and defining maximum height for visual obstructions for seated operators

Corrections: heavy outdoor clothing under buttocks (10 mm); sitting slumped (40 mm); seat cushion compression (variable)
Note: If an operator sits on a soft seat, it will sag under their weight, causing them to sink lower than they would on a hard surface. Most operators slump when relaxed

Sitting shoulder height	Men			Women		
	Percentile		SD	Percentile		SD
	5th / 50th / 95th			5th / 50th / 95th		
	540 / 595 / 645		32	505 / 555 / 610		31

Measurement: from bony tip on top of shoulder to point of contact between buttocks and seat surface
Application: determining position of controls for seated operators

Corrections: heavy outdoor clothing under buttocks (10 mm); sitting slumped (40 mm); seat cushion compression (variable)
Note: If an operator sits on a soft seat, it will sag under their weight, causing them to sink lower than they would on a hard surface. Most operators slump when relaxed. Controls used regularly should not be above shoulder height for a seated operator

Sitting elbow height	Men			Women		
	Percentile		SD	Percentile		SD
	5th / 50th / 95th			5th / 50th / 95th		
	195 / 245 / 295		31	185 / 235 / 280		29

Measurement: from underside of elbow to point of contact between buttocks and seat surface
Application: establishing working height of surfaces and equipment, and used to set armrest height

Corrections: heavy outdoor clothing under buttocks (10 mm); sitting slumped (40 mm); seat cushion compression (variable)
Note: If an operator sits on a soft seat, it will sag under their weight, causing them to sink lower than they would on a hard surface. Most operators slump when relaxed

2 Anthropometrics

Thigh thickness	Men				Women			
	Percentile			SD	Percentile			SD
	5th	50th	95th		5th	50th	95th	
	135	160	185	15	125	155	180	17

Measurement: from seat surface to top of thigh at its thickest point (close to abdomen)
Application: establishing the clearance required between a seat and the underside of a work surface
Correction: heavy outdoor clothing (35 mm)

Knee height	Men				Women			
	Percentile			SD	Percentile			SD
	5th	50th	95th		5th	50th	95th	
	490	545	595	32	455	500	540	27

Measurement: from floor to upper surface of knee
Application: establishing the clearance required underneath a work surface
Correction: shoes (25 mm)

Popliteal height	Men				Women			
	Percentile			SD	Percentile			SD
	5th	50th	95th		5th	50th	95th	
	395	440	490	29	355	400	445	27

Measurement: from floor to back of knees where lower leg meets thigh
Application: establishing the maximum height that a seat should be set above the floor
Correction: shoes (25 mm)

Buttock–knee length	Men				Women			
	Percentile			SD	Percentile			SD
	5th	50th	95th		5th	50th	95th	
	540	595	645	31	520	570	620	30

Measurement: from back of buttocks to front of knee
Application: establishing the clearance required between the seat back and obstacles in front of the knees

Corrections: heavy outdoor clothing (20 mm)
Note: This measurement is taken without the buttocks being compressed by something behind them, such as a seat back

Buttock–popliteal length	Men				Women			
	Percentile			SD	Percentile			SD
	5th	50th	95th		5th	50th	95th	
	440	495	550	32	435	480	530	30

Measurement: from back of buttocks to back of knee
Application: establishing the maximum acceptable length of a seat

Corrections: heavy outdoor clothing (20 mm)
Note: This measurement is taken without the buttocks being compressed by something behind them, such as a seat back

Shoulder breadth (bideltoid)	Men				Women			
	Percentile			SD	Percentile			SD
	5th	50th	95th		5th	50th	95th	
	420	465	510	28	355	395	435	24

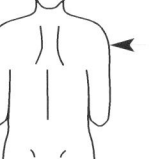

Measurement: across shoulders between the protrusion of the deltoid muscles
Application: establishing clearance at shoulder level

Corrections: indoor clothing (10 mm); heavy outdoor clothing (40 mm)
Note: The deltoid muscles protrude noticeably at the top of the upper arm where it meets the shoulder

Shoulder breadth (biacromial)	Men				Women			
	Percentile			SD	Percentile			SD
	5th	50th	95th		5th	50th	95th	
	365	400	430	20	325	355	385	18

Measurement: across shoulders between the acromia (bony points of the shoulders)
Application: establishing the lateral separation of the centres of rotation of the upper limbs and calculating the zone of convenient reach

Correction: none

Hip breadth	Men			Women		
	Percentile		SD	Percentile		SD
	5th / 50th / 95th			5th / 50th / 95th		
	310 / 360 / 405		29	310 / 370 / 435		38

Measurement: between hips when seated
Application: establishing clearance at hip height and maximum seat width

Corrections: light clothing (10 mm); medium clothing (25 mm); heavy outdoor clothing (50 mm)
Note: This measurement should be taken without the soft tissue of the hips being compressed by surrounding surfaces

Chest depth	Men			Women		
	Percentile		SD	Percentile		SD
	5th / 50th / 95th			5th / 50th / 95th		
	215 / 250 / 285		22	210 / 250 / 295		27

Measurement: from the point of contact between the back and a surface to the front of the chest or breast
Application: establishing clearance needed between the seat back and obstructions in front of the operator

Corrections: indoor clothing (10 mm); outdoor clothing (40 mm)

Abdominal depth	Men			Women		
	Percentile		SD	Percentile		SD
	5th / 50th / 95th			5th / 50th / 95th		
	220 / 270 / 325		32	205 / 255 / 305		30

Measurement: from the point of contact between the small of the back and a surface to the front of the abdomen
Application: establishing clearance needed between the seat back and obstructions in front of the operator

Corrections: indoor clothing (10 mm); outdoor clothing (40 mm)

2 Anthropometrics

Shoulder–elbow length	Men				Women			
	Percentile			SD	Percentile			SD
	5th	50th	95th		5th	50th	95th	
	330	365	395	20	300	330	360	17
	Measurement: from bony point of shoulder to underside of elbow **Application:** establishing elbow room around a workstation **Correction:** none							

Elbow–fingertip length	Men				Women			
	Percentile			SD	Percentile			SD
	5th	50th	95th		5th	50th	95th	
	440	475	510	21	400	430	460	19
	Measurement: from tip of middle finger, with fingers extended, to back of elbow **Application:** establishing forearm reach and defining the normal work area (NWA) **Correction:** none							

Upper limb length	Men				Women			
	Percentile			SD	Percentile			SD
	5th	50th	95th		5th	50th	95th	
	720	780	840	36	655	705	760	32
	Measurement: from tip of middle finger, with fingers extended, to bony point of shoulder **Application:** establishing maximum reaching distance to a control operated by the fingertip **Correction:** none							

Shoulder–grip length	Men				Women			
	Percentile			SD	Percentile			SD
	5th	50th	95th		5th	50th	95th	
	610	665	715	32	555	600	650	29

Measurement: from bony point of shoulder to centre of an object gripped in the hand with the arm straight
Application: establishing the working reach of the arm and defining the zone of convenient reach (ZCR)
Correction: none

Forward grip reach	Men				Women			
	Percentile			SD	Percentile			SD
	5th	50th	95th		5th	50th	95th	
	720	780	835	34	650	705	755	31

Measurement: horizontally from back of shoulder blades to centre of an object gripped in the hand
Application: establishing the maximum reaching distance
Correction: none

Vertical grip reach – standing	Men				Women			
	Percentile			SD	Percentile			SD
	5th	50th	95th		5th	50th	95th	
	1925	2060	2190	80	1790	1905	2020	71

Measurement: from floor to centre of an object gripped in the hand with arm extended above head
Application: establishing maximum overhead reaching distance
Correction: shoes (25 mm)

2 Anthropometrics

Vertical grip reach – sitting	Men				Women			
	Percentile			SD	Percentile			SD
	5th	50th	95th		5th	50th	95th	
	1145	1245	1340	60	1060	1150	1235	53

Measurement: from point of contact between buttocks and seat surface to centre of an object gripped in the hand with arm extended above head
Application: establishing maximum overhead reaching distance for a seated worker

Corrections: heavy clothing (10 mm); seat cushion compression (varies)

Elbow span	Men				Women			
	Percentile			SD	Percentile			SD
	5th	50th	95th		5th	50th	95th	
	865	945	1020	47	780	850	920	43

Measurement: between points of elbows when fingertips of both hands are touching at chest level
Application: establishing elbow room between workers

Correction: medium outdoor clothing (20 mm)

Arm span	Men				Women			
	Percentile			SD	Percentile			SD
	5th	50th	95th		5th	50th	95th	
	1655	1790	1925	83	1490	1605	1725	71

Measurement: between tips of middle fingers when arms are stretched out to the sides
Application: establishing dual reaching distance to either side of the body

Correction: none

Head breadth	Men			Women		
	Percentile			Percentile		
	5th	50th	95th	5th	50th	95th
	145	155	165	135	145	150
	SD: 6			SD: 6		

Measurement: maximum width of head above ears
Application: establishing clearance at head level
Corrections: ears (35 mm); hard hat (90 mm)

Hand breadth	Men			Women		
	Percentile			Percentile		
	5th	50th	95th	5th	50th	95th
	80	85	95	70	75	85
	SD: 5			SD: 4		

Measurement: maximum width of palm
Application: establishing the size of handles and grips and clearance through apertures
Correction: protective gloves (up to 25 mm)

Hand length	Men			Women		
	Percentile			Percentile		
	5th	50th	95th	5th	50th	95th
	175	190	205	160	175	190
	SD: 10			SD: 9		

Measurement: from tip of middle finger with fingers extended to crease at base of wrist
Application: establishing maximum reaching distance of hand and fingers, and clearance
Correction: protective gloves (up to 10 mm)

Foot length	Men				Women			
	Percentile			SD	Percentile			SD
	5th	50th	95th		5th	50th	95th	
	240	265	285	14	215	235	255	12

Measurement: from back of heel to tip of longest toe
Application: establishing clearance for the feet and in pedal design
Corrections: shoes (30 mm); safety footwear (40 mm)

Foot breadth	Men				Women			
	Percentile			SD	Percentile			SD
	5th	50th	95th		5th	50th	95th	
	85	95	110	6	80	90	100	6

Measurement: across the widest point of the foot
Application: establishing clearance for the feet and designing and locating pedals
Corrections: shoes (30 mm); safety footwear (40 mm)

Summary

- Anthropometrics is concerned with the subject matter of body measurements.
- Body measurements of interest include body size, shape and strength.
- Anthropometrics allows designers to accommodate populations with varying weight, shape, bulk, size and proportion.
- Designers should use anthropometrics to match the physical form of the workspace to the characteristics and capabilities of the workforce.
- Designers should not aim to accommodate the 'average' person, as this disadvantages too many people.
- Frequency distribution provides an indication of the range of dimensions within a population for a particular feature.
- Frequency distribution is often displayed on a graph as a bell-shaped curve.

- People who fall centrally within the population for a given characteristic are referred to as the 50th percentile. People at the smaller end of the scale are referred to as the 5th percentile (where 95 per cent of the population are bigger than they are) and people at the other extreme are referred to as the 95th percentile (where 95 per cent of the population are smaller than they are).
- Standard deviation is used to denote the variability within a population.
- Knowing who the target population is helps the designer to choose the correct set of data for their environment.
- Constraints will have an impact on the design criteria; there are four types of constraint – posture, reach, clearance and strength.
- The limiting user is the size of individual the designer has to accommodate with a design.
- Anthropometric tables provide lists of data relating to the dimension of humans, such as arm length, shoulder width, leg length and so on.
- Adjustments are needed to anthropometric data as they were recorded without clothing or footwear and when the subject was standing or sitting erect.
- Once designs have been established, they should be trialled before full introduction to determine whether modifications are required.

References and further reading

Bridger R S. *Introduction to ergonomics* (third edition). CRC Press, 2009.
Kroemer K H E. *Extra-ordinary ergonomics.* Taylor & Francis, 2006.
ISO 15534-3:2000 *Ergonomic design for the safety of machinery – Part 3: Anthropometric data.* ISO TC 159/SC 3.
ISO/TR 7250-2:2010. *Basic human body measurements for technological design – Part 2: Statistical summaries of body measurements from individual ISO populations.*
Pheasant S and Haslegrave C M. *Bodyspace: anthropometry, ergonomics and the design of work.* Taylor & Francis, 2006.
Pheasant S. *Anthropometrics: an introduction.* British Standards Institution, 1990.
Tilley A R and Henry Dreyfuss Associates. *The measure of man and woman. Human factors in design.* John Wiley & Sons, 2002.

3 The design process

Introduction

Those who design workplaces have a significant influence on operators' wellbeing and performance. Unfortunately, many designs are driven solely by the desire to achieve an end result, whether it be the processing and inputting of data from thousands of slips of paper, the production of a chocolate gateau, or the assembly of a fridge. As a result of this approach to design, the operator is often the last element to be considered in the equation, frequently being fitted in towards the end of the process. This short-sighted approach will almost certainly result in mismatches between the final design and the intended user population.

Errors, poor quality, near misses, general dissatisfaction and ill health such as backache and upper limb disorders (ULDs) can often be traced to poor workstation and equipment design. However, having identified the source of such problems, it is usually the case that it would be too difficult, and costly, to change them. The logical conclusion is to develop the right designs from conception, as opposed to after construction.

Ensuring that designs are suitable, usable and safe requires consideration of the individual's characteristics and abilities, and the job requirements. It is important to take a combined approach to design. And, as this chapter is concerned mainly with the ergonomics of design, it is essential that designers refer to relevant regulations and standards before determining any final specifications.

The person

Human operators have certain basic needs that must be met if they are to function efficiently, comfortably and safely at work. Many of these needs are derived from personal characteristics such as body size, and personal qualities such as fitness and strength. These factors should be examined before items of equipment or workstations are designed for use by the operator.

Posture

Operators will commonly adopt a posture which is dictated by the design of their workstation or equipment. Such postures are not necessarily the most comfortable or the least fatiguing. For example, it is not unusual to have control panels in production areas which are set at such heights from the floor that operators have to raise their hands to, or above, shoulder height when inputting information. They also have to look upwards for extended periods to read the displays. Working in such unnatural postures can lead to pain and sometimes injury, and their significance cannot be overlooked or excluded from the design process. No designer should use the excuse 'we've never had any complaints before' as a means to carry on regardless and ignore the issue. Just because operators are not vocal about concerns, or because there are no recorded injuries or increases in absence levels, does not mean that the workplace is free of problems.

In general, all designs should aim to promote good working postures which do not require high levels of static effort to sustain them. Static effort results from the tensing of muscles for an extended, uninterrupted period. You can experience this easily by stretching your arm out in front of your body and holding it in that position. This becomes hard work very quickly. Working posture should allow an operation to be completed effectively with the minimum of muscular effort.

Decisions regarding the use of sitting or standing postures should be made early in the design process. The designer should remember that standing requires levels of static muscle work to keep the joints of the knees, feet and hips in a fixed position. Such static muscle work is eliminated when the operator is seated. There are also other benefits:
- the weight is taken off the legs
- the chances of adopting an irregular or unnatural body posture are reduced
- the operator has greater stability
- jobs requiring fine, precise or manipulative movements may be carried out more easily, particularly if the arms are supported
- energy consumption is reduced
- demands on the cardiovascular system are reduced.

Despite these benefits, there are some disadvantages to sitting at work – in particular possible increases in backache. However, it must be said that backache is often directly related to poorly designed chairs and/or the inappropriate use of chairs. Both of these areas are dealt with later in this chapter.

If a workstation is specifically designed to be used by a seated operator, it should not, at a later date, be used from the standing position unless it has been altered accordingly. More often than not, the height of a seated workstation will be lower than that for a standing workstation, so standing operators will spend their time leaning forwards as they reach down towards the work surface – a common cause of backache. However, a workstation designed for the standing operator can always be used by the seated operator, providing the work allows it and the workstation design is compatible with the chair use. One of the most important considerations in this situation is a height-adjustable footring or footrest, as the operator will be sitting higher up than usual in relation to the floor.

There are several basic rules which, if incorporated into a design, will ensure that an operator can work comfortably and effectively whether sitting or standing. These are:
- the operator should be able to adopt an upright and forward-facing posture
- if standing, the body weight should be borne by both feet equally
- the posture should be balanced so that additional muscle activity is not required to support or stabilise the body as a whole, or individual limbs, such as would result from leaning forwards
- the head should remain reasonably upright or slightly inclined to the front
- the limbs, trunk and head should be positioned during the work activities so that the joints are not forced to go beyond their mid-point in terms of their range of movement
- the hands should not have to pass above elbow height regularly or for extended periods of time
- the largest (appropriate) muscle groups should be used to apply necessary forces in a direction which is compatible with their structure, eg using the leg muscles to operate a foot control in place of using a hand control
- the workload should be shared out equally/evenly across the body as a whole and between individual limbs
- the work should be capable of being carried out when the operator is in varying postures (and this should be achieved without a change in the quality of performance or comfort of the operator).

To ensure that such general principles can be applied in the workplace, it is important that designs suit the size and shape of the user population. Only then will operators be able to adopt and maintain natural, comfortable postures.

Anthropometrics
Anthropometrics is concerned with body size (see Chapter 1). The main point to remember during any design process is that designs should not cater for the 'average' person, since a large number of potential users will be put at a disadvantage when using the workstation or equipment. Consideration of body size and related influential factors, such as sex, will enable the designer to calculate appropriate dimensions when determining

acceptable reaching distances, overhead clearance, working heights and so on. The word 'calculate' is used deliberately because the decision regarding dimensions is not, or should not be, a hit and miss or trial and error affair with the designer assuming that because a dimension 'fits' them, it will suit everybody – in the same way that no-one would assume that just because a jacket fits them comfortably it will fit everybody else equally well.

Using the concept of anthropometrics, the designer can plot dimensions which are important to the user of a workstation or piece of equipment.

Access
Before an operator can even take up position alongside their workstation or equipment, they must be able to come within range of it easily, without any deviations from their upright posture and without having to extend their reach. To ensure ease of access, the design should provide enough space for the largest possible operator who may work in that area. This means considering factors such as operator stature, shoulder and hip width, and dimensions relating to hand and arm size. Additional allowances will have to be made for the movement of tools and other equipment or components by the operator, as well as for the storage of other items in the area. Individual differences will have to be taken into account where appropriate or necessary. For example, access requirements for a person in a wheelchair will be different to those for someone who walks to and from an area.

Designers should also acknowledge the fact that the equipment or workstation will probably not function perfectly 100 per cent of the time it is in use. They need to take account of the fact that there will probably be breakdowns at some stage in the workstation's or equipment's lifetime. Therefore, when working on the concept of access, consideration should be given to the requirements of maintenance personnel. Allowances should be made for the largest parts of the equipment or workstation that may have to be moved during repair or rework, as well as any tools that may have to be used. Of course, the operator may also be expected to respond to equipment breakdowns. For example, it is common practice in the food industry to 'bulk off' when a line malfunctions. For obvious reasons, food cannot be left lying around on conveyors until the line is up and running again. It has to be removed quickly and placed in chiller areas (ie the bulking-off process). However, more often than not, access along the conveyor will not have been built in at points where operators are required to remove the food. As a result, they will spend the bulking-off period reaching across large side casings on the conveyor, or over ingredient hoppers, or across conveyors of such a width that their upper body is almost perpendicular to their lower body as they attempt to stretch to the far side. Allowing for such events should be a fundamental part of the design process.

Clearance

Once in the work position, the operator should have clearance in all directions. Overhead or vertical clearance will ensure that the operator does not have to stoop. When determining this factor, the designer should cater for the tallest operator who could be expected to work in the area. Having reviewed the dimensions relating to stature, consideration should be given to the use of headgear and footwear, as both will have a significant impact on the level of overhead clearance.

Side-to-side and forward–backward clearance is also important. Again, the designer should cater for the largest operators who could be expected to work in the area, making allowances for some movement during the activities. Hip and shoulder width and trunk dimensions are important. In addition, the use of any other equipment will have to be taken into account.

Foot clearance is commonly overlooked in the design of workplaces. If a recess is not provided at floor level so that the foot can move beneath a workstation frame, the operator will be held back from the leading edge of the work surface. The operator will overcome this deficiency by leaning or reaching forwards. Further allowances should be made if a pedal is in operation.

If it is intended that operators sit down when working, it is important that they are provided with adequate clearance for their knees. When determining the required clearance, consideration should also be given to hip width and the width of the seat being used. The provided clearance should cater to the longest thigh. As it is unlikely that the operator will adopt a fixed position when working, an allowance for leg movement should also be incorporated into the design, which will require a review of overall leg and foot lengths. Vertical clearance between the seat's surface to underneath the work surface should not be ignored. An allowance should be made for leg crossing or the use of pedals, which may result in the raising of the knee. Again, the largest thigh should be taken as the benchmark. If undersurface clearance is not provided, operators will be held back from the work surface and will have to lean and reach forwards when completing an operation. Alternatively, operators faced with a lack of undersurface clearance may choose to sit sideways to the workstation and twist their upper body in the required direction. Lack of knee room is usually the major shortfall in a workstation which was designed for the standing operator but which is used later by a seated operator.

Reach

When determining reaching distances, the aim should be to allow the operator to grasp an object without excessive body movement or energy expenditure. This is particularly important in the case of seated operators who cannot move towards an object or work area. When examining reaching distances, the 'zone of convenient reach' and the 'normal working area' should be considered.

Zone of convenient reach

The zone of convenient reach is sometimes referred to as the secondary work envelope or maximum reaching distance. Areas which can be reached easily when the arms are fully extended sideways, forwards and upwards fall within the zone of convenient reach. The illustration below shows two intersecting curves. The radius of each curve is the length of the arm (a) and the centre of each curve is separated by the biacromial width of the shoulders (b). The sagittal plane (sp), transverse plane (tp) and coronal plane (cp) are also shown.

Zones of convenient reach Reproduced from Bodyspace – anthropometry, ergonomics and the design of work (Pheasant & Haslegrave 2006, Figure 4.4, page 95)

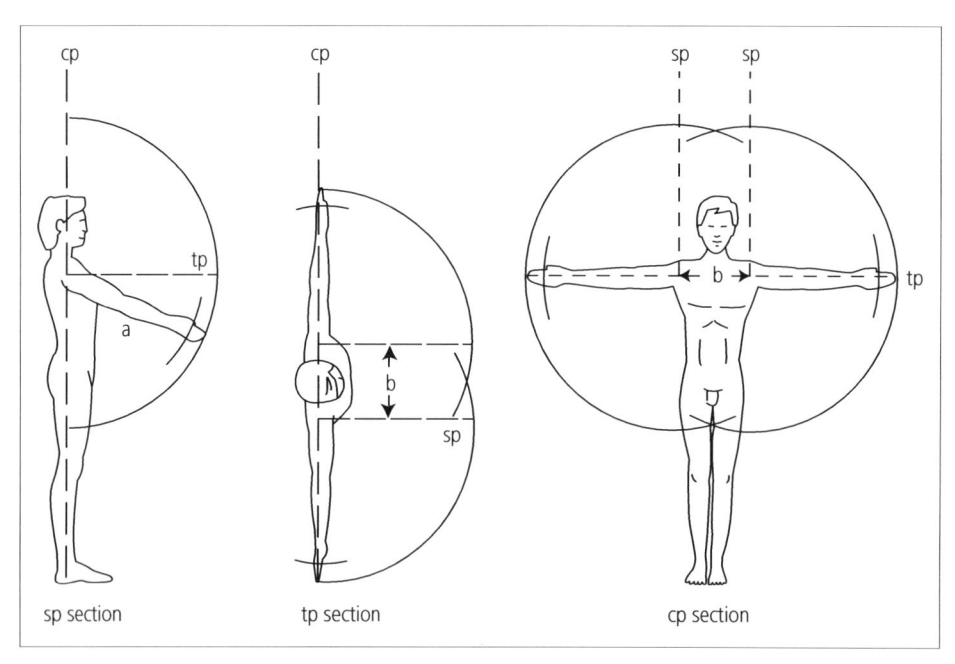

A work area or an object required during an operation should not be located beyond the zone of convenient reach. However, working with the arms at their maximum range of extension repeatedly or for prolonged periods is fatiguing and can be damaging for the limbs. Equally, operators should not be required to work with their hands and arms towards the rear of the body, nor to complete repetitive or sustained operations with their hands above shoulder height. While it is acceptable to undertake occasional activity within the zone of convenient reach, sustained work needs to be carried out much closer to the body.

Normal working area
The normal working area is sometimes referred to as the primary work envelope or optimum reaching distance. It is smaller than the zone of convenient reach and is defined as the area that can be swept comfortably by the forearm when there is a 90° angle at the elbow and the upper arm is hanging down naturally. Objects required frequently or actions that are undertaken for sustained periods should be kept within the normal working area. The zone of convenient reach and the normal working area are shown below.

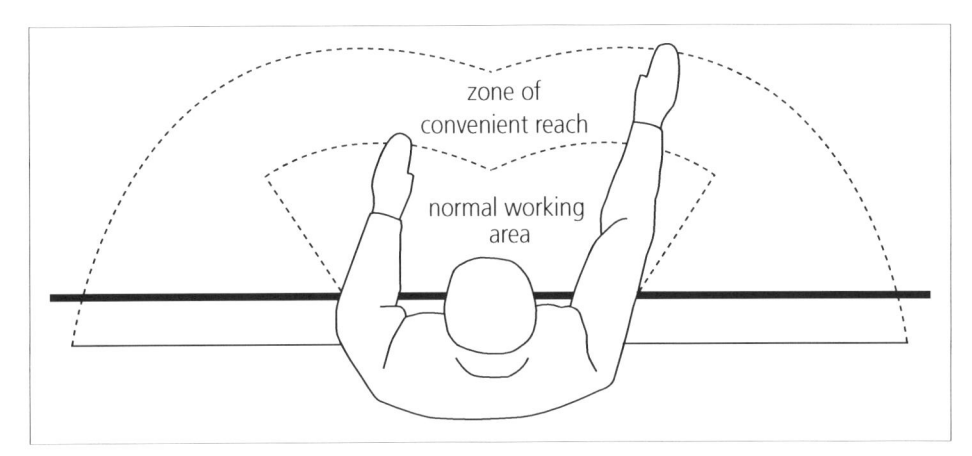

The relationship between the zone of convenient reach and the normal working area

When setting dimensions for optimum reaching distances, the main consideration should be given to the shortest arm length (includes upper arm, forearm, hand and fingers). If dealing with extended arm length (to the end of the fingertips), the designer should recognise that this dimension is reduced if the operator grips an object, due to the fact that the fingers are closing into a fist and enveloping the object.

Dimensions for British adults aged from 19 to 65 years are included in the 'Anthropometrics' chapter. Using these data will allow calculations of the zone of convenient reach and normal working area.

Reaching distances can also be applied to feet and legs, particularly if a pedal is being operated from the seated position. The designer should cater for the shortest leg length as well as the longest. Adjustability in pedal location will be of great benefit.

Personal space

When designing several workstations with the intention of locating them in close proximity, the designer should recognise the effects of 'territoriality' or personal space. Invasion of an individual's personal space may undermine the acceptability of a design. 'Personal space' is defined as a portable, invisible boundary which surrounds an individual and into which entry is restricted. This boundary is divided into several zones, each of which is determined by levels of social interaction. For example, people on an intimate level will be allowed closer than those on a purely friendly level, who in turn will be allowed closer than those on a wider social level, and so on. If someone invades a zone within another's personal space which is not appropriate to their relationship, it can cause stress or anxiety. For example, most people will accept accidental elbow contact with family members when eating a meal at home but will be uncomfortable when similar contact occurs with a stranger sitting in close proximity in a restaurant.

Personal space is not an evenly spread zone which surrounds the body on all sides. For example, personal space zones can be invaded to a greater extent from the sides than from the front. Consider a passenger standing on a crowded bus – a stranger will be more acceptable when standing at the side than if in front and facing them. The latter is deemed to be much more threatening. In addition, the appraisal of acceptable 'uninvaded' space changes if the space above alters: if a ceiling is low, people will increase their personal space outwards away from the body.

Handedness

Operators who use a workstation or piece of equipment may not be right-handed. Consideration should be given to producing designs, if practicable, which can be used equally well by either left- or right-handed operators. Designs which force an operator to use their non-dominant hand may cause problems.

If a design is intended to be used by either right- or left-handed people, its layout should facilitate such usage.

Disabilities

The Disability Discrimination Act 2005 defines disability as: "A physical or mental impairment which has a substantial and long term adverse effect on a person's ability to carry out normal day-to-day activities." In this context, 'impairment' includes:
- physical impairments affecting the senses, such as sight and hearing
- mental impairments, including learning disabilities and mental illness.

Disabilities arise from 'impairments' which themselves are considered to result from the interference of normal functioning or structure. Such interferences can derive from illness, injury or genetics. The introduction of the Disability Discrimination Act has significant implications for employers, service providers and others. For example, in the workplace a designer may have to take into account the specific needs of wheelchair users, or operators who have lost limbs or who have impaired vision or hearing. There are other levels of disability (eg backache or arthritic conditions) which may not be covered by the legislation but which may also need to be considered.

Specific data are available to assist in designing for wheelchair users (see, for example, Kroemer 2006). As is the case when designing for able-bodied operators, it is much more efficient and cost-effective to design for disabilities in the early stages rather than to try to alter an environment after construction.

Although disabilities come in many guises, employers should be able to produce a working environment that suits the needs of someone with a disability in the same way that they would for an employee without disabilities. That is not to say that it will be a particularly straightforward process. However, if an employer takes the time to investigate what the limitations are of a particular individual's disability, while at the same time investigating what specialist equipment is available on the market, they can lessen the impact of the disability when the person is at work.

Anyone with a disability will have very specific needs and the employer should try to get to grips with the impact each form of impairment might have on how the work is done. For instance, some people may have reduced strength, co-ordination, mobility and control of their hands and fingers, so manipulative tasks, such as operating controls, may be difficult for them. If an individual's upper body strength is poor and they have a limited range of movement, they will be unsuitable for any tasks involving lifting or where they have to apply force, such as during an assembly-type task. They will also be limited in the extent to which they can reach forwards or upwards. If the person has difficulty in controlling their limbs, more specifically their arms, they will find grasping, positioning and controlling an object difficult. In a situation where the person has difficulty in controlling the movement of their head, this will make any task where they have to monitor a screen or process or read information much more difficult, due to the repositioning of the head required. Visually impaired people will have difficulty in reading documents and displays on screens, as might be expected. A hearing impairment has implications in situations where the person has to be part of a system of communication, such as in training or team briefings. If the person has a cognitive impairment, they may have difficulties with understanding what is being presented to them either verbally or in writing. By understanding exactly what the impairment means in terms of its impact on the person's performance, the employer can find individual solutions – it is unlikely that off-the-shelf solutions will suit.

Employers should aim to find out what assistive and adaptive products or equipment are available. Assistive technology relates to products or equipment that can maintain, improve or increase the functional abilities of someone with a disability. Adaptive technology relates to the hardware or software that is developed or altered to enable someone with a disability to use a computer system. Whatever form of assistance the employer provides, it should increase the person's independence in the workplace and enable them to complete their work more efficiently. It should be easy to use and should be compatible with any other systems in use at the person's workstation or within the work area. Whatever aids are used, they should be flexible enough to cope with variations in the work system, if such variations are a normal part of the work routine. Consideration also has to be given to whether any specialist equipment used by the person should be portable so that they can take it to different areas of the workplace if needed. In order for any assistive or adaptive technologies to work effectively, it is important that the employer confirms that the user is not only physically comfortable when using it, but they are 'emotionally' comfortable using it in front of their colleagues.

The physical layout of the workplace may need to be altered if someone comes to work in a wheelchair. Apart from the expected parking, access, light switch placement, washroom and handrail issues, additional consideration will need to be given to how the wheelchair will 'fit' alongside a desk, workbench or other workstation arrangement. Standard leg clearance provided under desks and workbenches is unlikely to be sufficient for wheelchair users, which may cause them to reach when working if adaptations are not made. Wheelchairs without joysticks need a work surface height of at least 725–750 mm to provide sufficient clearance. If the wheelchair incorporates a joystick, a work surface of about 800–850 mm will be needed for clearance. However, this higher level work surface will cause the individual to work with their arms raised and this may prove to be tiring. The most effective way of ensuring that a work surface suits the dimensions not only of the wheelchair but also the user is to run trials and to consider providing a degree of adjustment in the workstation. Electrically powered height adjustment would be more suitable for users who have difficulty in gripping adjustment levers or who lack strength to press or rotate controls forcefully.

To increase the likelihood of the user being able to work comfortably alongside a work surface, it is advisable to discuss with them whether they can use foldback or removable armrests on their wheelchair. If the armrests can be removed, this will allow greater access to the work surface. If they cannot be removed and the armrests prevent the user from getting close to the leading edge of their work surface, consideration should be given to providing a tray that can be attached to the wheelchair to function as their work surface.

Greater space will be required around workstations where wheelchair users work than would normally be the case with operators who can walk. This is because of the turning circle required when a wheelchair-bound operator leaves their workstation. They will need a clear space of at least 1,000 mm directly behind them to enable them to push back and rotate left or right before moving forwards. If two wheelchair users are likely to be working back to back, the clearance between them should be at least 1,550 mm. This should be increased still further if it is likely that a third wheelchair will pass between them when they are working. If a wheelchair user is required to remove parts from various bins in a storage area, they should have an unobstructed space of at least 1,500 × 1,500 mm to be able to turn around to face different sections of the storage facility. However, it should be kept in mind that reaching to retrieve objects from shelves and storage bins is fatiguing for many wheelchair users and should be kept to a minimum.

Additional consideration needs to be given to floor coverings, as some surfaces may make it more difficult to move a manually propelled wheelchair. Carpets with a deep pile may make it difficult for people with walking frames or sticks to move from one area to another. Floors that have a high-gloss finish may cause a walking disabled person to think that they may slip, thus undermining their confidence, even if the floor is unlikely to cause slipping problems. Carpets or wall coverings with busy patterns give visually impaired people a distorted perception of distance. Also, if they work where there is glare from surfaces, they often find it confusing as they move about the area. Glare and reflections also make it more difficult for people with hearing difficulties to lip read and interpret sign language.

The task

A task may require an operator to work in a particular manner, to use certain tools, to operate controls and to read information. These requirements will dictate elements such as the height of the work surface, reaching and viewing distances, and the shape and location of controls.

Therefore, before designing any workstation or piece of equipment, the designer should have a clear understanding of the task demands. To ensure that a clear profile of all these requirements is developed, a detailed task analysis should be carried out.

Task analysis
A task analysis allows the job to be broken down into parts, enabling the identification of all the sub-routines involved in an activity. This allows the designer to map out all movements, postures and forces required during the activity, as well as the information required by the operator. It is only by completing such a detailed and accurate task analysis that the designer can develop a suitable specification which matches the job requirements.

During the task analysis, information can be gathered using a range of sources:

- **Current documentation**, such as operational manuals, training manuals or previous reports relating to the work. This will usually provide detailed accounts of how work should be completed. However, operators do not always follow instructions in a manual, so an examination of documents should be supplemented with other forms of analysis.
- **Observation.** The observer should watch the operation and document the activities using a checklist, flow chart or description. Timing of the operation is necessary but only as a means of determining priority or duration of tasks. This is not an exercise to try to find ways of shaving a few seconds off the processing time.
- **Recording with cameras and videos.** This has the advantage that the work can be studied repeatedly, if necessary, without having to spend long periods at the work site or without asking the operator to repeat the same portion of the operation.

When completing a task analysis, consideration should be given to any unseen activities which may occur irregularly – for example, maintenance or other work completed on unobserved shifts. These activities should be reviewed before any final conclusions are drawn. There is a more detailed account of task analysis in Chapter 9 on risk assessment.

Working height
Working height is defined as the level at which the hands work. This is not always the same height as the work surface. As a general rule the operator should be able to complete their activities with their hands at, or slightly below, elbow height, whether they are seated or standing. Therefore the elbow height of the operator should be used as a guideline for determining work surface height.

If the user population presents the designer with a range of varying elbow heights, the taller operators should be catered for and platforms or duckboards should be provided for shorter operators.

Some designers may raise objections about having to provide a range of platforms of different heights. Given that operators can generally work in the range that falls at or slightly below elbow height, if the most appropriately dimensioned platform is used, operators of different statures using this single platform should find that it allows them to work somewhere within that optimal range. Therefore, it may not be necessary to provide platforms of varying heights.

By providing platforms, further problems, such as tripping and hampering the transport of items around the area, are introduced. In addition, other practical issues, such as the cleaning of these platforms, their manual movement and the additional workspace required to position them, will have to be taken into account.

The need or desirability of presenting a work surface at elbow height is not the only consideration when determining working heights. The following are examples of other factors that need to be considered:
- If operators are involved in an assembly operation, they may place the components for assembly on their work surface. If the work surface has been set at elbow height, the addition of the parts to the work surface increases the working height above elbow height. This working height is increased further if the parts are placed in a jig and if the operator uses a tool, such as a drill, during the assembly process. It is quite common to walk around an assembly area and find that most operators are working with their shoulders raised and their elbows sticking out to the sides. Such postures are indicative of a working height which is too high.
- The force requirements of a task will also influence the appropriateness of work surface height. If operators have to apply a large degree of manual force when assembling a part, or if they are using a tool such as a hammer, they may find that a work surface set 10–15 cm below elbow height is more acceptable. However, the work surface should not be set so low that the operator ends up stooping. If the heavy work is only one part of an overall operation, it may be necessary to provide the operator with two surfaces of different working heights.
- If the operator is carrying out fine or precise work, they may require the work surface to be raised above elbow height. In such cases, a work surface set 5–10 cm above elbow height may help. Tasks requiring high levels of visual acuity may need to be performed slightly below shoulder height so as to avoid the need for the operator to lean

forwards and downwards towards the workpiece. Padded supports for the arms, hands or wrists should be provided in such a situation to reduce the loading on the shoulder muscles and to steady the hands. The design of these supports should be such that they do not hinder the operator. A level of adjustment in the pads may be advisable. In addition to raising the work surface for fine work, consideration should be given to tilting the surface towards the operator. This will further minimise the need to lean forwards towards the work area. It will also reduce the potential for seated operators to raise their arms and bend their wrists when working.

Visual requirements
The visual demands of a task will have a direct bearing on head and neck postures. If operators are required to read or inspect an item during the course of their work, it is important that the object of attention is presented in an appropriate orientation. If it is not, the operator will have to alter their posture to complete the task.

The eye usually adopts a downward cast of about 15° below the horizontal when resting and when the operator is seated. When standing, the downward gaze is usually about 10° below horizontal. These ranges represent the normal line of sight. However, the eye has a total range of movement of about 60° below the horizontal. The most comfortable viewing is achieved within the band ranging from horizontal to 30° below the horizontal. This range has been referred to as the preferred zone for visual displays but it has been recognised that the zone covering up to 15° below the horizontal is the best area for attention, scanning, viewing objects at a distance and viewing details and colours.

Non-priority visual tasks can be performed in the less favourable visual zones, ie outside the 30° range, and can involve occasional but small head and eye movement. Very low priority tasks, carried out on an irregular basis, can also call for the movement of the trunk. The priority of the task determines the location of the source of information and the postures to be adopted by the eyes, head, neck and trunk. Therefore, given its importance, the priority of the task should be quantified early in the design process.

A viewing distance of 350–500 mm is considered acceptable, but this range should be reduced if the work is detailed and extended if the object is large.

Efforts should be made to ensure that obstacles do not block free viewing by the operator. Designers should take account of operator stature, both seated and standing, when determining the effect of obstacles, as objects in the visual field may become obstacles as an operator's eye height is reduced; in other words, a short operator may not be able to see over other objects in the visual field to focus on the target object.

As a general rule, high priority, frequent or sustained work, or work requiring high speed scanning or high levels of accuracy, should be positioned so that it can be read or attended to when the head is upright (or slightly inclined), facing forwards and in a relaxed position. Where there is a need to look at very detailed work, magnification should be considered.

Controls

If the task requires operators to use controls during their activities, these controls should be given as much consideration as any other workstation or equipment element. Controls are the means with which operators interact with the system; if operators are to respond appropriately to work demands, they need to be able to use the controls efficiently and accurately. And, given the critical nature of control use in some situations, it is obviously essential that operators are able to differentiate between controls, adjust them to the appropriate degree and operate them correctly even (or especially) in emergency situations.

As in the case of designing a workstation or piece of equipment, a task analysis is required to determine the final form a control should take. The task analysis will allow knowledge of significant aspects such as the forces used, the speed and accuracy required, the pattern and priority of usage, and the frequency and duration of use. These will guide both the design and location of the control. The following important aspects should be considered during control design.

Force

If limited or low levels of force are required, such as to operate an on–off switch, then a toggle switch, push button or key-lock would be acceptable.

If greater degrees of force are required, the design should allow for the force to be applied easily. In such situations reliance on the fingers alone to complete the action would not be appropriate, so the control should take a form which allows for the application of force using the whole hand, such as in the case of hand-push buttons, levers, joysticks, cranks, pedals and handwheels.

The duration of the effort should also influence the final form that the control takes, and consideration should be given to the 'weakest' operator, taking into account age, sex, fitness and training.

Feedback

The guidance of a machine is likely to be more accurate if it moves in a direction and at a speed that corresponds to the movement of the control. If the operator experiences high levels of resistance when using a control, or if there is little obvious movement or sensation of movement in the control, the operator may not be sure that the desired movement has been achieved. However, if this is corrected by making a control more sensitive, it should not then be set at a level which permits accidental activation.

Layout

High priority controls should be located in the primary work envelope directly in front of the operator. If they are intended to be used by both upper or lower limbs simultaneously, they should be located so that they can be accessed easily and equally by both limbs. If the intention is that both left- and right-handed operators will use the controls, they should be located centrally. This will also allow for use by either hand by any given operator.

Function

Controls with a similar function should be grouped together, in order of priority. However, they should not form more than a row of three and a column of three. Controls in a group should not interfere with each other during use.

If controls are used in sequence during an operation, their layout should match the sequence and their usage should be accomplished smoothly. A standardised left-to-right, top-to-bottom order is the most acceptable. If the sequence is unchanging, consideration should be given to interlocking the controls which will make their operation more efficient and will control the potential for errors. If particular controls are to be left out of a sequence on occasion, the potential for erroneous inclusion in the sequence can be avoided by coding the control (see below).

Expectations or stereotypes

Expectations will influence the acceptability of a design and the error rate associated with its use. Operators may expect or assume that a control will be in a particular location. As a consequence, any 'blind' search and use may lead to errors. Cultural stereotypes will 'train' an operator to expect certain responses from a control; for example, flicking the switch upwards typically turns the system off in Europe but on in the United States.

Designing contrary to stereotypes and expectations can lead to critical situations, particularly during emergencies, when the operator is subject to stress and prone to reverting to the stereotype. Such designs may also lead to longer training times and a reduction in speed and accuracy during early usage – and, even with experience, reaction times will be slower.

Compatibility
Operators will expect controls to move in a direction which is compatible with the layout of a display or system. They will also expect controls on similar machines to operate in a similar manner. Compatibility is particularly important in situations where:
- the operations are complex
- training has not been extensive
- sequences of use are not always the same
- the operator is responsible for monitoring and interacting with a range of machines
- where any mistakes are costly or dangerous.

Coding
Controls can be coded by adding features which allow them to be distinguished more easily. For example:
- **location** – as already discussed, operators have expectations of where they think a control should be located
- **shape** – it has been shown that in conditions of stress, an operator can still distinguish up to 12 different controls by their shape, especially when the shape of the control offers an indication of its function
- **size** – it has been shown that operators can distinguish up to three different sizes of control in moments of stress, suggesting the use of small, medium and large controls
- **colour** – different colours may be used to distinguish controls. However, such a system has disadvantages: it will only work efficiently in well-illuminated environments; it takes longer for the operator to respond as the meaning of the colour has to be interpreted before action can be taken; and cultural stereotypes may interfere with appropriate reactions (eg red generally represents 'danger' or 'stop' in the UK while in China it is associated with happiness). Thought should also be given to the effects of colour blindness in operators
- **labelling** – written labels can describe the function of a control. To be effective the label should be capable of being read easily when standing or sitting in the position where a control will be used, and should be read from left to right (vertical instructions take longer to read). Labelling has its disadvantages: labels may not survive in a legible form in a very dirty or wet environment (embossed labels should be used); the success of the instruction will be determined by the literacy level of the reader; and (as with colour coding) the information has to be interpreted before action can be taken, hence increasing reaction time

- **relation to displays** – controls and their related displays should be positioned so that both can be viewed simultaneously without the need for adopting an irregular posture. To facilitate this, controls should be close to the display or at least grouped in a similar pattern to that of the display. Layouts of groups of controls and displays should be compatible, so that, for example, the bottom left control refers to the bottom left display. Relationships can be highlighted by borders around displays and their related controls, or by placing both on a coloured panel.

Displays

The important requirements of any display are that the desired information can be read and understood easily, rapidly and accurately. Therefore, to produce the appropriate design, thought should be given to the type of information being presented, the levels of interpretation and response required and whether the information has to be memorised. The location and layout of displays should be given similar consideration to that for controls (discussed above). There are additional points to consider:

- **Dials** can carry a wide range of information but are not considered appropriate for providing warnings or complex information.
- **Lights** can convey information as a stand-alone light, as the illumination for a button or as part of colour coding. They are useful for drawing attention to urgent information or warnings, particularly when flashing.
- **Digital displays** are useful in situations where information changes slowly, numerical data are presented, high levels of accuracy are required and the duration of reading bouts is short. Digital displays have disadvantages, particularly when information is changing rapidly and when the direction of change or ranges of movement are important.
- **Annunciators** (devices which give a visual indication as to which of a number of electric circuits has operated, such as an indicator that identifies exactly which area of a burglar alarm has been triggered) can be useful to confirm that a particular control has been activated, or to provide a signal that action is required.
- **Auditory displays** are commonly used as a means of providing warnings. Their frequency and intensity should be compatible with the environment. Alternatives to sound include systems which are based on tactile (touch), kinaesthetic (movement) or olfactory (smell) information; these are particularly effective if deaf or partially deaf operators are working in the area.

Labels

The most effective label is one that carries information which is short and to the point while still managing to convey a full message. If a message is too long it may not be read. If a message is written in positive terms it is more likely to be acted on than one written in either passive or negative terms. For example: "Pushing the red button will stop the conveyor" (positive); "The conveyor can be stopped by pushing the red button" (passive); and "Pushing the green button will not stop the conveyor" (negative).

The most difficult label to understand is the negative one, as the reader has to understand first what they are not supposed to do before they can work out what they are supposed to do. An everyday example of this is a road sign which states that parking is not allowed between certain hours. This takes longer to comprehend than a sign which outlines when parking is allowed.

A label should be capable of being seen and identified easily even in the poorest working conditions. The reading of the message should be facilitated by using appropriate letter/number size, typographic style, layout and spacing. Jargon or a 'bureaucratic' style should be avoided. Simple words and sentences should be used. If abbreviations have to be included, they should be readily understood by all operators. Etched and embossed labels will probably last longer than painted or printed ones.

Symbols
In some cases, a symbol may be more appropriate than a written message as it will carry information much more succinctly. In addition, symbols should be more readily understood by operators who do not know the relevant language well or who cannot read.

One of the disadvantages of symbols is that, although they may draw an operator's attention to a problem situation or provide advance warning about states of functioning, they do not always convey what action is required once the situation has been recognised. In addition, symbols are completely redundant if the reader has not received any training relating to their meaning and the necessary actions required. In this context, there may be some advantages to using pictograms where the appropriate action is demonstrated as part of the graphic.

To ensure that symbol use is successful, the design should use widely agreed and accepted standards, such as those produced by the International Organization for Standardization. An example of an internationally accepted symbol is that used in a car to indicate which control operates the fog lights.

Additional design considerations

Future use
Many workstations or pieces of equipment are not used as originally intended. This is usually as a result of an alteration in product design or processing procedures. The consequence of this change in use is that many operators are forced to work in highly irregular postures, or apply higher levels of force than was originally planned, simply because the designer had only thought in 'here-and-now' terms and neglected to consider the possible future uses of the design.

If designers are able to build a degree of flexibility into their specifications, the system will be capable of manipulation at a later date without compromising the safety and wellbeing of operators.

Adjustability
The best method of ensuring that the majority of the working population can use a design without undermining health and safety is to make it adjustable. The adjustment feature does not have to be complex or sophisticated to work, nor have to operate through a gas-lift mechanism, crank handle or electrically powered control panel. Workstations can be fitted with adjustable legs or feet which can be unscrewed to extend their length. This is particularly effective if the same operator will use a workstation for a period of time and it does not have to be altered frequently for other operators. Some workstations can be made from a frame which can be unbolted and adjusted, then bolted together again. The greater the degree of adjustment and flexibility offered to operators, the more likely they are to be comfortable when they work. The easier an adjustment is, the more likely it will be made by the operator. The appropriate tools should be available to adjust a workstation (eg the right size of spanner).

Sharp edges
Workstations and equipment commonly do not have rounded edges. Operators often lean on these edges and, apart from the obvious outcomes such as bruising or abrasions, compression of the skin will reduce the blood flow into the hands and can contribute to the development of ULDs over time. To minimise the likelihood that cumulative damage to the limbs will result, contact edges should be rounded or padded.

Cold surfaces
Working in, or coming into contact with, low temperatures can contribute to the development of ULDs. Therefore, if operators use work surfaces which are cold to the touch, such as stainless steel inspection and packing

lines in the food industry, they should be discouraged from leaning on them. If operators cannot be prevented from coming in contact with these surfaces, the surfaces should be padded.

Seating
Generally, seats in industry appear to be viewed simply as perches for taking the weight off one's buttocks, legs and feet. It is quite common to find operators using chairs which are in such a poor state that they are taped together, or have had packing materials stapled onto them to make them more comfortable. If more effort is put into the design and selection of seating, operators will be less likely to suffer from backache and more likely to remain comfortable throughout the day.

If an operator is required to sit down when working, and to use equipment in the most efficient way possible, it is essential that:
- the chair is adjustable for height
- the backrest has independent height adjustment
- the backrest can be altered for inclination
- the backrest is adequately shaped and includes a distinct lumbar support
- the seat can accommodate the largest hips
- any armrests are padded and, preferably, adjustable for height
- adjustments are easy to reach and use from the seated position
- the chair is (ideally) capable of being moved towards or away from the work surface by the operator rather than being fixed in one location
- if the chair is raised to a high point, an adjustable footrest or footring is provided
- any pedals are capable of being adjusted for height in relation to the operator's feet
- the workstation design is compatible with the use of the seat.

Safety
Although the emphasis has been on designing to suit the individual, consideration should also be given to safety issues. When determining appropriate workstation or equipment dimensions, an additional allowance has to be made in some situations to ensure that the operator is at a safe distance from hazards. Such hazards may include parts of a machine which saw, press, spray, weld, cut or eject parts.

When determining safe distances, consideration should be given to whole or part body movement during reaching and leaning, the insertion of a limb through an aperture, or the squeeze point where part of the body is pushed through an access point, eg pushing the leg through a gap between two pieces of equipment.

It is essential to study all relevant national and international standards carefully during this phase of the design process.

Selection and use

Having developed the workstation or equipment design to the point where it is ready for construction, the designer should consider a mock-up and subsequent trial before committing to full introduction of the change to the working environment. This also applies to purchasing decisions regarding a design provided by a supplier. Decisions should only be made following the design's use in a near-normal situation.

Mock-ups

In the first instance, a chipboard mock-up should be assembled to test dimensions and layouts. A range of operators of varying sizes should be asked to try the mock-up to determine whether it is suitable for use. It is recommended that a level of adjustment is built into the mock-up at this stage so that operators can try out various settings. This will assist in finally deciding on any single setting if the workstation is to be non-adjustable. If adjustments are to be built into the mock-up, they should be capable of being made quickly so that the operator can make a sound comparison of settings.

At the end of this stage, the designer will have an indication of maximum and minimum acceptable working limits and areas of convenient reach and comfort that suit the likely range of operators.

Trials

Having established the acceptable working limits and layouts during the mock-up phase, prototypes can be developed and used in a full trial phase. During the trials, as many operators as possible should use the design under near-normal working conditions. The operators should be representative of the normal user population in terms of skill, age, size and background. However, allowance for 'individual differences' will have to be made. Such individual differences can result from personality, attitude and level of alertness.

During the trials, operators should alter one dimension at a time (eg working height) between minimum and maximum acceptable levels, making comparisons between each. All comments regarding the design should be recorded in full. Informal verbal feedback which has not been recorded is not a sufficient basis on which to change a design. The designer, or trial manager, also needs to act as an 'action interpreter' during the trials, as operators may carry out movements or change settings without providing feedback or without realising that they have actually done something. All this information should be collected and evaluated.

Once operators have worked with the prototype and provided feedback on acceptable and unacceptable working limits, a degree of overlap should be found between the preferred settings. This will indicate the level at which a dimension can be set. If such an overlap is not apparent, it may be necessary to redesign the workstation or equipment or to provide a level of adjustment in the final design.

If a workstation or piece of equipment is provided by an outside supplier, it should be placed in the working environment and used 'normally' for several weeks by a range of operators. All feedback should be recorded and analysed at the end of the trial phase.

Layout
Having developed a workstation design, consideration should be given to the layout of its surface. Items should not be put on a surface in a random position. Their location should be determined by their use. A distinction is recommended between primary and secondary items. Primary items are those that are used frequently, and secondary items are those that are used less frequently. Primary items are placed within the primary movement envelope of the operator, ie the area that falls directly in front, within their optimum reaching distance. Secondary items are located in the secondary movement envelope, which falls outside the primary envelope but does not exceed the maximum reach of the operator. Determining the primary and secondary layout of items will apply to books, files, telephones, tools, waste bins, components and controls. It may also be beneficial to consider laying out work items to suit sub-tasks as well as the overall task.

Training
In order to achieve the most from any new workstation or equipment, it is essential to give operators full instruction on use. If such instruction is not given, operators will develop their own way of using the items which may not be the most suitable or safest method. In addition, there is the possibility that without training on how to use the workstation or equipment, operators may refuse to use them.

Supervision
Having trained the operators in the use of a workstation or equipment, it is important that proper use is maintained. This can be achieved through adequate supervision. Supervisors should encourage the continued and

appropriate use of any new items and should discourage any misuse or neglect of them. Feedback from supervisors to designers is an important element in continuing good ergonomics design.

Maintenance and housekeeping

New designs introduced into the workplace should be maintained satisfactorily. If this does not happen, the item's condition may deteriorate and eventually undermine its effective use. Operators, in turn, should ensure that poor housekeeping does not result in the new design being more difficult to use. Again, this is an issue for supervisors to deal with.

Environmental conditions

If maximum effective use of a design is to be achieved, the environment in which it will function should be appropriate for the operators and their tasks. Consideration should be given to noise levels, the thermal environment, lighting and vibration.

Noise levels

'Noise' is any unwanted sound. From a legal standpoint, in order to avoid hearing impairment noise should not exceed 85 dB(A) during a working day. But hearing impairment is not the only reason that noise control is important. Excessive noise can affect concentration and attention, and can impede communication between operators. In addition, warning sounds such as truck horns or fire alarms can be masked. Noise can also act as a general stressor.

Noise can be controlled at source in a variety of ways, including:
- placing heavy, vibrating equipment on a separate, rigid structure
- using sound-isolating joints between vibrating equipment and the floor
- using vibration isolation mounts
- using damping materials, mufflers and acoustic screens.

If the intensity of sound cannot be controlled at source, then operators should be provided with some form of protection, such as ear defenders or ear plugs. The fact that some defenders and plugs are not selective in reducing noise exposure – and may reduce an operator's ability to hear warning sounds – should be taken into account.

Thermal environment

The thermal environment can result in a decrease in the quality of performance if it does not suit the operator and the task they are completing. If it is too hot or cold, operators can become irritable, lose concentration and become uncomfortable through perspiring or shivering.

As physical activity tends to generate body heat, consideration should be given to the type of work being completed before temperatures are set in the environment. If operators are involved in heavy manual work, they will require a cooler environment than sedentary workers (eg keyboard users). As temperatures start to dip below 16 °C, manual dexterity will be impaired. This can eventually contribute to the development of ULDs and operators should therefore have appropriate protective clothing.

Humidity (the level of moisture in the air) and air flow will also influence operators' wellbeing and should be controlled as far as possible. Adjustments to temperature or humidity settings may be required as more people move into an area and as further equipment is introduced.

Computer-controlled temperature settings should be monitored carefully as they tend to work on 'averages' in an area. For example, the average temperature in an office may be 20.5 °C but this may be maintained by blasts of cold air through two air vents located in the corners of the room. This may prove to be unacceptable to the operators who sit at these points.

Lighting
Lighting at an appropriate level will help to maintain acceptable levels of quality and performance, as well as avoiding operator discomfort, eg headaches and eye fatigue. The required level of illuminance – the amount of light falling onto a surface – should be determined by the task demands (eg visual display unit (VDU) work requires a lower lighting level than a written or inspection task). Luminance – the amount of light emitted from a surface – should also be controlled, as excessive luminance can cause glare. Glare should be eliminated as far as possible from the environment because of its effect on visual performance.

The location of the light should also be considered. Siting lights on the ceiling or walls may not be the best option. Again, the task requirements will dictate where lights should be located.

Vibration
Vibration is associated with the development of ULDs and back injuries, and operators should be protected from it as far as possible. Operators can be exposed to whole and part body vibration through the use of vibrating tools, when driving trucks and from working with and leaning against vibrating machinery. The methods discussed above for reducing noise levels will also have the effect of reducing vibration in many cases.

Summary

Posture
- Postures should not require high levels of static effort to sustain them.
- Variations in working posture should be permitted but not at the expense of operator comfort or performance.
- Designers should consider the use of either sitting or standing postures early in their decision-making.
- Sitting down while working reduces the degree of static work required of the body.
- The operator should be able to adopt an upright and forward-facing posture.
- If standing, the body weight should be borne by both feet equally.
- The posture should be balanced so that additional muscle activity is not required to support or stabilise the body as a whole, or individual limbs, such as would result from leaning forwards.
- The head should remain reasonably upright or slightly inclined to the front.
- The limbs, trunk and head should be positioned so that the joints are not forced to go beyond their mid-point in terms of the range of movement.
- The hands should not have to pass above elbow height regularly or for long periods.
- The largest (appropriate) muscle groups should be used to apply necessary forces in a direction which is compatible with their structure.

Anthropometrics
- Designers should consider the body size of the user population.
- Designs should not be based on the 'average' person.

Access
- Operators must be able to reach and use their workstation or equipment easily.
- Access dimensions should cater to the largest operator who may need to work in an area.
- Allowances should be made for the use of any tools or other equipment in the area, as well as space requirements for storage of items.
- Allowances should be made for maintenance operations and the personnel who will carry out repair work, the tools they may use and the largest parts of the machine or workstation that may have to be moved.
- Consideration should be given to the work to be carried out by operators following any system failure – access should be provided at relevant points in the work area.

Clearance
- Vertical or overhead clearance should cater for the tallest operator who will work in an area – allowances for any headgear or footwear should be included.
- Side-to-side and forward–backward clearance should also cater for the largest operator who may work in an area.
- Foot clearance is required at floor level so that operators can move closer to work surfaces or equipment (if necessary, adjustments should be made for pedals).
- Seated operators should be provided with knee clearance that caters to the largest hips, the width of the seat and the longest thigh, and permits forward or upward leg movement.

Reach
- Frequent or sustained work should remain within the operator's optimum reaching distance (defined as the area that can be swept easily by the forearm when there is a 90° angle at the elbow and the upper arm is hanging naturally at the side of the trunk).
- Designs should cater to the shortest arm length and allow for the fact that the dimensions for extended arm length are reduced if the operator grips an object.
- The reaching distances to items such as pedals should be matched against user leg lengths.

Personal space
- Personal space should be taken into account when designing several workstations or pieces of equipment to be located in close proximity for use by several operators.

Handedness
- Consideration should be given to the use of designs by both left- and right-handed operators.
- The ability to use two hands simultaneously or alternatively should be incorporated into the design.

Disabilities
- Disabilities should be considered and catered for during the design process.

Task analysis
- Task requirements must be fully understood before the design process. They should be identified via an in-depth and accurate task analysis.

Working height
- Working height may be different to work surface height and is defined as the height at which the hands work.
- When setting surface heights, the work should generally be presented to the operator at or slightly below elbow height unless the task requirements demand a different level.
- Adjustments should be made to surface height to allow for the addition of parts, jigs and tools to the work surface.
- Consideration should be given to other task requirements – such as the forces required and the precision of the work – which may also dictate an alteration in work surface height.

Visual requirements
- The most comfortable viewing is achieved within the band that ranges 30° below the horizontal eye level.
- Tasks which require attention, scanning or viewing at a distance, in detail and of colours, should be located in the zone which covers up to 15° below the horizontal.
- Non- or low-priority tasks can be located outside the 30° from horizontal range and can involve head, neck and trunk movements.
- High priority, frequent, sustained, high speed or accurate work should be carried out when the head is upright, facing forwards and in a relaxed position.

Controls
- The design and layout of controls should be based on task requirements.
- The force and duration of force will influence the shape of the control.
- If the movement of the control corresponds to that of the machine its operation will be more accurate.
- High priority controls should be directly in front of the operator and located for use by the appropriate hand(s).
- Controls with a similar function or sequence should be grouped together but with no more than three per row and three per column.
- Stereotypes will influence acceptability of a control design and levels of errors during its use.
- There should be compatibility between controls on similar machines and between controls and related displays.
- Coding can be used to distinguish between controls.

Displays
- Displays should be located in a similar manner to controls.
- The type of display should match the requirements of the task and how the information has to be used.

Labels
- Labels should carry short, pertinent information which conveys the full message.
- Information should be in a positive form.
- The label should be constructed to remain legible in the working conditions.
- The style and layout of text should facilitate easy reading of the message.

Symbols
- Operators should receive training in the interpretation of symbols and the actions required following identification of the given situation.

Future use
- A degree of flexibility should be built into a design to allow for future changes of production which may necessitate different use of the system.

Adjustability
- A good range of simple-to-use adjustments will make it more likely that the operator will be comfortable.

Sharp edges
- Operators should be prevented from leaning on sharp edges of equipment or the edges should be padded or rounded.

Cold surfaces
- Operators should be protected from cold surfaces by either preventing them from leaning on them or by padding them.

Seating
- The chair should be adjustable for height.
- The backrest should have independent height adjustment.
- The backrest should be adjustable for inclination.
- The backrest should be adequately shaped and include a distinct lumbar support.
- The seat should accommodate the largest hips.
- If armrests are supplied they should be padded and, preferably, height-adjustable.
- Adjustments should be easy to reach and use from the seated position.
- The chair should be capable of being moved to and from the work surface (rather than being fixed).
- If the chair is raised to a high point, an adjustable footrest or footring should be provided.

- Any pedals should be capable of being adjusted for height in relation to the operator's feet.
- The workstation design should be compatible with the use of the seat.

Safety
- Safety considerations should be incorporated into the design process.

Mock-ups and trials
- Before full introduction of a new design into the workplace, it should be tried out, with as many operators as possible testing the various settings.

Layout
- Items used regularly should be located close to the operator to avoid regular or sustained reaching.

Training
- All operators should have thorough training in the use of their new workstation and/or equipment.

Supervision
- Supervisors should ensure that operators continue to use their new workstation or equipment in the intended manner.

Maintenance and housekeeping
- Designs should not be permitted to deteriorate over time.

Environmental conditions
- Environmental factors such as noise, lighting, heating and vibration will all influence the acceptability of a new design. They should be set at levels which suit the operator and match the requirements of the task.

References and further reading

Bittner A C and Champney P C (eds). *Advances in industrial ergonomics and safety VII*. Taylor & Francis, 1995.

Bridger R S. *Introduction to ergonomics* (third edition). Taylor & Francis, 2009.

Collingsworth J and Rehahn A (eds). *Design for disability: a handbook for students and teachers*. London Guildhall University, 1993.

Corlett E N and Clark T S. *The ergonomics of workspaces and machines*. Taylor & Francis, 1995.

Delleman N J, Haslegrave C M and Chaffin D B. *Working postures and movements. Tools for evaluation and engineering.* CRC Press, 2004.

Grandjean E. *Fitting the task to the man* (fourth edition). Taylor & Francis, 1988.

Health and Safety Executive. *A pain in your workplace? Ergonomic problems and solutions*, HS(G)121. HSE Books, 1994.

Health and Safety Executive. *Sound solutions*, HS(G)138. HSE Books, 1995.

Helander M. *A guide to the ergonomics of manufacturing* (second edition). Taylor & Francis, 2006.

Jones J C. *Design methods.* Van Nostrand Reinhold, 1992.

Kroemer K H E. *Extra-ordinary ergonomics. How to accommodate small and big persons, the disabled and elderly, expectant mothers and children.* Taylor & Francis, 2006.

Pheasant S. *Ergonomics – standards and guidelines for designers.* Taylor & Francis, 1987.

Pheasant S and Haslegrave C M. *Bodyspace – anthropometry, ergonomics and the design of work* (third edition). Taylor & Francis, 2006.

Roebuck J A. *Anthropometric methods: designing to fit the human body.* Human Factors and Ergonomics Society, 1995.

Sheridan T B (ed.). *Analysis, design and evaluation of man-machine systems.* Elsevier Science, 1995.

4 Hand tool design and use

The use of hand tools can be traced back to the Stone Age. Their purpose was to extend the use of the hand, allowing it to complete tasks which it would not be capable of normally. Tools allowed the hand to centralise and deliver power, resulting in the slicing, cutting, smashing, piercing or scraping of an object. That purpose and capability remains unchanged today – but, of course, today's tools are made from different materials and many are power-driven. Unfortunately, the modern adaptation of the basic tool design has resulted in an increase in the potential for injuries. But that is not to say that a simple tool, such as a hammer, is without its problems.

Injuries occur as a result of a tool being designed solely from a function perspective, which ignores the effect its form can have on the user. Obviously, meeting the requirements for use is important but this does not have to be achieved at the expense of the user. If a poorly designed tool is used day in, day out, this could result in decreased productivity as well as injury.

In some cases, users are not provided with any tools and find that they have to use their own hands. For example, it is quite common for workers involved in assembly operations to use their hands like mallets when pushing components into position. This practice can have a destructive effect on the limbs and should not be allowed to continue.

The hand

The starting point when designing a tool should be an examination of the hand, as this is the means by which the user will hold and operate the tool.

Gripping

The hand is a versatile, flexible tool in itself and possesses a neuromuscular power unsurpassed by any other part of the body. It can be used for extremes of function ranging from the primitive grabbing of an object, such as a spanner, to the delicate manipulations required during a fine motor task, such as making delicate pieces of jewellery. The hand's use of such power grasps or precision grips will be determined by the characteristics of the object being gripped and the task demands.

To understand the concept of the power grip, imagine the hand making a fist where the fingers are wrapped around one side of an object and the

thumb around the other, eg when gripping the handle of a hammer. There are three separate categories of the power grip, distinguished by the direction of the force:
- parallel to the forearm, eg when using a plane or saw
- at an angle to the forearm, eg when using a mallet
- rotating about the forearm, eg when using a screwdriver.

The precision grip is used for precise manipulations which require the object to be held between the fingertips and thumb. Examples of precision grip tasks include picking a loose hair from clothing, turning a key in a lock or using a pen. The precision grip can be either internal or external. Holding a pen is an example of an external precision grip, because the object is outside the palm. Holding a knife when eating a meal is considered an internal precision grip as the knife handle is held inside the hand.

Often, a combination of both power and precision grips will be used to complete an operation. For example, when returning the lid to a soft drink bottle a precision grip is used to hold and locate the lid carefully before switching to the power grip for final tightening to ensure that it is secure. It is considered (Putz-Anderson 1988) that the power grip provides the individual with five times the gripping strength of the precision grip, which suggests that the strength requirements of an activity can be reduced if the task can be completed using the more powerful grip. In terms of tool design, if individuals can use a power grip to hold a tool they can use a lower percentage of their overall gripping strength, which will in turn be less fatiguing for their muscles.

Force

The hand can exert the most force when in a neutral, or near neutral, position (ie when a line runs virtually straight from the elbow through the forearm and wrist and into the hand). Once the hand is bent downwards or to either side of the wrist, the grasping power of the hand is reduced. The loss of grip strength following deviation of the wrist is illustrated below.

It would appear, therefore, that in order to allow the hand to work most effectively it should be allowed to adopt a neutral posture. This should be taken into consideration during tool design or selection.

Design features

Hand or arm injuries following the use of tools may indicate inappropriate tool design or improper use. Such injuries can range from something as simple as a callus or blister, to something more severe such as a ULD. In most instances, injuries can be avoided by ensuring that tools are properly designed, taking both the user and the task into account.

Handle design
One of the most common complaints made by workers is that they have to bend their wrist when using tools. For some reason, designers have until recently designed most tools with straight handles and heads. As a result, when the tool user works on or against a flat surface, they will usually have to bend their wrist.

The user experiences a loss of grip strength from working with a bent wrist. To overcome this problem, and to control the tool fully, the pressure of the grip may be increased. Increasing the grip pressure will speed up the rate at which the muscles fatigue. Therefore, to avoid the reduction of grip strength and subsequent acceleration of muscle fatigue, maintaining a straight wrist should be a primary design and selection consideration. This can be achieved easily in many work situations by bending the handle (see below).

In some situations, bending of the wrist can be eliminated by providing a pistol grip tool where the handle is bent by 70–90°. However, this design is only acceptable if used in an appropriate orientation. In general, pistol grip tools should only be used when the tool axis is horizontal. If the tool axis is vertical or the force is applied perpendicularly to the work plane, a straight grip should be used. Examples of wrist posture, tool design and orientation of use are shown below.

Handle construction
If users have to work with a tool which has a smooth, hard handle constructed of a material such as flat metal or plastic, they may experience difficulty in stopping their hand from sliding across the handle as they apply force. To prevent the hand from moving, the user will increase the pressure of the grip – this situation is made worse if their hands are hot and sweaty.

Care should be taken if the handle is designed with flutes or ridges (eg a screwdriver). If these flutes or ridges are too deep or have sharp edges, they may increase the pressure placed on the soft tissue of the hand when the user grips the handle and this may result in discomfort and pain. Soft oval indents on a handle are preferable – they allow improved purchase without causing pressure points.

If handles are made of metal, they may remain cold throughout the course of the shift. Exposure to colder temperatures may increase the possibility of a user developing a ULD, so the use of metals in handle design should be avoided.

It is recommended that soft, compliant and textured materials are used on handles so that they are easier to grip, although care needs to be taken that these cannot be damaged easily, subsequently presenting sharp edges.

Application of force
If users have to apply downward force when working with a vertically oriented tool, such as a drill fitted with a parallel sleeve, they may find that their hands tend to slip downwards during the operation. In an attempt to prevent this, they will increase the force used to grip the sleeve. The need to use this level of additional force could be controlled by simply fitting a moulded collar to the bottom of the sleeve. This would prevent the hand from moving and would allow the user to apply the downward pressure necessary to operate the tool without the need to increase grip pressure. A similar approach could be taken to the design of handles on tools such as pliers, where thumb stops could be added to prevent the hand from slipping. Any such alterations will obviously be dependent on the particular operation being performed.

Contouring
Contouring along the handle may not achieve the intended result of helping the user to hold it firmly and comfortably. Contouring, particularly finger grooves, should be avoided altogether unless the design is based on anthropometric dimensions and will actually fit the users' hands sufficiently. If the finger grooves have not been based on anthropometric dimensions, users may find that their own fingers do not fall in line naturally with the grooves, necessitating an alteration in their natural gripping position to suit these contours. Deviation from the comfortable or natural gripping position of the hand will result in a reduction in grip strength and an increase in pressure exerted by the user to ensure that they hold the tool firmly.

Handle size
Grip strength required to complete a task will also be influenced by the diameter of the handle. It is not uncommon for a small tool to be provided with an equally small handle. However, reducing the size of the handle makes it more difficult to grip. This is also the case if the handle is too big to fit comfortably into the hand. In both cases, users will have to increase the pressure of their grip to ensure that they maintain a firm hold of the tool and control it during use. It has been recommended that the diameter of a single-handle tool should be approximately 40 mm, which will be suitable for most purposes. However, in situations where torque is

exerted about the axis of the handle, as in the case of using a screwdriver, it may be advisable to provide a handle with a larger diameter, possibly up to 65 mm. Although there may be a decrease in grip strength as a result of going beyond the optimum handle diameter, this may be offset by the increase in mechanical advantage. As general rule, the handle should be of a size that allows for a slight overlap of the thumb and fingers when the tool is gripped by a small individual.

If the handle of a tool is too short, it may press into the palm of the hand during use. This is quite common when using tools such as pliers or paint scrapers. The palm is rich in nerves and blood vessels, and compression by the handle can lead to a reduction of blood flow and nerve damage. Many users working with short-handled tools report feelings of numbness and tingling, and this can become more serious with long term use of the tool. The handle should be at least 100 mm in length. To provide users with some freedom in terms of where they place their hand along the handle, a length of 115–120 mm is preferable. The desirable handle length will be influenced by the use of gloves; a further 10 mm should be added to the length if they are worn. In some circumstances it may be appropriate to fit an extending handle to a tool to eliminate the need for the operator to work with their arms raised above shoulder height or for them to work with their arms extended fully forward, such as if assembling a large, bulky item.

Double-handle tools
A number of tools – such as buffers, grinders, drills and sanders – may have two handles or the facility to position the second hand on the tool unit. The advantages of such a design are that it shares the demands of the operation out more evenly between the hands and may improve the positioning and control of the tool, particularly for fine, precise or delicate work. However, it is hard to find double-handle tools which have two handles of equivalent size and construction. For example, many angle grinders require the user to grip the main body of the grinder (which houses the motor) while the other hand grips a much thinner plastic handle set at 90°.

Clearly, the general requirements and specifications for handle design covered in this chapter apply equally whether there is one handle or two.

Handedness
Designers typically develop tools for use by right-handed users, which causes problems for left-handed users (who represent 10 per cent of the workforce). If left-handed users attempt to use their right hand they may find that their non-dominant hand does not have the same level of

dexterity or the same strength capacity as their dominant hand. If they use the tool in their left hand they may find that any contoured finger grooves or apertures do not allow them to grip the handle easily and comfortably (eg scissors). It is therefore important to select tools, whenever possible, which allow for use by either hand. If this is not possible, left-handed users should be provided with tools designed specifically for their use.

Handle span

The span between two handles of a tool will influence the type of grip used and the strength requirement of the task. For example, the operation of nail scissors will result in the user applying a pinch grip to hold the scissors, which will reduce the effective grip strength by up to 25 per cent. To control the degree of effort required to close the handles, it was generally recommended in the past that the span should be 50–75 mm. Lee *et al*. (2009) have established more recently that users prefer a grip span of 50–55 mm. In their study, small and medium-handed users rated 50 mm and 55 mm as the most comfortable size to use in a maximum grip strength test and large-handed users rated 55–60 mm as the most comfortable. Lee *et al*. were able to show that the highest level of grip force was applied with a handle span between 50–55 mm and the lowest occurred with a grip span of 65 mm. The middle finger, which contributes the highest percentage of the total grip force when compared with the other fingers, showed lower level force when the grip span was above or below 55 mm. The least force was applied by all fingers when the grip span reached 65 mm.

If the tool is used repetitively, as in the case of using scissors to remove threads from clothing, it is recommended that the handles should be fitted with an automatic spring-opener. This will allow the use of the stronger hand-closing muscles and avoid the need for using the weaker hand-opening muscles. Care should be taken with the tension setting on the spring; the user should not have to exert excessive force to close the handles due to the resistance of the spring.

Aperture size

If the hand or fingers have to be inserted into an aperture, such as when using scissors or a saw, consideration should be given to finger and hand clearance. This is particularly important because of the sensitivity of the backs and sides of the fingers. Repetitive use of standard surgical-type scissors for a finishing task, such as removing excess material from moulded rubber components, will result in pressure on the backs of the fingers each time the blades are opened. In addition, the concentration of pressure around the joints of the fingers, due to the reduced dimensions of the finger apertures on the scissors, will compromise the functioning of the fingers. A finger ring with a diameter of 30 mm will allow for the comfortable insertion, removal and movement of a finger or thumb by most users. If the hand is to be inserted into an aperture, as when using a saw, a rectangle of 110 mm by 45 mm is recommended.

Triggers

The inclusion of a trigger on a tool introduces further problems requiring consideration. If the trigger is to be used repetitively, as in a production setting, it should be capable of being activated by more than one finger. This will allow the user to share the load more evenly across the fingers, thereby minimising the possible fatiguing effect on any single digit, while at the same time increasing strength capacity. To allow for activation by more than one finger, a trigger strip of 50 mm should be provided. If activation by one finger only cannot be avoided, the handle should be long enough to be capable of being gripped by the whole hand when the finger is off the trigger, outside the trigger guard. This will prevent accidental activation of the tool when it is being moved.

If the handle is so large that the user has to reach with the finger(s) to operate the trigger, they will only be able to flex (or bend) the tips of their fingers when applying the necessary force. This can cause pain and discomfort in the hand and fingers, and over time can result in the development of a ULD. The handle size should allow for activation of the trigger by the middle and end sections of the fingers simultaneously.

Triggers which are hard, or which have sharp edges, can also cause compression of the soft tissue of the fingers and may produce feelings of discomfort. The trigger should be covered with a similar material to that used on the main handle and should be rounded to eliminate any sharp edges.

The effort required to depress the trigger is also a consideration. The level of effort judged acceptable will change in line with the frequency of use. Generally, the more frequently a trigger is used, the less effort should be required. However, the degree of pressure required to activate the trigger should be compatible with avoiding inadvertent operation. Accidental start-up can obviously be hazardous but increases in static loading, resulting from the user deliberately holding their finger away from the trigger for fear of accidentally depressing it, can also lead to problems.

Static and dynamic work

Static muscle work is required to hold the tool, while dynamic muscle work is required to manoeuvre it into position and use it. Static muscle work requires the muscles to tense for an uninterrupted period of time. It is considered far more fatiguing than dynamic muscle work, which allows the muscles to rhythmically contract and relax during the operation. It has been suggested that muscles involved in dynamic work are more resistant to fatigue and possible injury than those involved in static work. Therefore, it is essential that the effects of static muscle work are minimised as far as possible. Both he weight of the tool and the distribution of weight affect static work.

Weight
A frequently used tool should weigh as little as possible. It has been suggested that it should be capable of being held in one hand and not weigh more than 0.5 kg. (It is possible to source alternative tool designs which complete a job efficiently while weighing only half as much as their regular counterparts.) If a tool weighs more than 0.5 kg, consideration should be given to using a counter-balance. If the tool is not counter-balanced, the user should be encouraged to put the tool down at every opportunity to allow the hand to recover from the static muscle work required to grip it during use. Even a break of a few seconds will make a difference to the fatiguing rate of the muscles. To encourage users to put their tools down they should be provided with a surface or holster close to the tool's area of use. Alternatively, if the tool's use, shape and weight allow it, straps around the handle, such as those found on ski poles, would allow the user slight relief from the static loading.

There are two exceptions to the rule of minimising tool weight: those tools which need a certain weight to prevent the transmission of vibration to the user's hands and arms; and those which enable equal pressure to be exerted over the surface being addressed (eg when using a buffer or grinder). If users find that the tool is too light to carry out the job efficiently, they may try to compensate by gripping harder and exerting more force.

The tool's centre of gravity should be close to the hand (the effort to grip the tool will increase as the centre of gravity moves away from the hand). Locating the handle close to the tool's centre of gravity should also minimise the possibility of the tool slipping out of the hand. However, when determining the location of the handle, consideration should be given to the influence of air hoses and any other attachments which might alter the distribution of weight. To control their influence, the length of any air lines and power cables should be kept to a minimum. The aim should be to eliminate the need for the arm muscles to compensate for inappropriate tool balance.

Air hoses

If users are working with tools with an air hose, they should be protected as far as possible from the cold blow-back from the tool. The cold air jet is often directed towards the hand and wrist area and the subsequent reduction in temperature may result in the reduction of blood flow into the hand, which is associated with the development of ULDs. In addition, when the hands become cold, the user will experience a loss of dexterity and grip strength, and as a result may have to increase the pressure of their grip. If gloves are used as a means to limit the effects of the cold air, several issues should be given careful consideration:

- the gloves should fit the hand properly so that they do not impair manual dexterity
- tight gloves may deceive the user, leading them to believe that they have a firm grip on the tool when they do not, which could result in tool slippage and an accident
- loose or bulky gloves may become caught up in rotating tool elements
- bulky gloves may interfere with tactile feedback, resulting in the user gripping the tool more firmly than is necessary
- additional clearance may be required for gloved fingers and hands.

Vibration

Workers can be exposed to hand–arm vibration through using hand-held power tools, by using hand-guided equipment such as a lawnmower, or by gripping materials being processed by a machine such as a grinder.

It is thought that regular exposure to hand–arm vibration can result in permanent health problems. These can include a range of conditions referred to as hand–arm vibration syndrome (HAVS), as well as more specific ULDs, such as carpal tunnel syndrome.

Typical signs that a worker is suffering from a vibration-induced condition include tingling and numbness in the fingers, strength reduction in the hands, loss of sensitivity in the fingers and blanching of the fingers, usually only the tips at the start. For most workers, the symptoms appear after a number of years of exposure to vibration and they tend to get worse with continued exposure. It is possible for these symptoms to become permanent. Harm can be caused to workers with as little as 15 minutes of exposure per day to some tools.

There are several industries that are considered to be the most likely to involve hand–arm vibration, including:

- construction
- forestry
- foundries

- mines
- vehicle repair
- estates management
- building and maintenance of roads and railways.

Some of the commonest types of tool that have the potential to cause health problems as a result of vibration include:
- chainsaws
- road breakers
- grinders (hand-held and pedestal)
- polishers
- power hammers and chisels
- hammer drills
- cut-off saws
- impact wrenches
- jigsaws
- brush cutters
- powered lawnmowers
- powered sanders.

This list is not exhaustive, so employers should keep in mind that any high-vibration tools or processes, particularly if they cause tingling or numbness in the hands during or after use, can present a risk. Processes that are considered to be high risk include:
- drilling and breaking rock, concrete and so on
- consolidating or compacting sand, concrete or aggregate
- riveting, caulking, hammering, clinching, flanging and hammer swaging
- preparing and dressing welds
- surface preparation, including scabbling, descaling and paint removal
- grinding, sanding or polishing wood, metal, stone, rubber, plastics and ceramics
- cutting metal, wood, grass, stone, bone and so on
- holding or supporting objects being worked on by machine
- component or product assembly.

The Control of Vibration at Work Regulations 2005 require employers to assess the vibration risk to their employees. To assess daily exposure, an assessor needs to find out the average magnitude of the vibration (ie the level of vibration) at the point where the hands and the tool come into contact. This is expressed as an acceleration value in metres per second squared (m/s^2). They also need to know the daily exposure time. If workers are likely to be exposed above the daily exposure action value (EAV), a series of control measures should be introduced to eliminate risk or reduce exposure as much as is reasonably practicable. The EAV is the daily amount of vibration exposure above which employers are required to take action to control exposure. For hand–arm vibration, the EAV is a daily exposure of 2.5 m/s² A(8). Employers also have to provide health surveillance for employers exposed above the EAV. If employees are exposed above the daily exposure limit value (ELV), the employer has to take immediate action to reduce the employee's exposure below the limit value. The ELV is the maximum amount of vibration an employee can be exposed to on any single day. For hand–arm vibration, the ELV is a daily exposure of 5 m/s² A(8).

During an assessment, the assessor should first make a list of all of the equipment that may cause vibration. Information relating to vibration risks should be gathered from the manufacturer's handbook that should have accompanied the tool. Assessors need to be aware that the values provided in the handbook will probably differ from real-life use, as the measurements listed in the handbook relate to tests carried out in laboratory settings. The assessor should then identify all of the likely users of that equipment and how long they are actually operating each piece of equipment for throughout their shift. This will allow employees to be divided into three groups:
- the high risk group exposed above the ELV, which would include employees who regularly operate hammer action tools for more than one hour per day or who use rotary or other action tools for at least four hours per day
- the medium risk group exposed above the EAV, including employees who regularly operate hammer action tools for more than 15 minutes per day or who use rotary or other action tools for more than one hour per day
- the low risk group.

If an assessor arranges for measurements to be taken of the vibration, they need to be aware that the results can vary depending on the condition of the tool and how it has been maintained, how the worker uses the tool, the materials against which the tool is being used and how the measurements are made. As it is quite difficult to achieve precise values, the assessor should look to record the average vibration magnitude. If both hands are exposed to vibration, the assessment should take account of the hand with the greater exposure.

As far as means for reducing the risks from hand–arm vibration are concerned, the first thing that should be considered is whether the vibration can be eliminated altogether by introducing a different method of work. Alternatively, the work could be mechanised or automated. It is important that the equipment is suitable for the work it is intended to be used for and that the tool with the lowest vibration that is suitable and can complete the work effectively is used. If high vibration tools remain in use, the time for which they are used should be kept to a minimum. Comparison across tool ranges to identify more suitable models should be done before decisions are made about what to buy and employees should be made aware of the vibration reduction features in a tool. Once purchased, tools should be checked and maintained regularly. Workstations should be modified so that operators can achieve optimum working postures, and jigs and suspension systems should be used to limit the extent to which heavy tools need to be gripped. The length of time the tool is in use should be kept to a minimum and it may be necessary to have the tool in use for a number of short bursts rather than one longer burst of use. Job rotation should be considered if the task itself cannot be altered to reduce exposure time. Protective clothing should aim to keep the operator warm and dry so as to encourage good blood circulation. Although gloves help to keep the hands warm, they will not offer protection from vibration. Employees should be aware of the symptoms of hand–arm vibration and the need to report their appearance.

Torque response
It is not uncommon for users to experience upper limb pain caused by the kick-back from the recoil of tools such as nut runners. The abrupt snap response of the nut runner indicates that a nut has been driven to the required level of torque, and having achieved this the tool switches itself off immediately. Should the tool fail to switch off, the torque may be relayed to the user's arm, which can result in injury.

The sudden stress placed on the hands and arms by the tool switching off abruptly should, if possible, be controlled by using variable torque tools. These have a clutch mechanism which will automatically alter the effective torque as the required level of tightening is reached and will shut the tool off gradually, thereby eliminating the sudden snap-off, which can prove to be destructive over time.

Multifunctional tools
To eliminate the need for tool users to switch continually between a series of different items, repeatedly picking them up and putting them down, it may be advisable to design or select a multifunctional tool capable of carrying out several operations. However, the advantages of using one tool continually should be weighed against the benefits of allowing the hand to release one object and then grip an alternative shape or weight.

Domestic and off-the-shelf tools
It is not unusual for domestic tools to be introduced into a work setting, although many are not designed to be used for long periods or in a

repetitive manner and are therefore unsuitable for occupational use. For example, a domestic hand drill may wear out quickly and vibrate more than is considered acceptable.

Similarly, off-the-shelf tools are often used in inappropriate environments. As a result, the user may have to compensate with inappropriate limb postures and increased force. Only appropriately designed work tools should be used in a work environment.

Areas of use
Having given full consideration to the tools themselves, attention should also be focused on their area of use, as this will influence the ease with which a tool can be used and a task completed. Ideally, any surfaces or components which are being addressed by the tool should be oriented so that the user can remain in a natural, upright posture. They should not have to deviate their body or limb posture grossly in order to apply the tool.

Access to the application area should be made as easy as possible. Any obstacles between the user and the area of application should be removed so as to minimise unnecessary reaching.

If the tool user has to lean on a surface to steady a hand during work, consideration should be given to padding the surface to increase comfort levels and to reduce the possibility of contact with any sharp edges or cold surfaces.

In conclusion

It is considered that the handle is the easiest piece of the tool to alter, yet it is the part that is usually overlooked during design and redesign processes. A properly designed tool handle should enable full tool control and stability, increase mechanical advantage and reduce the amount of effort required. Poor tool design results in users having to adopt a series of irregular postures which allow them to hold and use the tool. Gross deviations in posture and subsequent increases in required effort result in an increased fatiguing rate and the possible development of discomfort, pain or injury. Tool designs should accommodate the user and enable them to work comfortably and safely – while allowing efficient completion of the operation.

Summary

Gripping
- At every opportunity, the user should be able to employ a power grip when holding a tool.
- The user should be able to use the tool when the hand is in the most natural position, with a straight line running from the elbow through the wrist and into the hand.
- To avoid bending the wrist, the tool handle or tool head should be bent.
- Pistol grip tools should only be used in an orientation which permits the wrist to be held straight (otherwise a straight grip tool should be used).

Handle design and construction
- A tool handle should not have a hard or smooth surface which will allow the hand to slip during use.
- When applying downward force with a tool (eg a drill), a moulded collar will prevent the hand from slipping as pressure is applied.
- Handles made from metal which may be cold should be avoided because they may reduce the temperature of the hand.
- The handle should be covered in a soft, compliant and textured material to make it easier to grip.
- If flutes or ridges are used on the handle, they should not be too deep or have sharp edges which may damage the soft tissue of the hand.
- Contouring on handles, such as finger grooves, should be avoided unless their design has been based on anthropometric data specific to the intended user group.
- A single-handle tool should be approximately 40 mm in diameter but an increase to 65 mm may be acceptable if torque is exerted about the axis of the handle (eg when using a screwdriver).
- The handle should be a minimum of 100 mm in length with a preference for 115–120 mm. A further increase of 10 mm should be made if gloves are worn.

Handedness
- Tools should be designed for operation by both left- and right-handed users. Alternatively, specifically designed tools for left-handed users should be provided as appropriate.

Handle span
- The span between two handles (eg with a pair of pliers) should be 50–75 mm.
- For repetitive use, an automatic spring-opener should be added to tools with two handles (eg scissors). The spring's tension setting should not demand excessive levels of effort to close the handles.

Aperture size
- Finger apertures in tools such as scissors should have a diameter of 30 mm.
- Hand apertures in tools such as saws should form a rectangle of 110 mm by 45 mm.

Triggers
- If a trigger is used repetitively, it should be designed so that it can be activated by more than one finger.
- A trigger strip of 50 mm is recommended to allow for activation of the trigger by more than one finger.
- If only one finger is used during trigger use, the handle length should be such that it can accommodate all the fingers when the trigger finger is not in use.
- The trigger and handle dimensions should be co-ordinated so that the trigger can be activated by the middle and end sections of the fingers, not just the tips.
- Triggers should not be hard or have sharp edges.
- The effort required to depress the trigger should be regulated and altered in line with the frequency of use.

Static work
- The static effort required to hold and use the tool should be controlled as far as possible.

Weight
- The tool weight should be kept to a minimum (except for those tools which require weight to prevent transmission of vibration and those which enable even pressure to be exerted over a surface).
- Heavy tools should be supported by a counter-balance or placed in a holster when not in use.
- Users should be encouraged to put the tool down when not in operation.
- The centre of gravity of the tool should be kept close to the hand.
- The length of air lines and other attachments should be kept to a minimum to limit the effect on the tool's balance.

Air hoses
- Users should be protected from the cold air blown back from an air tool.

Vibration
- Vibration should be kept to a minimum and users protected from it as far as possible.

Torque response
- The torque response of tools should be controlled to limit the effect on users.

Multifunctional tools
- Where appropriate, multifunctional tools should replace a series of individual tools.

Domestic and off-the-shelf tools
- Domestic and off-the-shelf tools should not be used in an occupational setting unless they are suitable.

Areas of use
- Access to the application area should be made easier by inclining surfaces when necessary, removing obstacles and padding any surfaces which may be leaned on.

References and further reading

Health and Safety Executive. *Whole body vibration. The Control of Vibration at Work Regulations 2005*, L141. HSE Books, 2005.

Health and Safety Executive. *Hand–arm vibration. The Control of Vibration at Work Regulations 2005*, L140. HSE Books, 2005.

Poole K and Mason H. *Upper limb disability and exposure to hand-arm vibration in selected industries*, RR667. Health and Safety Laboratory, 2008.

Lee S-L, Kong Y-K, Lowe B D and Song S. Handle grip span for optimising finger-specific force capability as a function of hand size. *Ergonomics* 2009; 52 (5): 601–608.

Delleman N J, Haslegrave C M and Chaffin D B. *Working postures and movements: tools for evaluation and engineering.* CRC Press, 2004.

Health and Safety Executive. *A pain in your workplace?*, HSG121. HSE Books, 1994.

Health and Safety Executive. *Vibration solutions: practical ways to reduce the risk of hand-arm vibration injury*, HSG170. HSE Books, 1997.

Health and Safety Executive. *Upper limb disorders in the workplace*, HSG60(rev). HSE Books, 2002.

Helander M. *A guide to the ergonomics of manufacturing.* Taylor & Francis, 1995

International Labour Office. *Ergonomic checkpoints.* ILO, 1996.

Pheasant S and Haslegrave C M. *Bodyspace – anthropometry, ergonomics and the design of work* (3rd edition). Taylor & Francis, 2006.

Putz-Anderson V. *Cumulative trauma disorders: a manual for musculoskeletal diseases of the upper limbs.* Taylor & Francis, 1988.

5 Job design and work organisation

The job design process

Providing workers with well-designed workstations, workplaces and equipment is not enough to ensure that they can work comfortably, safely and contentedly. Job and work organisation factors – such as speed of operation, rest breaks and rotation programmes – also need to be carefully designed, as they will determine how people relate to each other and with the production system.

There are three ways of looking at the needs of the organisation during the design process:
- **Production system framework** – the organisation is viewed as one flowing process whereby items, such as a product or service, are fed into the system and transformed into an output. To facilitate this framework, the job must be designed to meet the requirement for a high quality output. Therefore, the focus will be on generating efficient operations, maintaining equipment, recording processing information and controlling the quality of materials.
- **Miniature society framework** – this perspective views the organisation as a social institution consisting of individuals who act in response to shared experiences, expectations, rewards, conflicts, prejudices and so on. To facilitate this framework, the job design and work organisation must meet the needs of recruitment, training, co-ordination, communication and other related issues.
- **Individual framework** – this framework acknowledges the importance and contribution of the individual within the organisation. It recognises that each individual has a specific career path in mind and has personal expectations and aspirations. There is also a recognition that the individual's outlook does not necessarily focus solely on the organisation but certainly overlaps with it at intervals. An organisation is more likely to meet its own goals if it is able to design jobs and work systems which allow the individual to satisfy personal needs and achieve personal goals.

There are various desirable features which are important in job design if both the organisation and the individual are to satisfy their needs and achieve their aims:
- the work should be challenging and meaningful
- individuals should be able to learn on the job (this will necessitate an indication of specific performance criteria in advance and feedback following performance)

- individuals should have some control over decision-making and be permitted to use their judgment and discretion; achievements should be measured by evaluating objective outcomes
- there should be social interaction where individuals can call on each other for support, assistance and understanding
- each individual's contribution should be recognised
- individuals should be able to equate their work role with their role outside work
- individuals should perceive that they have a desirable future and are not stuck in 'dead-end' jobs
- the job should be flexible enough to accommodate individual differences, characteristics and circumstances.

The 'Quality of working life criteria checklist', linked to the list of desirable features listed above, presents individual needs in a succinct format. It provides a profile of the factors which are important to an individual and which influence their levels of satisfaction or dissatisfaction in the workplace.

Quality of working life criteria checklist (Davis & Wacker 1987)

Physical environment	Safety, health, attractiveness, comfort
Compensation	Pay, benefits
Rights and privileges	Employment security, justice and due process, fair and respectful treatment, participation in decision-making
Job content	Variety of tasks, feedback, challenge, task identity, individual autonomy and self-regulation, opportunity to use skills and capabilities, perceived contribution to product or service
Internal social relations	Opportunity for social contact, recognition for achievements, provision of interlocking and mutually supportive roles, opportunity to lead or help others, team morale and spirit, small-group autonomy and self-regulation
External social relations	Job-related status in the community, few work restrictions on outside lifestyle, multiple options for engaging in work (eg flexitime, part-time, job share, subcontracting)
Career path	Learning and personal development, opportunities for advancement, multiple career path possibilities

Motivation is an important consideration in designing jobs and structuring work organisation. An individual's effectiveness is influenced by their motivation; in a motivated state the individual is ready to perform better. Recognising the importance of motivation, most job designers draw heavily on theories such as that expounded by Maslow (1954). Maslow suggested that people have a hierarchy of needs and that five major needs direct their actions. These are:
- physical needs – consisting of primary needs such as food, water and sex
- safety needs – including protection from physical harm, ill health and economic disaster
- social needs – including the desire to feel part of a group and the need to establish a position in relation to others in the organisation
- achievement needs – consisting of the need for self-respect and a feeling of competence
- self-actualisation needs – including the need to achieve one's fullest potential in terms of self-development and creativity.

Maslow's theory on the hierarchy of needs is a dynamic one. His theory states that at any given time any one need may be operating. However, an individual responsible for job design can apply the theory by concentrating on the physical and safety needs first – providing appropriate rest break schedules, suitable heating, lighting, ventilation, opportunities to eat and so on. If these lower grade needs are not met, the designer cannot possibly hope to meet the higher grade needs.

Before designing the job itself, six separate decisions should be made:
- **What tasks will be completed by the workforce?** The organisation should first review workplace technology such as equipment, robots and materials, and determine which technical and organisational tasks remain for the workforce to complete. Technical tasks contribute directly to the production system. An example of this would be an operator who is required to remove boxes of pre-packed food from a conveyor belt and pack them into an outer case. The production system will have cooked the food, placed it in the container, sealed it and passed it onto the operator for packing. Organisational tasks involve the planning, training, problem-solving and co-ordination which supports the production process.
- **How will individual tasks be structured?** Decisions have to be made with regard to the complexity of each individual task. The job designer has to decide whether an operator will be given a series of complex sub-routines to complete, or a fragmented operation which they will repeat frequently.
- **How will a range of tasks be grouped together?** Consideration should be given to the grouping of tasks and whether it will be done simply to

facilitate the process or to provide the operator with a meaningful and interesting range of opportunities. The decisions will be influenced by constraints such as location of tools, equipment and controls. Such constraints will limit the range of movement of an operator or group of operators from certain work areas and workstations and the variety of work they can undertake.
- **How will the tasks be assigned to individuals?** Consideration has to be given to the abilities and limitations of the individual and these will be influenced by their personal characteristics, training and experience. The organisation's in-house approach to work distribution and worker responsibility will also have to be taken into account.
- **How will the work be co-ordinated?** Co-ordination of work creates a link between all individuals within an organisation. The generation of this link can be achieved through open communication, formal reporting procedures, meetings, team identities, hierarchical management and supervision, and informal personal relationships.
- **How will individuals be rewarded for their work?** Rewards can be financial but they can also come in the form of promotion, opportunities for further training or additional responsibility. However, performance has to be measured to allow for the adequate reward for work. Performance can be evaluated through supervisory or managerial evaluation, tests, achievement of goals and targets, piecework, educational achievements and so on.

Having made these decisions, consideration should be given to the mechanics of job design. This chapter discusses the characteristics of jobs and work organisations that determine the individual's level of satisfaction as well as their physical wellbeing.

Repetition
As a consequence of the trend towards specialisation, certain organisations have designed tasks which are highly repetitive. It is understandable with large organisations, producing numerous products in a given timescale, that the most 'efficient' way of ensuring that the desired number of items is produced to the appropriate standard is to break tasks down into small subcomponents and train an operator to complete one subcomponent. By doing so the organisation can virtually guarantee that the operator will become highly skilled in that operation and will almost always produce high quality work. This was the approach taken by car manufacturer Henry Ford in the 1920s. Such simplification of jobs is not unique to production line operations. It is also apparent in office work, where individuals are required to sit for long periods inputting information using a keyboard. The data-entry operator is a prime example of an office-based worker involved in highly

repetitive work. As discussed in Chapter 8, such rapid repetitive movements can have serious implications for an operator in terms of developing a ULD.

Putz-Anderson (1988) has provided a system for determining whether a task can be classified as 'high repetitive' or 'low repetitive'. He has suggested that a task with a cycle time of less than 30 seconds, or one where more than 50 per cent of the cycle time involves performing the same kind of fundamental cycle, can be classified as high repetitive. (A fundamental cycle is a work cycle that has a sequence of steps or elements that repeat themselves within the cycle.) A long cycle time does not necessarily mean that the job is not repetitive. For example, the cycle time for a garment packer to pack three pairs of briefs into a plastic pack may be 45 seconds, which may suggest, using Putz-Anderson's criteria, that it would not be classified as high repetitive. However, as three pairs of briefs are packed, the fundamental cycle time is actually 15 seconds and the job should therefore be classified as high repetitive.

When designing any task, the ideal aim should be to offer as much variety as possible so that the work is not focused on one single part of the body, resulting in a possible overload of that structure. If there is greater job variety, the operator is also less likely to become bored or feel isolated. If the job content cannot be changed, the work could be reorganised. A programme of rotation could be designed which would allow operators to move away from repetitive tasks to other less repetitive or less demanding operations. The aim should be to provide the individual with an opportunity to recover from the stresses of the first operation. To achieve this, the subsequent activity should be qualitatively different to the first, so that a second set of muscle groups is used. This allows the muscles used during the previous operation to rest and recover.

Job rotation should not be undertaken without full consideration of all the tasks to be included in the programme and the activities involved when completing each task. It is only by doing so that each of the tasks can be included in a programme which offers regular recovery periods. If an operator is moved through a series of equally repetitive, short cycle tasks, they will not benefit because they will experience similar levels of musculoskeletal loading during each operation.

If operators are to be rotated, they should be fully trained in each of the tasks they are to complete during a rotation programme. Without the appropriate training, they may experience further problems as they attempt to complete an unfamiliar operation.

Worker flexibility – or 'multiskilling' – is a refinement of job rotation. With this approach the worker is trained to perform a number of jobs and is then deployed in different areas as circumstances dictate. Worker flexibility normally generates an increase in remuneration. This approach is seen to offer a more varied and interesting range of work experiences than would apply with traditional job rotation. Such multiskilling is of particular benefit to the organisation during sickness or holiday absences, as operators possess skills which enable them to move from job to job and cover for absentees.

An alternative way of tackling the issue of repetition is to consider 'job enlargement'. This approach increases the number of individual tasks an operator has to complete without a change in responsibility. Other benefits of job enlargement include reduced storage for work in progress and reduced handling time, as operators do not need an allowance for packing and repacking items as work is moved from one area to another. However, operators should not be allowed to divide their newly enlarged tasks into a series of sub-tasks and complete each sub-task repetitively for a period of time before moving onto the next sub-task. This approach undermines the purpose of job enlargement.

'Job enrichment' differs from job enlargement in that it gives the operators more responsibility over their own work and possibly a greater say in the decision-making process, particularly in respect of their own team or work group or their work activities. Quality control, testing of products and rework are examples of job enrichment. It can be introduced successfully in areas where there are (semi-) autonomous working groups. The development of such groups increases co-operation between group members, encourages a more positive approach to work, and reduces boredom, monotony, isolation and absenteeism.

Work rate

Typically, the speed at which an operator is expected to work is dictated by the production capacity of the equipment or machinery they are using. Organisations expect the machinery to pay for itself over a period of time – and want it to work at maximum capacity. However, increasing the speed of the operation serves only to increase the stresses placed on the operator. The aim should be to set the speed of operation to fall within the operator's optimum – not maximum – level of functioning. This can be compared to the physical states experienced when running or walking. Most people can run for a short time but will find it demanding and tiring. Walking at a comfortable pace, however, will probably allow a greater distance to be covered. It is the same in the workplace. Operators can probably work faster but to do so increases their fatiguing rate and the likelihood that they will suffer strain or injury.

If an acceptable work rate is agreed, it is important that it remain consistent throughout the course of the shift and the working week. Operators should not be expected – or allowed – to work faster at certain points in the day or week. Working faster may be a result of a change in demand, or the operator choosing to work that way. An operator with targets to meet by the end of the day may decide to work faster in the morning, meeting up to three-quarters of their target, so that they can have a slower, more relaxed afternoon. Bursts of activity such as this result in residual fatigue which standard rest breaks cannot counteract. Standard, regular breaks are designed to allow a rest from activities which are performed at a consistent pace across the course of a shift. Peaks and troughs in activity should be controlled as far as possible.

Workload
The workload is the amount of work an individual is expected to complete within a given timescale. Whatever level this is set at, there is usually one crucial factor which should be recognised: all operators require a period of time to become 'work hardened' or 'task fit'. This is similar in nature to the level of fitness required of a runner before entering a marathon – an athlete would not expect their body to perform at its best without a gradual build-up or acclimatisation period. A similar approach should be taken at work, particularly with new employees or those returning from sickness or holiday leave. Even long term employees will have lost some of their task fitness after a two- or three-week holiday. Therefore, to avoid overload of the musculoskeletal system, they should be allowed a gradual build-up period to become accustomed to the demands of the work again. New employees and those returning to work following an absence are particularly vulnerable to work-related injuries.

This level of vulnerability is also apparent in workplaces where work demands change suddenly as a result of seasonal adjustments or increased customer demand. It is not unknown for an organisation to double or treble its workforce's workload overnight because of an increase in demand. Unless the organisation takes on temporary workers to assist in meeting the increased demand, or the workload is increased gradually, it will probably be faced with a sudden increase in complaints of ULD-type symptoms from the permanent workforce.

Increasing the workload to the point of overload (ie where demand outstrips capability) may lead to mistakes, errors or accidents as the operator develops a 'trade-off' strategy where the work is completed but with compromises. An example of this is an assembly operation where an operator is supposed to fit four nuts to a part but because of the overall workload they decide to fit three to keep up with the speed of production.

Attempts by the operator to rectify any mistakes or errors will themselves increase the workload further as they have to maintain production levels while at the same time trying to resolve problems relating to previous tasks.

Rest breaks
Rest breaks are usually a major source of discussion within organisations. Generally, the focus is on the amount of time operators are allotted during a shift. However, frequency rather than duration of breaks is important. Short, frequent breaks are more beneficial than longer, irregular breaks. The aim should be to allow the person to stop work before they actually start to fatigue – so that when they stop work they will rest. When work is resumed they can pick up where they left off. If, however, operators work for long periods of time without a break they will start to fatigue and their performance will deteriorate. When they finally stop work they will be recovering, or recuperating, from the stresses of the activity and not resting. When they resume activities, they have to build back up to their original performance level.

It has been suggested (Grandjean 1988) that as a minimum in moderately heavy jobs, operators should have a break of at least 10–15 minutes both morning and afternoon, in addition to their lunch break. However, a few minutes' rest every hour has been shown to reduce fatigue and improve concentration. This is particularly effective in repetitive assembly line-type jobs.

For display screen equipment (DSE) operators, it is recommended that a break of 5–15 minutes in every hour is desirable if the work requires high levels of concentration and lasts a long time (Pheasant 1991). If the working conditions are appropriate and the task is interesting, five minutes in every hour would be sufficient. For boring or stressful DSE work, 15 minutes might be more appropriate. As a rough guide, an average of 10 minutes in every hour is advisable.

In addition to designing work so that the operator can stop altogether during standard rest breaks, consideration should be given to introducing 'micropauses'. These are very short rest periods, possibly lasting only a few seconds, which provide a brief respite from the stresses of the overall task. For example, a keyboard operator would stop to read their screen at regular intervals (perhaps every 10 minutes); or a welder feeding parts to welding machines would be allowed to stand and wait for the welding operation to finish before removing the part, instead of using the time to complete another operation.

Bonus and piece-rate systems

To ensure a high level of production, many organisations offer bonus or piece-rate payments. However, these simply encourage operators to work at speeds which move beyond their optimum level of functioning towards their maximum. Such systems increase the rate of repetition and sometimes decrease the regularity with which breaks are taken as operators work through them. Alternative systems of rewarding operators should be considered.

Overtime

Many operators view overtime positively as it provides an opportunity to increase their take-home pay. However, problems associated with overtime should not be overlooked. Overtime obviously increases an individual's exposure to their working environment. This extended exposure may cause problems if the normal shift involves repetition, force, deviation of the wrists, static muscle work, cold temperatures and so on. Overtime may also reduce the possible available recovery time. Therefore, overtime should be viewed not only in terms of the benefits for the organisation and the individual but also in terms of the disadvantages. If an individual is involved in a demanding, repetitive operation during a normal shift, it may not be appropriate to allow them to work overtime.

Work schedules

Schedules of work will influence an operator's attendance, motivation and commitment. The compressed working week results in longer working days on Monday to Thursday but permits the operator to have a three-day weekend. With flexitime, the operator is required to be present at work during core times but outside these periods may choose their own work schedule. Such a system gives employees greater control over their working hours and thus increases motivation. Job sharing, where two people share a single job, allows the individuals concerned to achieve goals related to both family and work life. The organisation also benefits from this arrangement because it can use the talents of two people, as well as having access to those who might otherwise not necessarily be motivated to go to work at all due to family or other commitments.

If using such work schedules, the organisation should ensure that operators are not overloaded due to a shorter working day, or are not working through breaks to make up time on the flexi schedule.

Shiftwork

Certain types of employment require job holders to work when most others are at home asleep (eg nurses, security guards, bakers). In the manufacturing and service industries, the 24-hour period is usually divided into three eight-hour shifts (06.00–14.00, 14.00–22.00 and 22.00–06.00). Most people dislike irregular, antisocial working hours. About two-thirds of shiftworkers suffer ill health of one form or another and about a quarter eventually give up shiftwork because of it.

It is evident that people who work on a night shift or who work in the very early hours of the morning encounter a number of problems, the most prominent one being a disruption of their internal body clock. This regulates how the body functions at any point in the day. For example, body temperature, blood pressure and heart rate are higher during daylight hours than at night. They change cyclically as day becomes night and then back to day again. This is referred to as the circadian rhythm. Certain external cues exert influence over the circadian rhythm, including regular bedtime, light levels outside, regular mealtimes, as well as regulated patterns of behaviour such as going to work or taking the children to school.

The internal body clock can adapt to changes in the way a person works. However, circumstances in that person's life make it impossible for the body clock to fully adjust if the person works a night shift. For instance, if the person does not work at the weekend and they fall back into the same getting up and going to bed times as their family, their body clock will readjust to fit that pattern. This makes it more difficult for the worker to get back into the routine of working the night shift once they go back to work. This has implications in the case of rotating shift work, where an individual may work one week on the night shift followed by days off or by working days. By constantly changing the way that they work, and at the same time changing when they are expected to be active and awake, their body may remain in a state of limbo where it cannot adjust completely to suit any shift pattern. This can lead to circadian dysrhythmia and sleep disturbance. This situation can also be experienced by temporary workers who have to fit in with whatever shift they are put on, possibly for only a short period of time.

People on shift work often find it difficult to sleep during the day. Those who can go to sleep are often woken by the rest of their family or the general community, who are carrying on normal daytime activities. Apart from the fact that daytime sleep is more likely to be interrupted, it has also been established that it does not have the same restorative powers as night-time sleep because it tends to be shorter and lighter. Ultimately, this results in poor quality sleep, which can have a negative impact on reaction time and memory. This has implications for safety-critical tasks. On that basis, employers may want to review when certain tasks are performed during the day, given that tasks requiring concentration and attention may be completed more successfully during daytime hours. This may also be worth considering in connection with training offered to workers. It is likely to be more successfully absorbed if it is offered to workers when they are on a day shift. Workers performing dangerous or safety-critical tasks should be warned about the increased risk of performing such tasks at night due to the decrease in their level of alertness.

If sleep continues to be disturbed, the worker can start to experience fatigue. If this happens, it will have an impact on their mental functioning and performance. This is most noticeable in situations where they are faced with a demanding workload. If they develop chronic fatigue as a result of excessive working hours and poor quality sleep, they can develop long term health problems, particularly digestive disorders and heart disease, while some workers may experience a deterioration of pre-existing health problems such as epilepsy, asthma, diabetes and some psychological illnesses. Even if shift workers do not develop serious health problems, it is common for them to experience less serious conditions more frequently, such as colds and flu. As a means to lessen the likelihood of workers experiencing symptoms such as indigestion, employers should offer their workforce the right type of food at night-time. Typically, canteens produce stodgy food such as pies and chips. However, at night time a worker's system is naturally trying to suppress food intake and it will struggle to digest heavy foods. Canteens should provide lighter, tasty food that is easier to digest. Workers should be given advice about changing their eating habits, particularly at night.

It is important that shift workers tell their GPs that they work shifts so that their doctor can consider whether it is a contributory factor in the development or worsening of any medical condition. Shift workers should be advised against taking medications to help them sleep during the day. There are other strategies that may be effective in helping them get to sleep without them resorting to taking drugs. They should not underestimate the value of working through the same bedtime routine as they would have at night, such as brushing their teeth, putting on pyjamas, closing the curtains and sleeping in their bed rather than napping on the sofa. They should also switch off phones and make sure that their family knows when they are asleep and should not be disturbed. To help them to get off to sleep quickly, they should avoid any caffeinated drinks several hours before they go to bed and they should not rely on alcohol to help them get to sleep. Carrying out household chores or watching television when they get back from a night shift before they try to go to sleep will only serve to stimulate them and wake them up, so they should try to go to bed as soon as they get home from work.

Workers should also be advised against relying on legal stimulants to help them remain vigilant through a night shift. Both drugs to aid sleep and stimulants can have a negative affect on performance and this could cause problems in safety-critical environments. As a means to ensure that workers' performance is not affected by shift work, supervisors and managers should be trained to recognise the signs that are suggestive of shift-related problems.

How individual workers cope with shift work is very much dependent on personal characteristics. For example, some workers find it very easy to go to sleep during the day, while others struggle to remain asleep for more than an hour or two, assuming they can get to sleep in the first place. Anyone who has experienced sleep disorders in the past is likely to find it extremely difficult to sleep during the day. People who normally feel refreshed after only five or six hours of sleep will cope better with shift work than those who need at least eight or nine hours to feel refreshed. People who are described as being at their best first thing in the morning struggle to adapt successfully to night work. It would appear that people over 50 years of age are more likely to struggle with night work. A person's general fitness level appears to determine how successful they are at working at night and sleeping during the day. People who are drug or alcohol dependent or who have mental health problems find it difficult to work through the night and sleep during the day. Someone who has a second job will also be less effective when working through a night shift.

It would appear that rotating shifts on a weekly basis is the most disruptive schedule. This is because it does not provide a suitable opportunity for the body clock to adjust properly before reverting to other working hours. At the same time, it allows sleep deprivation to mount up. Although it may appear distasteful to some, a very short rotating shift pattern of one or two days, or a longer pattern of three weeks or more, causes fewer problems for the worker. A clockwise rotation of shifts where the individual works days, followed by evenings, followed by nights results in better adaptation than working a counter-clockwise shift system where they work nights, then evenings, then days.

Eight-hour shifts tend to result in a consistently higher performance at work and for that reason safety-critical tasks should be limited to eight hours, as should tasks requiring high levels of alertness, accuracy or concentration. Performance is significantly affected if a person works more than 12 hours in a shift. These workers are also more susceptible to illness. If the shift is split, so that the person works part of the shift in the early part of the day then returns later in the day to complete the shift, it is possible that they may experience increased fatigue if they do not have sufficient time to rest in between the two parts of their shift.

Ideally, workers should have two full nights of sleep in between switching between day and night shifts, and vice versa.

Other organisational issues

Automation

Automation is a fundamental part of progress in modern businesses. The movement towards it has been encouraged by the increasing cost of the human workforce, the existence of operations which are difficult or hazardous for the individual to complete, the lack of sufficient appropriately trained labour and the desire for increased competitiveness through reduced costs. However, factors such as the cost of automation, the lack of appropriate automation technology, internal organisational forces such as unions, and the lack of a market to necessitate the increase in production, may influence the development of automation. Few organisations have fully automated systems. Many use partial automation coupled with human input or effort. In these cases, it is important that the people and machines complement each other.

When the operator is expected to interact with equipment during a process, its design should not overly stress them physically or mentally. Ideally, the equipment designer should be able to develop a 'win–win' situation, where the automated process eliminates the dangerous, repetitive or mundane tasks previously completed by the operator. The biggest drawback of automation is machine-pacing, which removes the control an operator has over their speed of operation and method of work. Some studies have shown that operators who prefer machine-paced work are less intelligent and more 'humble', practical and group-dependent. Those who prefer self-paced work are more intelligent, assertive, imaginative, shrewd and self-sufficient. Findings such as these underline the importance of basing recruitment and selection decisions on an individual's suitability for the task.

Certain job characteristics should be considered before the introduction of new manufacturing technology. These will influence the performance of the operators and the new technology, as well as the levels of job satisfaction and dissatisfaction experienced by the operators. Characteristics to be taken into account include:
- **control** – how much control does the operator have over the process in terms of how a job is completed, and what happens at the boundaries

where the system takes over or where another operator assumes responsibility?
- **cognitive demand** – most advanced manufacturing technology requires the attention of flexible, sophisticated operators who can interact with the system as they watch over it, diagnosing and solving problems as they occur. Production systems demand rapid responses to problems and the selected operators have to be capable of reacting in an appropriate manner
- **responsibility** – clear lines of responsibility for the system and any output should be identified in advance
- **social interaction** – what are the opportunities for, and what is the quality of, interaction between people associated with the introduction of the new manufacturing technology?

The biggest mistake made by organisations when introducing new technology is to ignore, or give insufficient attention to, implications for both the individual and the organisation as a whole. The success of the introduction is tied up with these elements. Organisations commonly assume that previous infrastructures will be suitable for the change in technology. This is not necessarily the case.

Managing change
Changes can occur in an organisation for a number of reasons. They can be the result of the economic climate prevailing at the time, competition, changes in technology, the political situation and general social trends. These can push the organisation into acquiring new levels of knowledge and skills and offering new forms of training. At the same time, previous skills and knowledge may become superfluous. Changes may be seen in an alteration in the pattern of work at a site or the whole site may be relocated. Because of the inevitability of change, the workforce needs to be flexible enough, and willing, to cope with whatever demands are placed on them. If the workforce is to be helped to accept change, the organisation needs to plan the implementation of the changes carefully and anticipate any likely responses, particularly the negative ones.

Change brings with it uncertainty. Workers feel threatened by change and become unsettled as many will fear the unknown. They will feel particularly vulnerable if they know they have to acquire a new set of skills or knowledge base. Some may dread the thought that they will have to work with people who they have never dealt with before. Some people may not want to change engrained patterns of work behaviour that have developed over years. Others may resist change because they feel there is no need to change, while some may worry about a loss of power, authority or even their job in a restructured organisation. Most resistance comes from the perceived personal loss that will follow the change.

If an organisation wants to introduce changes successfully, it needs to recognise that its workforce will probably not move with the changes unless they are influenced to do so by others. This influence can come through information about what is happening. The workers will be more likely to accept the changes if they feel they have some input and are being listened to, if change has occurred successfully previously, if they understand what the outcomes are going to be and that they are predictable outcomes, but also if there is full support from higher levels in the organisation's hierarchy.

An organisation may find that its workers exhibit a wide range of different reactions to the prospect of change. Some may hand in their notice immediately. Others may resist it by refusing to accept it or may agree to accept the changes only on their terms. Some workers may try to enlist the support of colleagues and encourage them to walk out in protest or present a series of objections to plans. Once groups of individuals resist together, it becomes more difficult for individuals to agree to the changes because they may fear being ostracised. Some workers may not demonstrate their opposition so clearly but may offer quiet resistance in the form of slowing down the transition process through not completing tasks on time or as required but blaming other reasons for doing so. There will be others who just accept the changes even though they may not agree with them, and some will see the positives to be gained by fully supporting the changes.

Organisations can increase their chances of introducing changes more successfully by taking steps to reduce the resistance to change. In the first instance they should educate and inform their workforce. Although this is time-consuming and may tie up several people in the organisation, it is worthwhile as the workforce will understand the benefits brought by the changes. Having the workforce participate in the discussion groups also enables information to be passed on about the consequences of the changes. In addition, it allows the change agents to gain a more accurate insight into the impact of their proposed changes on the workforce and what their concerns are so that they can be addressed.

Using the right people to provide information plays a major part in how successfully the changes can be introduced. Both in-house personnel and outside assistance can help. In-house personnel are familiar faces and know well how the organisation functions. They are also on hand when needed and are a lower cost option than outside consultants. However, it has to be recognised that the workforce may consider them to be biased and not impartial. Change agents from outside the organisation can take a more objective stance and will probably have a broader range of experience of making changes. They will also have the right types of contact as the organisation's requirements grow through the process of change.

Having introduced the changes, the organisation should strive to reinforce new skills, knowledge and attitudes through appropriate managerial and supervisory support.

No process of change is complete without an evaluation. Progress should be measured and followed up to assess the effectiveness of the changes. Feedback will enable effort and behaviour to be directed towards the desired outcomes. Since positive results may take some time to appear, evaluations should be carried out over a long period. The evaluations should be viewed as an integral part of the change process. To achieve an overall balanced work system, adjustments or modifications will invariably be required and it will probably take some time before many changes are fully implemented.

Summary

Job design
- Motivation is of primary importance in job design.

Repetition
- Repetitive tasks should be avoided.
- Where repetitive tasks exist, job rotation should be used to reduce the risk of injury, boredom and monotony.
- Each task included in a rotation programme should be qualitatively different from the preceding and succeeding operations.
- Multiskilling is a refinement on job rotation where the operator is trained to complete any operation within a given area. This offers greater variety than traditional job rotation.
- Job enlargement can also be used as a means to combat the effects of repetitive tasks. This increases the number of individual tasks an operator completes without a change in responsibility.
- Job enrichment gives the operator more responsibility for their own work and a greater say in the decision-making process.

Work rate
- Operators should be encouraged to work at a consistent rate throughout the course of a day and from day to day. Peaks and troughs in activity should be avoided.

Workload
- Operators should be given an opportunity to become accustomed to the demands of any new or recently altered task before they are expected to produce a set level of output. This enables them to develop a level of 'work hardening' or 'task fitness' which will reduce the risk of injury.

Rest breaks
- All operators should have regular rest breaks.
- Short, frequent breaks are more effective than longer, irregular breaks.
- Micropauses, lasting only a few seconds, should be designed into tasks if possible.

Bonus and piecework systems
- Bonus and piecework systems of payment are not ideal. They encourage operators to work faster, for longer periods of time and with few, if any, rest breaks.

Overtime
- Overtime extends an individual's exposure time to their working environment. If this environment is a stressful or physically demanding one, overtime will increase the likelihood that problems will occur.

Work schedules
- Schedules of work influence attendance, motivation and commitment.

Shift work
- The body clock never fully adjusts when a person works on night shifts because of circumstances in their life.
- If the body clock does not adjust, it can lead to circadian dysrhythmia and sleep disturbance.
- Night shift workers find it hard to sleep during the day and should be offered strategies for going to sleep.
- Strategies to go to sleep include following the usual night-time routine of brushing teeth, putting on pyjamas and closing the curtains.
- Poor quality sleep can have an impact on reaction time and memory, which has implications for safety-critical tasks.
- Workers who suffer from chronic fatigue can develop long term health problems.
- To lessen the chances of night shift workers suffering from indigestion, canteens should offer light, tasty food rather than traditional stodgy meals.
- Shifts that change every week are the most disruptive. Shifts that change every one or two days or after at least three weeks are the least disruptive.

- A shift pattern that starts on days, then moves to evenings followed by nights results in better performance than one that works in reverse.

Automation
- The effects of automation on the workforce should be considered (eg changes in levels of control and responsibility, changed demands and interactions with other operators).

Managing change
- Any changes should be managed and introduced with care – this process will influence the level of acceptance among the workforce.
- Once changes have been made, they should be evaluated to ensure that they have become part of a balanced work system.

References and further reading

Bridger R S. *Introduction to ergonomics* (third edition). McGraw-Hill, 2009.

Davis L E and Wacker G J. Job design. In: Salvendi G (ed.). *Handbook of human factors.* John Wiley, 1987.

Grandjean E. *Fitting the task to the man* (fourth edition). Taylor & Francis, 1988.

Haslegrave C M, Wilson J R, Corlett E N and Manenica I. *Work design in practice.* Taylor & Francis, 1990.

Hayashi M, Chikazawa Y and Hori T. Short nap versus short rest: recuperative effects during VDT work. *Ergonomics*, 2004; 47 (14): 1549–1560.

Josten E. *The effects of extended work days.* Royal Van Gorcum, 2002.

Kroemer K and Grandjean E. *Fitting the task to the human* (fifth edition). Taylor & Francis, 1997.

Lund R T, Bishop A B, Newman A E and Salzman H. *Designed to work: production systems and people.* Prentice Hall, 1993.

Maslow A H. *Motivation and personality.* Harper & Row, 1954.

McKenna E. *Business psychology and organisational behaviour* (fourth edition). Psychological Press, 2006.

Monk T H and Folkard S. *Making shiftwork tolerable.* Taylor & Francis, 1992.

Moon S D and Sauter S L (eds). *Beyond biomechanics: psychosocial aspects of musculoskeletal disorders in office work.* Taylor & Francis, 2007.

Pheasant S. *Ergonomics, work and health.* Macmillan Press, 1991.

Putz-Anderson V. *Cumulative trauma disorders: a manual for musculoskeletal diseases of the upper limbs.* Taylor & Francis, 1988.

Statt D A. *Psychology and the world of work*. Palgrave Macmillan, 2003.
Wilson J R and Corlett E N (eds). *Evaluation of human work* (third edition). CRC Press, 2005.

6 Manual handling

Introduction

Generally speaking, when people think about 'manual handling' they picture a heavy load being lifted by a stocky man in an industrial setting. This naive view of manual handling operations is one reason behind the serious problem of manual handling injuries at work.

In order to control the number of handling accidents and injuries, it should be recognised that:
- women as well as men may be involved in the handling of loads
- it is not only the weight of a load which is problematic
- manual handling is not restricted to industrial sectors – people are involved in handling activities in a variety of environments, including offices, hospitals and schools.

There is a tendency to overlook much of the manual handling carried out behind the scenes by individuals such as post room workers dealing with a variety of incoming and outgoing mail; canteen workers moving cans, pots and bowls full of liquids and foods during meal preparation; and porters and maintenance personnel who are expected to move an unpredictable variety of objects in the course of a working day. Frequently, the manual handling elements of work are unrecognised and those carrying out the work are untrained and unaided.

The HSE has provided figures for injuries sustained by people involved in manual handling in Great Britain for 2007/08. They show that manual handling injuries are still the most common kind of over-three-day injury, accounting for 40 per cent of all such injuries. These cases accounted for an average of 134,200 days lost, with an average of seven days lost per case. Although a large number of these cases will appear to have a sudden onset following the movement of a single object, many of them are likely to be cumulative in nature, resulting from months or years of overuse (or abuse) of the body. Sadly, the outcome of these injuries can be physical impairment or permanent disability.

The cost of work-related accidents and ill health

In addition to the figures reflecting the number of accidents resulting from manual handling operations, the 'cost' factor can be easily illustrated. Employees need to be made aware that a handling accident can have an impact on their quality of life as well as financial implications. The affected person may not enjoy life as before – and could find that they have changed from being a healthy and happy individual to being incapable of putting on their own shoes.

From the financial point of view, there is a loss of income in the short term as the individual recovers from the injury. In the longer term they may not be able to return to the same job – or to work at all. There may be additional expenses, such as drugs and other treatment, and alterations to their home or car to ease their discomfort or accommodate a disability.

The costs to the employer are more clearly defined. The most immediate outcome following an accident in the workplace is loss of output. This can result from the absence of the injured party or others stopping work to assist their injured colleague. Equipment could have been damaged during the accident, which may also affect production. Falling behind schedule can be remedied by overtime but this in itself is costly.

The organisation may be unable to meet its contractual obligations as a result of falling behind schedule (and financial penalties are not uncommon). In addition, in a competitive marketplace, the loss of the client's goodwill or damage to the organisation's reputation should not be overlooked.

Assigning people to investigate the accident and prepare a report, along with organising the repair or cleaning of the accident area, also have cost implications.

The costs directly related to the injured party will include additional administration and the recruitment and training of replacement workers. The employer may be responsible for providing extra medical treatment, such as physiotherapy, and a level of compensation may be required. Although the employer's liability insurance will cover such compensation payments and the associated legal fees, these extra costs will be reflected in increases in the annual premiums. Finally, there could be fines or other penalties (including imprisonment), again with associated legal costs.

It has been estimated that the indirect and uninsurable costs of accidents (which include investigation costs, recruitment and training and loss of goodwill) are at least eight times the direct insured costs (which include sick pay, repairs and compensation payments).

Tackling the problem of manual handling

It is unlikely that the problems associated with manual handling operations will ever be completely eliminated. For as long as people use their own body to lift, carry, push, pull, throw, drop or support an object, there will always be the possibility that they may injure themselves. No handling operation can, or should, be viewed as 100 per cent 'safe'. However, the risks associated with a manual handling operation can be reduced to minimise the possibility of injury. Following sensible guidelines should help to reduce risks – such guidelines are presented throughout this chapter.

Positive steps to tackle the problems associated with manual handling include:
- identifying areas where objects are manually handled
- acknowledging that there may be the potential to cause harm
- recognising that it is within both the employer's and employee's power to combat potentially damaging manual handling problems.

The Manual Handling Operations Regulations 1992 as amended by the Health and Safety (Miscellaneous Amendments) Regulations 2002 provide employers with a means to assess and control the risks associated with manual handling activities.

The Manual Handling Operations Regulations 1992 as amended by the Health and Safety (Miscellaneous Amendments) Regulations 2002

The Regulations came into force on 1 January 1993. They implement European Directive 90/269/EEC on the manual handling of loads.

The Regulations lay out a series of logical steps that an employer should follow. If a general assessment carried out under Regulation 3(1) of the Management of Health and Safety at Work Regulations suggests that a handler may become injured as a result of their work, the first thing that should be considered is whether the manual handling operation can be avoided. If this is not considered reasonably practicable, a suitable and sufficient assessment of the operations should be completed. Following the assessment, steps should be taken to reduce the risk of injury to the lowest level reasonably practicable. Employers are also required to provide information relating to the weight and weight distribution of a load where it is reasonably practicable to do so.

Employers should note that they are not required to provide information on the weights of loads if the effort involved in doing so would be much greater than any health and safety benefits that might result. Generally speaking, the HSE takes the view that it is much more effective to reduce the risk by providing lifting aids, making loads smaller and by limiting the amount that is carried at one time, rather than relying on the provision of weight markings.

If weight markings are attributed to loads, they can be to the nearest kilogram. The intention is to give handlers a quick and reliable warning of the weight they are about to handle if the load is considered to be heavy. To ensure that handlers can benefit from the weight markings, they should be positioned in an obvious location on the load and should be understood easily. On that basis, marking a packing case as containing 24 items at 300 g per item is not particularly helpful as it does not give the handler an immediate indication of the weight. Employers should also consider whether they need to provide a range of weights for an item that might get heavier or lighter under certain conditions. For instance, wooden pallets will become heavier if left in the rain.

Employers who have a workforce who speak a variety of languages, or who employ people with learning difficulties or who just have poor literacy skills generally, may need to consider alternative types of warning, such as colour coding or images.

The weight indicator does not have to be attached to the load itself but can be provided in other forms. For instance, employees can be given a verbal reminder (but this should be recorded formally as having been given) or they can be provided with posters in their work area. Alternatively, employers can place the details on information sheets already in use, such as picking sheets in warehouses. If the items are pushed around on a trolley, as opposed to being picked up and carried, weight information does not need to be provided.

The employer's duty to avoid or reduce the risk of injury will be satisfied within the confines of 'reasonably practicable' if they can show that the cost of any further preventive steps would be grossly disproportionate to the further benefit that would be gained from their implementation.

Interpretation
The Regulations provide a specific interpretation of the terms 'injury', 'load' and 'manual handling operations':
- **Injury** refers to injuries sustained by any part of the body – not just the back. Examples of the types of injury which can occur include those caused by picking up a load which is too heavy, by cutting the hand on a sharp edge, or by dropping the load onto the foot as a result of slippery packaging.

- **Load** refers to a 'discrete moveable object' such as a box, printer, product component, animal, person, or material supported by a fork or shovel. It is important to recognise that an implement, tool or machine is not considered to be a load when in use for its intended purpose. An example of this would be a large welding gun used in a car body factory. Although suspended overhead, these guns are renowned for being extremely heavy and difficult to manoeuvre. In this situation, the use of the welding guns would not be assessed under these Regulations. However, if a consignment of such guns arrives at the plant on a lorry and have to be unloaded by people, they would then be viewed as a load.
- **Manual handling operations** refer to the movement of a load by human effort (as opposed to using a crane or forklift truck). This effort can be applied directly, such as when gripping a load with the hands, or indirectly, as when tying a rope around a load and pulling on it. The hands do not have to be used at all during the handling of the load – the operator can use other parts of their body, such as the foot or shoulder, to move an object.

The term 'manual handling operation' includes what would be viewed as 'typical', ie picking an object up from one place and locating it elsewhere. It also includes other activities such as:
- supporting the load without moving it
- intentionally throwing or dropping the load
- pushing and pulling (which means the load does not have to leave the supporting surface).

Even if operators are provided with mechanical assistance to move the load, they will still be required to move, steady or position the load during its relocation. Therefore, the operation will still involve an element of manual handling.

Duties of the employer – Regulation 4
Generally, the employer is expected to reduce all risk of injury so far as is reasonably practicable. Having introduced measures to reduce the risks, the employer is expected to monitor the interventions to see whether they have achieved the desired effect. If not, they must review their decisions and develop alternative strategies for risk reduction.

All assessments should be kept up to date, bearing in mind that the balance of the reasonably practicable equation may alter as a result of changes in technology, reductions in the cost of handling aids or alterations to the workplace. Assessments should be reviewed if there is a change in the handling operations which could alter previous conclusions or if a reportable injury occurs.

Employers are obviously responsible for employees who work at their own site. But they are also responsible for employees who are working away from their own premises. Although it is difficult to exert control over the conditions in these other working environments, the employer does have control over the training given to employees and, possibly, control over the task and load. For example, if employees are sent to another site to carry out maintenance work, the employer can ensure that they pack their tools and equipment into several manageable loads rather than one or two very large loads. The employer can also ensure that employees are aware of the need to work at a suitable pace with regular rest breaks. Employers in control of premises at which visiting employees have to work have duties towards them under the Health and Safety at Work etc Act 1974, the Management of Health and Safety at Work Regulations 1999, and the Workplace (Health, Safety and Welfare) Regulations 1992, to ensure that the premises and plant provided are in a safe condition.

Anyone in the organisation can undertake the assessments on behalf of the employer. Whoever is given the responsibility of making the assessments should have a clear understanding of the types of handling operation performed, the range of loads which will be handled and the environments in which the handling operations occur. Outside assistance can be sought, particularly with problem areas, but the final responsibility for the assessment lies with the employer.

It is recommended that employers do not ignore the valuable input of employees and their safety representatives. Those directly involved in handling operations are more likely to know exactly where the problem areas are and may be able to give recommendations for change.

Information from records kept by the employer can offer an insight into areas which may require immediate or more thorough assessment. Records from the medical department may show areas with a high incidence of injuries, and personnel records may indicate areas with frequent absences. Further sources of information include those relating to productivity, quality, rejects and damage. This information should only be used to augment other assessment methods.

Assessments will be judged 'suitable and sufficient' if they address in a considered way all the handling operations carried out at the site. Employers should bear in mind that they can carry out 'generic' assessments which will pull together the common threads of many similar operations. A sample checklist is provided within the guidance to the Regulations to assist in the assessment procedure. The assessments should provide a profile of the risks to which employees are exposed and assist the employer in constructing preventive steps where necessary. They should be carried out with reference to relevant findings resulting from other assessments made under Regulation 3 of the Management Regulations and with reference to the results of any health surveillance provided in compliance with Regulation 6.

In general, the significant findings of the assessment should be recorded and kept for as long as they are relevant. However, the assessment does not need to be recorded if the task is simple and obvious and can be easily repeated or explained at any time, or if the handling operation is of low risk, straightforward and lasting only a very short time, and as such the time taken to record the findings would be disproportionate.

When a more detailed assessment is necessary, it is recommended that the assessor should examine the operation under five separate categories:
- **the task** – what the person is doing during the handling operation (eg lifting the load at a distance from the body, whether they are stooping, whether they are sitting)
- **the load** – the characteristics of the load itself, such as its weight, shape and packaging
- **the working environment** – the area in which the person is handling the load (elements such as the floor surface, steps, temperature and space constraints should be taken into account)
- **individual capability** – personal characteristics (ie the physical suitability of the employee to carry out the work, their clothing, footwear or other personal effects, their knowledge and training, whether they are part of a group identified as being especially at risk)
- **other factors** – for example, the effects of using personal protective equipment when carrying out a manual handling operation.

Having assessed the operations, the employer is expected to reduce the risks by adopting a similar structured approach in considering the task, load, working environment and individual capability. Methods for reducing risks associated with manual handling operations are discussed later in this chapter.

Finally, to assist employers in reducing the risk of injury, where the originators of loads (ie manufacturers or packers) are aware that the products are likely to be manually handled they may have relevant duties under the Health and Safety at Work etc Act 1974 and as such should consider making a load easier to grasp and handle and to marking it with the weight and centre of gravity.

Duty of employees – Regulation 5
Employees are required to make use of any equipment provided for them, such as a handling aid, and use it in the manner instructed. Employees are also required to follow the appropriate systems of work laid down by their employer to make handling operations safer.

Exemption certificates – Regulation 6
In the interests of national security, the Secretary of State for Defence may exempt home forces.

Extension outside Great Britain – Regulation 7
The Regulations apply to offshore activities, such as those connected with oil and gas installations.

Repeals and revocations – Regulation 8
The Regulations replace a number of outdated provisions which concentrated on the weight of the load alone. The provisions referred to are listed in Schedule 2 of the Regulations.

Manual handling injuries

Although the main concerns tend to focus on injuries involving the back, other less serious injuries resulting from crushing or trapping the fingers or feet, or from tripping or slipping, should also be addressed.

In addition, it is worth bearing in mind that it is possible to develop a ULD as a result of a handling operation (ULDs are discussed in detail in Chapter 8).

The back
It is estimated that approximately 70 per cent of people will experience backache at least once in their life and this will last for a short period. However, it has also been recognised that the recurrence rate is very high – possibly 60 per cent of affected people will suffer from backache again within one year.

The primary reasons for the condition of the back deteriorating are:
- the natural ageing process
- disease
- illness
- overuse
- general wear and tear.

The pain which can be experienced takes many forms and can be acute, dull, located in one particular area of the back or all over it. Back problems can also create painful sensations from the buttocks down to the feet.

To appreciate why the back is so vulnerable to manual handling injury, it is necessary to have a basic understanding of what it is made up of and how it functions.

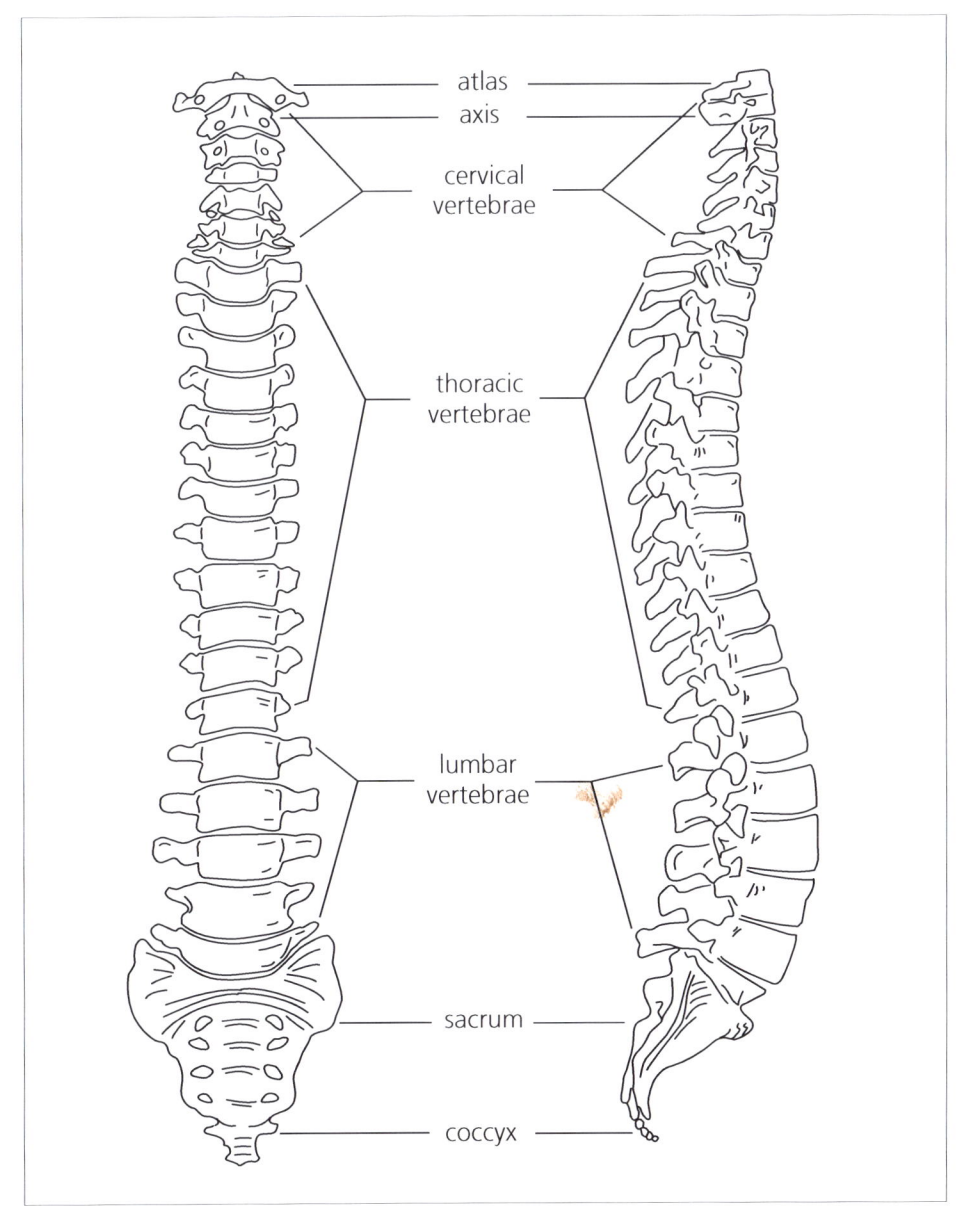

The spinal column
Reproduced from Hollinshead's functional anatomy of the limbs and back *(Jenkins 1998)*

There are 33 vertebrae (or bones) in the spine and these are divided into a number of distinct areas:
- the coccyx
- the sacrum, which consists of five fused vertebrae
- the lumbar region, which most people are familiar with and consists of five vertebrae
- the thoracic vertebrae, which consist of 12 vertebrae in the chest and rib area
- the cervical vertebrae, which consist of seven vertebrae in the neck.

As the weight borne by the lumbar region is greater than that carried by either the thoracic or cervical vertebrae, and as the spine undergoes the highest degrees of leverage at this point, such as when the person leans forward or sideways, the lumbar region is the part of the back which is subjected to the highest levels of stress.

The discs (see opposite) sit between the vertebrae and act as shock absorbers. They also give the back flexibility, allowing the person to lean forwards, sideways or even backwards. The discs tend to be thicker towards the bottom of the spine than at the top and they tend to be thicker at the front than the back in the lumbar and thoracic regions, which contributes to the forward curvature of the spine in these areas. The discs are made up of a fibrous outer band (the annulus fibrosus) with a fluid-filled centre (the nucleus pulposus). Normally, when a person sits or stands upright the pressure coming down through the spine (caused by the weight of the upper body) is evenly spread across the surface of the discs, allowing them to retain their disc-like shape. However, because of its make-up the disc can change its shape easily, such as when a person leans forward or sideways. When they do so, the fluid-filled centre becomes wedge-shaped, with the narrowest part of the wedge being on the same side as the bend, where the greatest pressure is being applied. An easy way to picture what happens to the disc as a person leans forward is to imagine a small, round, ripe camembert sandwiched between two slices of bread. If someone was to place this 'sandwich' on the palm of one hand and they pressed down evenly on the top slice of bread with the other hand the camembert would probably bulge slightly and evenly all the way around its perimeter. If, however, the person exerted greater pressure on one side of the upper slice of bread, the camembert would bulge more on the side opposite where the greatest amount of pressure was being applied.

The annulus fibrosus can bulge or even rupture if it is subjected to excessive stress, particularly during bending. Bulges or ruptures (ie a prolapsed disc) tend to happen in the posterior region, as this is where the

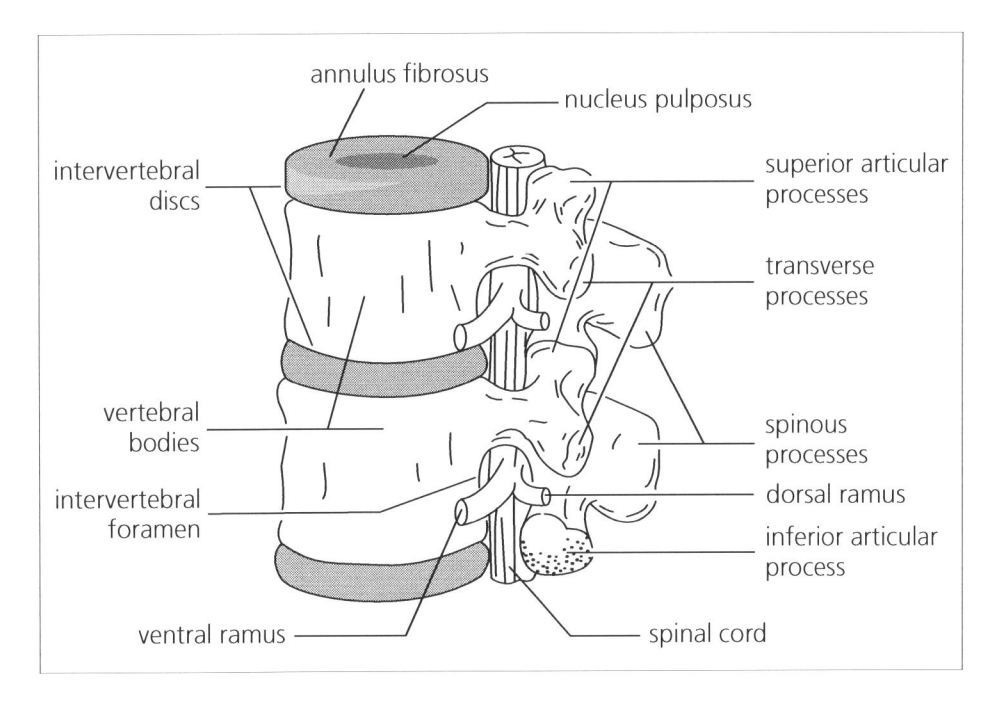

Intervertebral discs *Reproduced from* Hollinshead's functional anatomy of the limbs and back *(Jenkins 1998)*

discs are at their thinnest. Bulges and ruptures are also more common in the lumbar and lower cervical regions.

People who experience a prolapsed disc will usually report that it occurred suddenly. This will usually occur because of an acute failure in the annulus fibrosus. When this happens the person will experience pain, usually quite severe. They do not experience this pain as a result of the rupture because the disc does not have its own nerve supply. They will be experiencing pain because of the pressure being exerted on a nerve root or spinal nerve by the actual bulge or rupture and the pain will be centred in the region served by the nerves. For instance, it is not uncommon for problems in the neck to cause discomfort in the hand and some people who have problems in the lumbar region will experience pains in their thighs or lower leg. If they are experiencing discomfort in a buttock that also travels into the thigh and possibly down to the feet, they are likely to be suffering from sciatica, which can be triggered by a disc problem in the lumbar region. It is believed that the development of good handling techniques, and good posture generally, will go a long way to avoiding problems involving the discs.

The muscles of the spine are the main means by which the spine is kept upright and can be rotated. When a person stands upright, the most challenging task faced by the muscles is resisting the pull of gravity. If the person remains in an upright, balanced posture, the muscles have to do little to maintain stability. However, if a person leans forward, such as when raising a load from the floor, they rely on the muscles contracting to prevent them from falling forward. They also rely on the muscles to allow them to lean forward seamlessly and smoothly. The further the person leans forward, such as if stretching across a desk to pick up a monitor, the more active their back muscles have to become. As the person returns to the upright position, the same muscles assist in the change of posture. Throughout the process of leaning forward and returning to the upright position, the back muscles work in conjunction with the stomach muscles, which also assist in offering stability. This is one of the main reasons why people with back injuries are given stomach strengthening exercises during physiotherapy sessions.

Once a person adopts a sitting or standing position, they rely on static muscle work to maintain that position over any period of time. Static muscle work occurs when the muscles contract over an extended, uninterrupted period of time. This is in contrast to dynamic muscle work, which involves the contraction and relaxation of muscles to achieve movement. What some people may find surprising is that static muscle work, where no apparent movement is visible, is actually more fatiguing than dynamic muscle work. For that reason, it takes workers longer to recover from the effects of static muscle work than from the effects of dynamic muscle work. This underlines the importance of people in apparently sedentary tasks, such as at desks, taking regular breaks away from their workstation.

The ligaments virtually run the whole length of the spine and assist the muscles in providing stability when the person is in an upright position. They can be described as leathery straps that stretch between the bones, offering passive resistance and limiting movement as the joint reaches the end of its normal range. Ligaments, as well as muscles and tendons (which anchor muscle to bone), are susceptible to injury as a result of stretching, such as when an individual bends forward at the waist, and twisting. Twisting commonly occurs if handlers do not move their feet when transferring loads between two surfaces, such as between the end of a rollerbed and a trolley or pallet. Typically, they rely on rotating their trunk during the transfer of the load, causing twisting at the waist. Simply learning to move the feet when transferring a load will instantly eliminate any twisting and thus any unnecessary stresses placed on the back.

Hernias
Hernias are often associated with manual handling because the lifting action is accompanied by an increase in pressure in the abdominal cavity.

The abdominal wall can have weak spots or gaps and sometimes during the lifting operation – particularly when the body is bent at the waist, compressing the internal organs – a loop of intestine may be forced out through a weak spot. A hernia is the protrusion of this loop through the abdominal wall. Poor lifting techniques which involve the operator bending at the waist are known to increase the risk of hernias.

Other injuries
Other injuries may include cuts, bruises and fractures. They typically result from poor housekeeping where tripping hazards are present, from poor lighting, from dropping or spilling of the load, or from crushing or entrapment by the load.

Mode of movement

The manner in which a load is moved will determine how the body is stressed, how quickly it fatigues and the possible injuries that can occur. Lifting an object results in increased compressive force on the spine, which can affect the discs, ligaments, tendons and muscles.

When pushing and pulling loads, both the abdominal and back muscles are called into play, thereby increasing the reactive compressive force on the spine. Pushing in particular increases the loading on the shoulders and breathing is made more difficult by the subsequent rigidity of the rib-cage.

Once an object is supported in a fixed position or carried across a distance, static muscle work is required. Such work arises from having to hold the muscles tensed for an uninterrupted period and is extremely fatiguing for the muscle groups concerned.

Avoiding the risks of a manual handling operation

Obviously, the surest way of reducing risks is to avoid the handling operation altogether.

Direct delivery
Some working environments lend themselves to the safe movement of loads by mechanical means. For example, loads such as flour, starch, grains and liquids could be pumped directly to the area of use, thereby eliminating the interim storage areas where loads are held temporarily before being rehandled and taken to the final area of use.

Other loads could remain on pallets at all times, with the complete pallet being moved to the area of use via a forklift – rather than splitting the pallet and handling items individually.

Increase in volume
Many loads are on the borderline between 'tempting' and 'unmanageable' (eg 35 kg sacks of salt and 250 kg drums of detergent). Operators may attempt to move this type of load and as a consequence injure themselves. It may be worth considering the delivery of products in volumes which are impossible to move by hand. The only option open to operators in these situations would be to use forklift trucks. This is contrary to the view that making a load smaller makes it safer to move, but it does remove the temptation experienced by some operators to 'have a go' and attempt to manage a load unaided.

Mechanical transportation
Conveyor lines, rollerbeds and chutes will eliminate the need for the operator to move an object manually from one area to the next.

Trolleys also eliminate the need to carry an object between two locations. However, that is not to say that the task will necessarily be made easier for the handler. The movement of a trolley always requires a degree of effort on the part of the handler to move it and this will be influenced by the characteristics of the trolley and its wheelbase. Maintenance is an important feature and every trolley should be subject to regular checks to ensure that they are functioning effectively. Wheels and castors may become worn or damaged and will increase the stresses placed on the handler.

When selecting a trolley, consideration has to be given to the load that will be moved and the environment in which it will be moved. The trolley should have sufficient levels, or tiers, to accommodate the varying loads easily but these should not be so high that they impede the handler's view as they push the load. The wheels should be capable of coping with the total load weight that is likely to be placed on the trolley. They should also suit the surface over which they are likely to move. Some trolley wheels are intended specifically for use over carpeted surfaces, while others are intended for use on vinyl or concrete surfaces. This has implications in sites where trolleys tend to get borrowed from their original area of use and end up in a completely different type of environment. All wheels do not work equally well on all floor surfaces. Nylon or cast-iron wheels will move more easily across a hard, smooth floor surface such as concrete. They will struggle if they are pulled over bumpy ground or a surface with potholes. In these situations trolleys that have rubber wheels will move more easily as the rubber helps to absorb some of the shock. Pneumatic tyres are probably the most effective when used over uneven floor surfaces, but that assumes they have the correct pressure.

Few people involved in purchasing trolleys will consider the impact of the size of the wheel on the effort involved in moving it; nor are they likely to give much thought to how many wheels they need. Larger wheels make it easier for the handler to push a trolley over uneven or broken floor surfaces as they have lower rolling resistance. Small wheels are best suited to lighter loads being moved over shorter distances. Narrow wheels work effectively on hard surfaces, whereas broader wheels make the movement of a trolley across a carpeted floor or a broken surface less arduous.

If the mechanical aid has only two wheels, such as a sack truck, it must be recognised that as the load is tipped back the handler bears some of the weight of both the trolley and the load. For that reason, using a two-wheeled mechanical aid is probably not advisable over long distances. In these situations, platform trolleys would be beneficial. They are also more suited to bigger, bulkier loads. If platform trolleys are being used, handlers need to be reminded that they should avoid bending when placing items on the lower level. Having drop-sides on these trolleys also makes the loads more accessible when removing them. Rather than lifting a load over the side of a shelf, the handler can drop the side and slide the load towards them before picking it up.

Not many people know whether they should have swivelling wheels on the front of the trolley or the rear, whether all four wheels should swivel or whether two should swivel. If the trolley will be used in a confined space or in a congested area where it will have to be manoeuvred around obstacles, four swivelling wheels are recommended. It should be fitted with handles at both ends so that it can be steered from either end. However, as more effort is needed to control and steer such a trolley it should only be used over short distances. In addition, this type of trolley may start moving sideways on a slope, making it difficult to control. If the trolley is being moved on a slope, the handler should always be uphill of it so that it does not collide with them if they lose control of it.

If the handler has to move a trolley over a long distance and the journey is expected to involve slopes, they should have a trolley with two fixed and two swivelling wheels. If slopes are a frequent feature of the route, the trolley should be fitted with a brake. This is because a slope with a gradient of more than 2 per cent will require a significant increase in effort to control it both during ascent and descent. Brakes can be either hand- or foot-operated. They need to be easy to reach and use and should not require excessive force to engage or disengage. If a foot brake is fitted to the trolley it should not be positioned so that it comes in contact with the handler's feet or legs when they walk.

A long trolley with two central fixed wheels and a set of swivelling wheels at each end will make it easier to manoeuvre around corners. However, locating it neatly against a wall is more difficult.

The height and positioning of handles contributes to the ease with which a trolley can be moved. Allowing the handler to grip a handle of a suitable diameter between waist and shoulder height should be the aim, as this is most likely to allow them to stand upright when applying the necessary forces. Cylindrical handles with a diameter of 25–40 mm are considered to be the most suitable, particularly if they are covered in an insulating material such as rubber. This not only prevents heat exchange, but also reduces the likelihood of the hand slipping. Using vertically positioned handles allows the user to grip the handles at a point which suits their stature. These types of handle work best on narrow trolleys. Locating them about 450 mm apart is likely to be most effective. If the trolley has to be manoeuvred precisely then horizontal handles make the task easier. As it is desirable for the handler to be able to push a trolley through a doorway without grazing or crushing their knuckles, the trolley should be about 80 mm narrower than the narrowest door it passes through. Handles should be set in from the outer edges of the trolley to ensure that there is always clearance for the hands when walking through doorways and along narrow corridors. Doorways should not encourage the handlers to abandon the trolley and carry items. Efforts should be made to ensure that trolleys can pass easily through doorways, so automatic door opening facilities should be considered or perhaps a simple wedge to temporarily hold the door open.

How the handler chooses to move the trolley will influence the degree of stress associated with moving the trolley. If they choose to drag it behind them one-handed, they will twist to one side and the workload will be focused on one side of the body, in particular the arm involved in gripping the trolley. Using two hands to move a trolley enables the handler to stand upright and maintain a more symmetrical posture. They are also able to share the workload out more evenly across their body as two arms/hands are being used to control and steer the load.

It is always preferable for a handler to push a load in front of them. However, this will be dictated to an extent by the height of the load on the trolley. If the upper load on a trolley is no higher than 1,400 mm above the floor, even the smallest woman should be able to see over it.

The only way to ensure that excessive forces are not required to move a trolley is to actually measure the forces involved. This feature is often overlooked during manual handling risk assessments. Some assessors rely on the 'feel' of the trolley if they test it. This is not acceptable. When measuring the effort involved, two separate pieces of information should be collected: the effort involved in starting the movement of the load from a standstill and the effort involved in keeping the load moving. It is essential that several sample measurements are taken to ensure that accurate readings have been recorded. The measurements should also be taken in a range of typical environments and this may include taking measurements on different floor surfaces or when pulling the trolley around corners or up slopes. If a trolley is taken into a lift, measurements should be made at the point where the trolley enters or leaves the lift in case a difference in floor level causes an increase in effort required.

Finally, specific mention should be made at this point of a particular type of load movement using mechanical aids. Many patients who have mobility problems or disabilities are now moved in hospitals, care homes or in their own residences with the use of hoists. The movement of people makes manual handling a much more complex operation. The complexity is influenced by the body size of the patient, their weight, how co-operative they are (and this is influenced by their cognitive skills, injury or disability, personality and so on) and how capable they are of bearing their own weight. It has been reported (Rice *et al.* 2009) that compared to manually moving a patient, using a floor-based or ceiling-mounted hoist significantly reduces the physical stresses experienced by handlers. When use of these types of handling aid was compared, Rice *et al.* found that the forces required when pushing, pulling and rotating the hoist (such as when changing direction of movement) were significantly less when using an overhead-mounted (ie tracked) hoist. Marras *et al.* (2009) have found that the stresses of using a floor-based hoist peaked at a level that caused concern when the hoist was turned, particularly in a confined space such as a bathroom. It is also likely that the forces required to move the floor-based hoist would significantly increase when operated across less optimal flooring, such as rough wood or carpeting, which are typical in many care homes and private residences; this should be taken into account during risk assessments.

Handling aids

The provision of specifically designed aids should assist in handling operations. However, such aids can be expensive and serious consideration should be given to their design and use before they are transformed from paper to prototype.

The following are examples of issues that the designer or purchaser may need to address when considering a handling aid:

- **Will the handling device reduce the physical effort required to move the load?** It would be self-defeating if the effort required to move the handling aid into position was similar to that required to move the load manually.
- **Will its introduction cause any new problems?** If a handling device is being used alongside a production area where operators have to carry out other activities, it could become an obstruction, reducing their freedom of movement and interfering with their adoption of safe working postures.
- **Will it be easy to operate?** If a handling aid is too complicated or awkward to use, operators will tend to work without it when moving the load.
- **Will it function adequately in terms of speed and flexibility once introduced to the work area?** This is particularly important if the handling device will interact with a continually moving production line.
- **Will operators be satisfied with its use?** If operators are not satisfied with the design or introduction of a handling device, they may not use it.
- **Can operators use it comfortably when wearing PPE (particularly gloves)?** If the handling aid becomes difficult or more complex to work with because operators are wearing PPE, they may work either without the aid or without their PPE.
- **How much training will operators need?** This should be worked out before the handling aid is introduced so that enough time is set aside. If appropriate training is not given, the safe operation – and continued use – of the handling device cannot be guaranteed.
- **Will the supplier provide the training?** If so, the employer should ensure that training is adequate.
- **What will happen to the device when it is not in use?** It may need to be moved out of the immediate area to provide additional work space. The device should allow for this movement.
- **Does the device include a facility to allow it to be locked off?** If the handling aid is free-moving (eg on an overhead gantry) efforts should be made to ensure that it cannot move around when not under the direct control of an operator.
- **Can the device be misused or abused?** A facility may need to be built into the handling device to prevent operators from abusing it.
- **Will the device damage or drop the object it should be moving?** For example, if a vacuum lifter is used in a dusty environment it might drop the load if the dust affects its contact with the load.

All these issues should be considered before designing or purchasing a handling aid. If they are not, it is possible that the (perhaps costly) handling aid will reside unused by the side of the work area. It is advisable to try out a device before introducing it fully into the workplace to determine whether there are any teething problems.

Reduction in degree of handling

There are other methods of reducing risks involved with manual handling. In certain cases it may be possible to reduce the degree of handling involved. For example, many machines which prepare food products deposit the food into a container at the out-feed end. The operator commonly lifts the container and carries it to the weighing scales before carrying it to a pallet. Simply incorporating the scales into the bench at the out-feed end of the machine would remove the need to carry the load to the scales before depositing it on the pallet (which should be located close to the bench).

Of course, eliminating or reducing the degree of handling involved is not always possible, or practical; therefore, other ways of reducing the risks should be found.

The problems of manual handling

Typically, it is assumed that the weight of the object is the most problematic aspect of the manual handling operation (hence the common assumption that the weight will be implicated if an injury occurs). However, in many cases the weight of the load is not the key issue. If appropriate preventive strategies are to be devised to combat the risks, a clear understanding of all contributory factors is required. The simplest way to examine the risks is to use the categories referred to earlier – task, load, environment and individual.

The task
When considering the task, the focus should be on what the person is actually doing as they move the load – attention should not be focused on the load itself at this point.

Posture
Posture is of great importance. The operator should achieve the appropriate posture before they attempt to take hold of the load. If they do not locate their feet so that they have a stable base, or if they do not

take hold of the load in the best place using a strong grasp, they cannot hope to control the load properly once it clears the supporting surface. Appropriate lifting postures put the operator in a position of strength where they can control the load more easily during its movement and where they are less likely to injure themselves. Correct foot placement is the key to safe lifting. Training in good lifting techniques is discussed later in this chapter.

Twisting while lifting significantly increases the stresses placed on the lower back and is known to be particularly hazardous. Continual twisting is likely to act cumulatively rather than immediately in terms of aggravating the back. This action is typically seen when an operator moves an object between two surfaces located close together, such as between the end of a conveyor belt and a pallet. Instead of repositioning the feet to move closer to each surface in turn, the operator will often pick from the conveyor and twist at the waist to deposit on the pallet.

Untrained operators often bend over at the waist when picking up a load, or lean forwards when reaching to grasp a load at a distance from the body. Both actions increase the stresses on the lower back because once the operator throws their trunk forwards it becomes an 'unintended load' which adds its weight to the weight of the 'intended' object the operator is trying to move. In effect, two weights are being moved – the upper body and the intended load. This will be tiring, particularly if carried out repeatedly or for long periods.

Reaching
An operator may lift an object located at a distance from their body by stretching their arms out rather than moving the object closer. Lifting a load in this manner, when it is at arms' length, is five times more stressful for the back than lifting the same load close to the body. In addition, once the load is at a distance from the operator's body it is much more difficult to control and the friction between the load and the operator's clothing, which helps to hold the load in position, is lost.

The aim should be to have all the objects that need to be moved within a zone that can be reached easily by the sweep of the forearm when there is a 90° angle at the elbow. Of course, this is not always possible, so when working at a surface such as a desk, the heaviest and most frequently used items, such as reference folders, should be sited closer to the operator, while the lighter and easier to move objects are stored on the outer edges.

Obstacles should be removed so that the operator does not have to reach over them to access the load. It is not uncommon to see operators reaching over boxes or pallets stored at floor level (which may be irrelevant to the operator and their task) when retrieving an object from a storage space directly behind them. In this situation, the risk of the handling operation is significantly increased. By moving close to the load, the stress on the operator's lower back will be reduced.

Operators will often be seen reaching across a pallet, stillage or work surface to retrieve or deposit a load rather than moving to a more appropriate position. Operators should be encouraged to move closer to the appropriate side of the storage container or work surface so that they are closer to the load. This will, of course, only work if there is enough space around the sides of the storage container or work surface to allow them to move freely.

In some instances, simply tilting a storage container will bring a load closer to the operator, thus reducing the need for them to bend at the waist and reach forwards. If one side of a storage container can be removed, it would make the retrieval of items stored towards the rear much easier. The operator responsible for delivering storage containers to production areas should ensure that they are delivered the right way round (there is, of course, no point in having a container with removable sides if the appropriate side is the furthest from the operator).

Working height
If the operator has to reach upwards to retrieve an object, stresses on both the arms and the back are increased. If the object is above head height, such as when reaching to an upper shelf or rack, operators cannot be sure that they have in fact grasped the uppermost object. Once they pull the load towards them they may find that something else, previously unseen, is situated above it. This other object may fall and injure the operator.

If items are to be stored on shelves or racks, they should be positioned in a manner which reflects their weight and the ease with which they can be handled. The greatest strength is found between knuckle and shoulder height and the heaviest or more difficult to handle items should therefore be stored on shelves or racks that fall within this range, preferably at waist height. Lighter or easier to handle objects could be stored on shelves which fall outside this range.

To ensure that items are consistently sited on the appropriate shelves, it may be advantageous to label the shelves to indicate the range of items which should be stored there. These labels could also provide information on the weight of the object so that operators will know whether they need a second operator or a handling aid to help move it.

For shelves which are located above shoulder height, an inexpensive platform or duckboard will make removal of objects easier – particularly for shorter operators. If platforms are introduced, they should not be so small that people can fall from them easily. Care should also be taken to prevent the platform from becoming a tripping hazard when other operators move around the area.

Stacking heights of goods on pallets should be controlled so that operators do not work above shoulder height. Pallets are typically stacked to a level well above head height, which increases the risks involved in handling loads.

It is preferable for operators not to have to lift from floor level, as this encourages stooping. Delivering loads directly onto tables or benches rather than onto the floor should be considered. Placing loads in raised storage containers or on benches with feet will allow the operator to position their feet under the supporting surface, which moves them closer to the load.

Locating a loaded pallet on top of another base pallet will raise it and make it easier for the operator to lift any loads on the pallet safely.

If it is not possible to raise the load off floor level, it would be preferable for the operators not to have to lift the load beyond waist height. If the load must go beyond this point, it would be more appropriate to provide an interim surface on which to rest the load during the lift. This would allow the operators to change posture and grip so that they are in a stronger position when raising the load to its final position. Although it would appear that the amount of handling has been increased, it is better to make two safe lifts than one unsafe lift.

Walking distance
The longer an operator is in contact with a load, the more likely it is that the handling operation will be fatiguing. If, having picked up a load, the operator has to walk a significant distance (> 10 m), the time involved in the handling operation is extended, and hence the stresses of the operation are increased. It is not uncommon for operators to be required to walk unnecessarily long distances due to poor workstation layout – objects are typically stored away from their area of use and their location has not been determined by frequency of use or overall weight. Simple improvements in workstation layout, such as locating the heaviest or most frequently used items closest to their area of use and placing lighter, infrequently used loads at more distant points, should reduce the risk of injury.

Pushing and pulling

Being able to push or pull something, as opposed to lifting and carrying it, does not guarantee that a handler can work without injury. The HSE has shown that pushing and pulling were involved in 11 per cent of the manual handling-related accidents reported under the requirements of the Reporting of Injuries, Diseases and Dangerous Occurrences Regulations that it investigated. In 44 per cent of the cases, the back was the reported site of injury. The upper limbs were injured in 28.6 per cent of the cases investigated. The HSE found that 61 per cent of the accidents involved pushing and pulling of objects that did not have a wheeled base, such as a desk or bales. In 35 per cent of the cases investigated, the handler was pushing or pulling a wheeled object such as a trolley or cart.

The ease with which the operator can push or pull a load will be influenced by the condition of the floor, the type of footwear used and the nature of the load. Current HSE guidelines for pushing and pulling loads suggest that a force of about 20 kg (approximately 200 newtons (N)) for men and about 15 kg (approximately 150 N) for women for starting and stopping the load is acceptable. The HSE also suggests that a force of about 10 kg (100 N) for men and about 7 kg (70 N) for women for keeping the load in motion is acceptable. These figures are based on the assumption that the hands are kept between knuckle and shoulder height and the load is not pushed further than 20 m at a time without sufficient rest and recovery periods.

For very large loads that do not have wheeled bases, such as sliding doors or crates, the operator could put their back against the load and use their leg muscles to exert the required force. Obviously, an operator using this approach will not be able to see easily where the object they are pushing is going.

Sudden movement

Should the load resist movement by the operator and then suddenly move, the operator may be unprepared for this and lose control of the load. The unpredictable movement of a load (eg a trolley wheel sticking in a pothole or product components tightly packed in a storage container suddenly becoming free) may put the operator at risk.

Seated lifting

Not all operators stand upright to handle a load. The seated operator carrying out handling operations faces additional problems. The operator will rely on the arms to do the work and may ultimately lean forwards to come within range of the object. Once they lean forwards there is the possibility that their seat may move backwards away from them. The seated lifter should not be expected to lift as much as someone who is standing. The HSE has recognised that special consideration should be given to the seated lifter. It provides a guideline figure of lifting no more than 5 kg for men and 3 kg for women when the person is sitting upright with their elbows at a 90° angle. In addition, the movement of loads from floor level should be avoided as the person will bend at the waist to reach the object. They will also often twist their body if they are not using a swivel chair.

Team lifting
Assigning two or more people to the handling activity may not eliminate problems. In fact, once other people join in the lifting operation additional problems are encountered. For example, ascending or descending steps or slopes becomes a more complicated operation when several people are handling a load, particularly as each additional person may impede the view of their opposite number on the other side of the load. Further problems are encountered when the load's packaging is designed for one operator and only one set of handholds is provided.

When working as a team, the operators should ensure that the team members are of equal build and ability so that all are lifting under equal conditions. One of the team members should take control, co-ordinating the timing of the lift and the direction of movement. There should be sufficient room for all team members to move easily as they relocate the load. If handholds are available, there should be enough for all team members. The total weight which can be safely picked up by a team does not increase in direct proportion to the number of people in the team. The HSE suggests that as an approximate guide, the capability of a two-person team is two-thirds the sum of their individual capabilities, and the capability of a three-person team is half the sum of their individual capabilities.

The table opposite provides a conversion of the HSE's current numerical guidelines for single handlers so that they relate to two or three handlers working together.

Work organisation
Obviously the speed at which an operator has to work, the length of time they have to work before having a break, and the degree of repetition, will influence whether and when an operator will experience fatigue or discomfort. Even if the handling task cannot be changed in any way, the risk associated with the movement of a load can be reduced by rest and task rotation. Effective use of programmes incorporating these can limit the operator's exposure time to the situation, and so the risk of injury is reduced. A rotation programme should ensure that operators move

Body position	Two men Close to body	Two men Away from body	Three men Close to body	Three men Away from body	Two women Close to body	Two women Away from body	Three women Close to body	Three women Away from body
Above shoulder height	13.3	6.7	15.0	7.5	9.3	4.0	10.5	4.5
Elbow to shoulder height	26.7	13.3	30.3	15.0	17.3	9.3	19.5	10.5
Knuckle to elbow height	33.3	20.0	37.5	22.5	21.3	13.3	24.0	15.0
Mid-lower leg to knuckle height	26.7	13.3	30.0	15.0	17.3	9.3	19.5	10.5
Below mid-lower leg	13.3	6.7	15.0	7.5	9.3	4.0	10.5	4.5

Lifting guidelines relating to team handling (in kg)

between qualitatively different tasks – for example, moving from loading boxes onto pallets at the end of a quiche production line to loading boxes onto pallets at the end of a pie production line will probably not reduce the fatiguing effects nor reduce the risks of the handling operation.

The load

Weight
Often when attention is given to the risk presented by a load, the focus is on its weight. However, this is only part of the picture. Making the load smaller and lighter may be one solution for reducing the risk. If the load is smaller it will be easier to grasp and handle. But consideration should be given to whether reducing the weight or size of the load will lead to an increase in the number of times the smaller loads have to be moved. In addition, handling smaller loads may result in operators bending down to lower levels at certain times, such as when loading them onto a pallet.

If the weight cannot be reduced it may be beneficial to consider supporting the load in some way, particularly in a situation where a container such as a large jug is being used to fill other containers.

Shape
A bulky load is more difficult to take hold of securely and safely. As a result, operators will have to use more effort and therefore will become tired more quickly. In addition, if the load is difficult to hold it is more likely to be dropped.

Size
If a load is large it may not clear the floor when lifted, which may mean it has to be dragged. If the load is lifted so that it does not have to be dragged, it may interfere with vision. In both cases the risk of tripping or falling is increased.

Centre of gravity
The centre of gravity of an object is particularly important, yet it is a commonly overlooked factor. If an operator attempts to pick up a package which looks symmetrical, but has been packed in such a way that the majority of the weight is on one side, they may find that they are thrown off balance because the heaviest side is further away from their body than they anticipated. Even when a load is manageable, it should be carried with the heaviest side towards the body to reduce the forces acting on the spine.

Sudden movements
If the load moves suddenly because it lacks rigidity (eg in the case of an unconscious person or animal) or because it has not been packed tightly within its outer packaging, operators will be at increased risk because they will be unprepared for the movement and the additional stresses it produces.

Grasping and moving the load
The outer condition of the load may make it difficult to move safely. If the edges are sharp or the contents are very hot or cold, operators may use gloves to protect their hands from cuts and burns. Using gloves can impair dexterity, making it more difficult to grip the object securely.

Making the object easier to grasp should be a major consideration. If the load itself cannot be altered it could be placed in a container with appropriate handholds – bearing in mind that adding a container increases the overall weight. Some seemingly 'lightweight' plastic containers (eg used to carry foods, nuts and bolts or documents) can add 2–3 kg to the total weight being moved.

The location and design of handholds will influence how easy an object is to move. The size or the centre of gravity of a load will influence where the handles should be located. The handholds should be designed so that they accommodate the operator's hands (which may or may not be protected by gloves). If the object is to be carried from the base, it may be advantageous to cut finger wells into the bottom surface to prevent the fingers being trapped when the load is put down.

Packing material used in containers should not add unnecessarily to the weight of the load and should prevent the contents from moving around freely during their relocation. (Popcorn can offer a more environmentally friendly alternative to polystyrene shapes or similar packing materials.)

If, as in the case of moving powders or liquids, packing cannot be used to prevent the shifting of contents, the containers should be filled as far as possible to limit the degree of movement. Should the contents still move around uncontrollably during relocation, it may be safer to use a handling aid.

Labelling

If organisations are responsible for the packing of their own loads into containers, and these will be handled by other operators in the facility, a labelling system to identify the important characteristics of the load may be appropriate. Labels could carry information relating to weight and distribution of weight, along with advice on how the load should be moved (eg 'with assistance', 'with a handling aid', 'with caution'). Colour coding and symbols could be used in place of a written description to provide a more immediate message that should be understood unambiguously by a greater number of people.

It may be possible to print appropriate information onto documents used in the production process. For example, in a warehouse setting it would be relatively simple to incorporate information into a computer-generated picking list which would advise the operator before they select an item that it may be heavy or bulky. Using symbols would be particularly useful in this situation.

HSE guidance

The HSE has generated guidance for the lifting and lowering of loads (see next page) which provides organisations with an indication of how acceptable their own working practices are in terms of the objects they expect operators to move during normal processing or production.

If this information is used as a basic guide for determining the acceptability of working practices, it should be borne in mind that these figures are based on the assumption that the operator is using both hands to pick up the load and that they are in a reasonable environment and are

Guidance for load handling
Reproduced from Manual Handling Operations Regulations 1992: guidance on Regulations (HSE 2004)

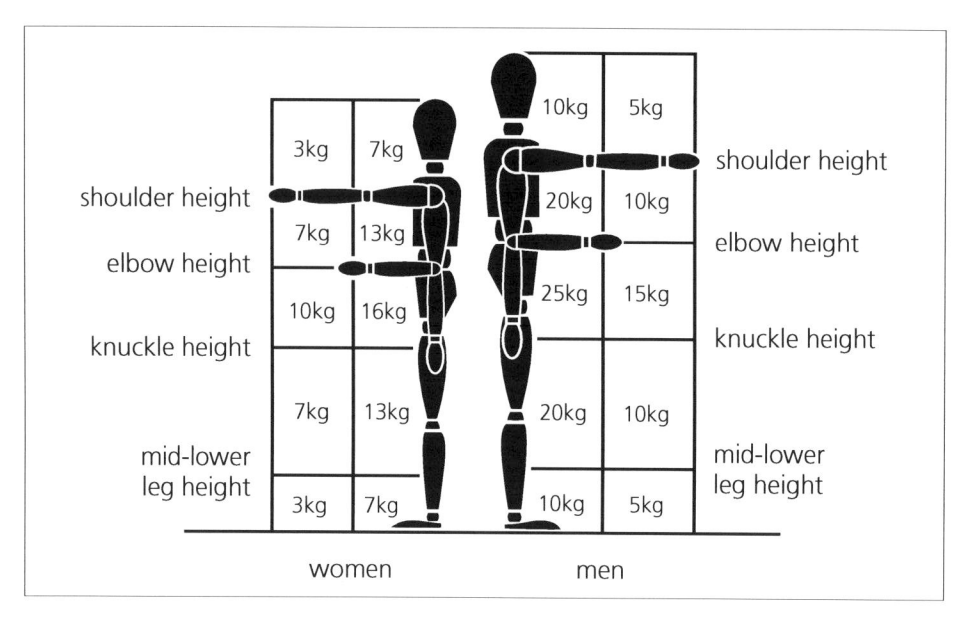

	women		men	
shoulder height	3kg	7kg	10kg	5kg
elbow height	7kg	13kg	20kg	10kg
knuckle height	10kg	16kg	25kg	15kg
mid-lower leg height	7kg	13kg	20kg	10kg
	3kg	7kg	10kg	5kg

using appropriate lifting techniques. Reductions should be made to the guideline figures in certain situations, such as when the operator is twisting or carrying out a repetitive operation.

The guideline figures are based on infrequent operations of up to 30 lifts an hour with provisos that the task is not a paced operation, it provides opportunities for rest and recovery, and that the load is not supported for extended periods of time. It is suggested that the figures should be reduced by 30 per cent if the operation is repeated once or twice per minute, by 50 per cent if the operation is repeated five to eight times per minute and by 80 per cent where the operation is repeated more than 12 times per minute.

The figures opposite and on page 128 show the numerical values once these reductions relating to handling frequency have been made.

Assessors should be careful that they apply the appropriate set of figures to their workforce. If women are likely to handle loads in the environment being assessed, the assessor should use the sets of figures relating to women as their guidance.

The HSE recommends that the figures should be reduced by approximately 10 per cent if the operator is twisting by 45° and by 20 per cent if the operator is twisting by 90°. The HSE figures are based on an assumption that when twisting the feet remain stationary and the upper body (particularly the shoulders) is rotated to one side.

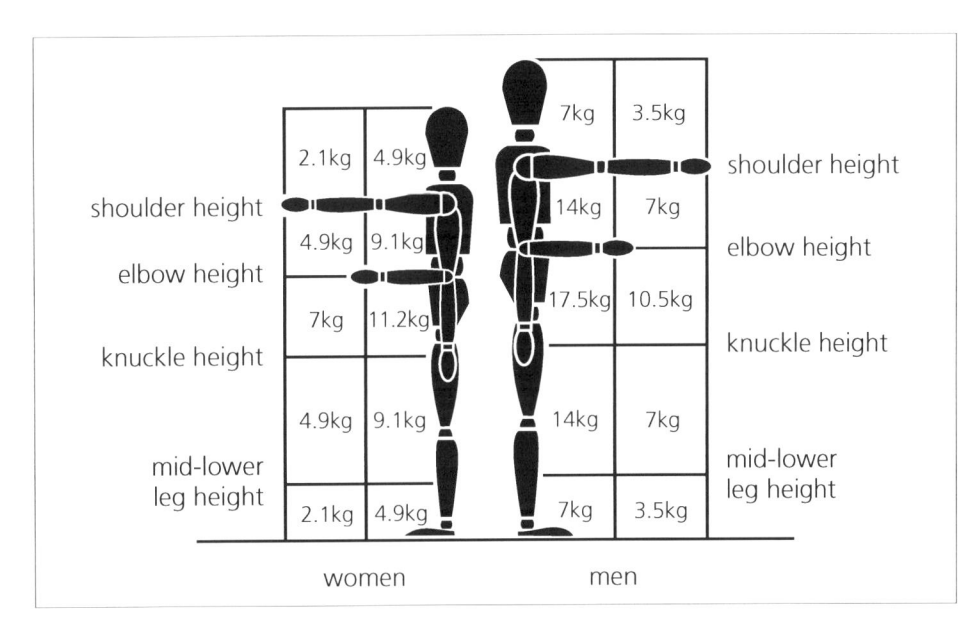

Guideline figures reduced by 30 per cent for an operation repeated once or twice per minute

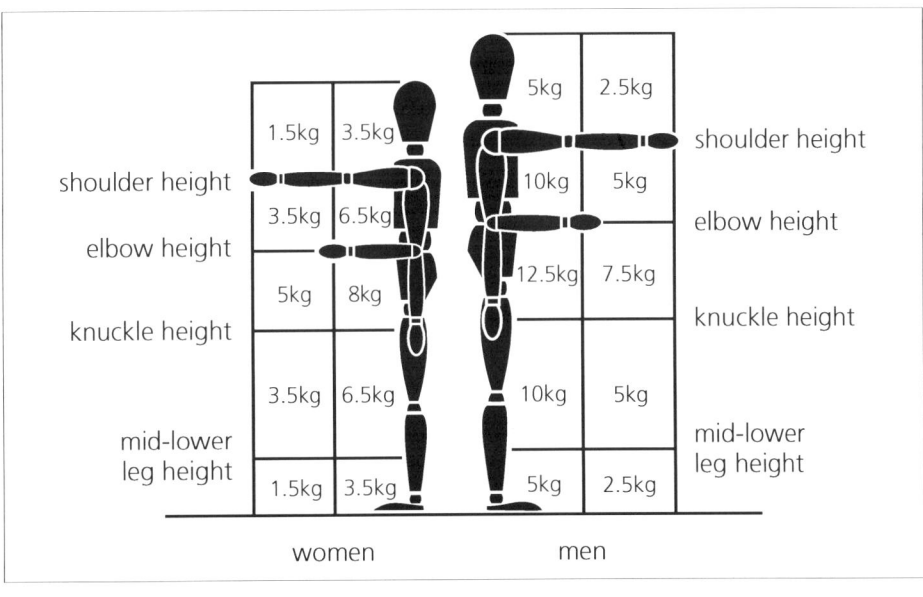

Guideline figures reduced by 50 per cent for an operation repeated five or eight times per minute

The HSE emphasises that these figures are only guidelines and are not limits. The figures can be exceeded but only if more in-depth assessment has shown that it is safe to do so.

National Institute for Occupational Safety and Health lifting guide
The NIOSH lifting equation is a tool to evaluate two-handed lifting tasks. The equation was developed by the US National Institute for Occupational Safety and Health (NIOSH) to help identify solutions for

Guideline figures reduced by 80 per cent for an operation repeated 12 times per minute

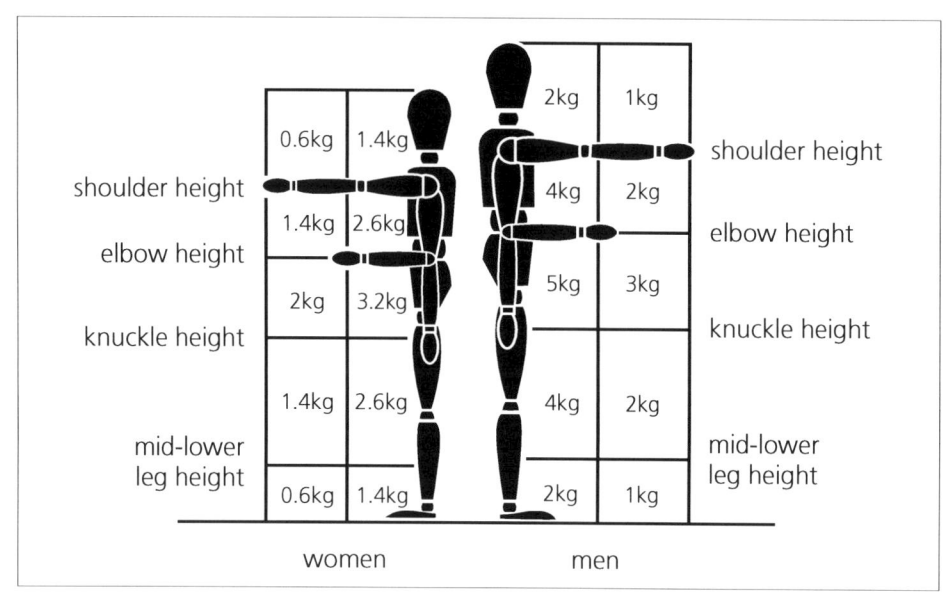

	women			men	
shoulder height	0.6kg	1.4kg	2kg	1kg	shoulder height
elbow height	1.4kg	2.6kg	4kg	2kg	elbow height
knuckle height	2kg	3.2kg	5kg	3kg	knuckle height
mid-lower leg height	1.4kg	2.6kg	4kg	2kg	mid-lower leg height
	0.6kg	1.4kg	2kg	1kg	

reducing the physical stress associated with manual lifting. In 1991 NIOSH published a revised lifting equation, which included for the first time the asymmetry multiplier. This meant that the equation now took into account that handling might not occur directly in front of the body but off to one side. The inclusion of the asymmetry multiplier reduces the Recommended Weight Limit (RWL) by around 10 per cent for each 30 per cent of asymmetry. The RWL is the weight of the load that nearly all healthy workers could handle in a specific set of task conditions over a substantial period of time (eg up to eight hours) without an increased risk of developing lifting-related lower back pain.

The revised lifting equation for calculating the RWL is based on a multiplicative model that provides a weighting for each of six task variables, namely the horizontal multiplier, vertical multiplier, distance multiplier, asymmetric multiplier, frequency multiplier and coupling multiplier. The equation does not apply in the following situations as it could either underestimate or overestimate the extent of physical stress associated with a particular lifting task:
- lifting or lowering with one hand
- lifting or lowering for over eight hours
- lifting or lowering while seated or kneeling
- lifting or lowering in a restricted work space
- lifting or lowering unstable objects (an unstable object or load is an object in which the centre of gravity varies significantly during the lifting activity, such as some containers of liquid or incompletely filled bags)
- lifting or lowering while carrying, pushing or pulling

- lifting or lowering with wheelbarrows or shovels
- lifting or lowering with high speed motion (faster than about 75 cm per second)
- lifting or lowering with unreasonable foot–floor coupling (< 0.4 coefficient of friction between the sole and the floor) that may increase the risk of a slip or fall
- lifting or lowering in an unfavourable environment (ie temperature significantly outside the range 19–26° C and/or relative humidity outside the range 35–50 per cent).

The working environment

Space constraints
The importance of maintaining good postures during the lifting and moving of a load has already been highlighted. However, the working environment may interfere with the postures adopted by the operator, which can place them at increased risk when they attempt to move an object.

Minimal space either around or above the operator will make moving an object difficult. Operators should be able to adopt reasonably upright postures when lifting and carrying objects. There should therefore be sufficient floor space. Ideally, they should not have to manoeuvre through narrow passageways. High standards of housekeeping should minimise the possibility of tripping or falling.

Overhead clearance should be provided in any workplace design to remove the need for operators to stoop when moving objects. This is particularly relevant when operators are working in storage areas with racks at different levels – they will have to stoop under upper racks when retrieving items from the floor-level storage area. If objects on the upper racks are not intended to be moved by hand, and are in fact lifted down on pallets by forklift, then these racks should be moved up out of the way. When setting the heights of the upper levels, consideration should be given to whether operators in that area wear head protection. The use of hard hats will, of course, increase the overhead clearance required.

If it is not possible to increase the height of the upper racking, operators should be encouraged to slide the load forwards until it clears the upper rack before it is picked up.

Variation in levels
Steps and slopes make the handling task more complex – particularly if the operator needs a free hand to steady themselves during the manoeuvre. Using steps is a particular concern.

Slopes should be as gentle as possible and steps should be well maintained and illuminated. It may be beneficial to provide operators with a small ramp to assist in accessing different levels (eg over a kerb). However, if the ramp has to be removed after its use, it should be treated as an additional load and its weight and point of storage should be taken into account during assessments.

If working between different work surfaces such as a conveyor and a workbench, it is recommended that they are of a uniform level to remove the need to lift or lower.

If operators have to push a load up a slope, it can be expected that the amount of force required will increase, which increases the risk of injury. The table below provides an indication of the increase in force required per 100 kg of load on different slope angles.

The impact of changing slope on pushing forces

Slope gradient (degrees)	Increase in force per 100 kg of laden trolley weight (kg force)
1	2
3	5
5	9
7	12
10	17.5

Floors

The floor surface will have an obvious impact on the safe movement of a load and it should therefore be kept level and in good repair. This is equally important whether working inside or outside. Torn lino or carpet, for example, can be a tripping hazard, while potholes and other rough surfaces increase the likelihood that the operator will have an accident.

Spillages such as oil, food, paint or water should be cleaned up as soon as possible. If the floor regularly becomes wet, slip-resistant surfacing should be considered.

Environmental factors

The temperature in the work area will have an effect on the handling operation. If the operator becomes hot, their hands may become sweaty and objects could slip out of them. If they become cold, they may start to lose some of their dexterity. This is particularly the case for those who work outdoors or in cold stores. Providing suitable clothing may reduce the effects of the cold but unless it fits properly it may hinder movement and make gripping more difficult.

It would appear that there is a significant variation between people in terms of their physiological responses to handling loads in either hot (29–39° C with 25–72 per cent humidity) or cold (0–10° C with 44–60 per cent humidity) environments. This makes it difficult to offer 'general' advice on how to reduce risk. The frequency of lift has a significant impact on physiological responses, as does the level of humidity in hot environments; this has implications if assessments of that environment only consider air temperature. People are also very poor at assessing their own level of physiological strain when handling in such extreme environments and many of them will overestimate their capabilities, so permitting them to pace themselves when working is a questionable strategy. For instance, operators working in a cold environment may choose to work at a more rapid rate in a bid to warm up.

Reducing the lifting frequency in a hot environment reduces the physiological strain placed on the individual by that environment. It is also beneficial to provide frequent opportunities for rehydration. If the worker is handling in a cold environment, they should have regular opportunities to move to another area to warm up. If there are long periods of inactivity, the risk of injury in the cold environment increases. Layered clothing provides the handler with opportunities to add or remove clothes to suit their thermal environment.

If a handler is absent from work for a long period of time due to illness or holiday, they may need a period to reacclimatise when they return to work. For this reason, they should not be immediately expected to work at the same rate on their return.

Poor ventilation will have a tiring effect on the operator. Sudden gusts of wind may throw the operator off balance when moving a large load (eg a sheet of glass or plasterboard). Action should be taken to reduce the possibility of this occurring – for example, taking a different route, using more than one person to move the load, using mechanical assistance, or repacking the load into a more suitable container.

Poor lighting will increase the likelihood that the operator will trip while carrying the load and will make it more difficult to locate and deposit the load quickly. By extending the time it takes to deposit the load, the fatiguing rate of the operation is increased.

The location of lighting is important. The ceiling may not always be the most appropriate position for the light source – for example, when using racking systems upper racks may cast shadows over lower levels. Wall lights may be more suitable.

Further environmental factors, such as excessive noise, rain, poor air quality or dust, may encourage operators to hurry their handling operation, which will increase the risks associated with moving the load. These other 'incidental' factors should therefore be addressed.

Individual capability
Sometimes it is the personal characteristics of the operator which increase the risk of the handling operation and these should be taken into account when assigning individuals to the task of lifting and moving loads. Some people may prove to be unsuitable for a manual handling operation.

Bearing in mind the high recurrence rate for back trouble, it would be advisable to consider carefully before asking operators who are known to have problems with their backs to get involved in a handling activity. This is also the case for those who have suffered hernias, ULDs or other health problems.

Sex
The different capabilities of men and women are a hotly contested issue. There is, generally speaking, a difference between men and women in terms of lifting strength, with men having a greater lifting capacity than women. However, there is some overlap, as some women can cope with a heavy lifting situation better than some men – this will mainly depend on factors such as age, fitness, health, build, training and experience. For example, most female nurses who have been trained in how to move patients will lift and move a load more safely than most male city executives who have sat behind a desk for 25 years lifting no more than a briefcase.

The HSE recommends that its numerical guidance aimed at male operators should be reduced by about one-third to provide the same degree of protection to approximately 95 per cent of the female operators who work in an area.

The effects of pregnancy and childbirth should also be considered. Once an employee becomes pregnant, the hormonal changes her body experiences will affect her ligaments, making her more susceptible to injury. In addition, as the pregnancy progresses she may start to experience postural problems which will put her at an increased risk of injury. (Similar problems may be associated with obese employees.) Manual handling during pregnancy combined with long periods of standing and/or walking is now considered to have significant implications for the health of the woman and the foetus.

Once a woman informs her employer that she is pregnant, the risks to the health and safety of both her and her unborn baby must be assessed. To ensure that employers comply with their duties under the Management of Health and Safety at Work Regulations 1999, they should have a plan on how to respond to the pregnancy. This plan could include:
- reassessment of the task to determine whether improvements could be made
- training to recognise changes in capabilities as the pregnancy progresses
- possible job-sharing opportunities, relocation to another area or suspension on full pay if an appropriate alternative cannot be found
- communication with the GP
- monitoring of the employee before and after the birth.

Consideration should also be given to women returning to work after childbirth.

Age
Age is also an issue that may engender some debate. It is believed that an individual reaches their peak in terms of physical ability in their early 20s, followed by a decline during their 40s which becomes more marked beyond this age.

Many organisations which have an older workforce should not be unduly concerned that their employees may appear to be more at risk than a younger workforce. Older operators have the benefits of experience and maturity, which should reduce the risks and may outweigh the benefits to be gained by having a younger, less experienced and more immature workforce. However, older operators should be made aware that although they may believe themselves to be fit and healthy, they should appreciate that they may become injured more easily and may take longer to recover from injury.

Disability
The Disability Discrimination Act 2005 places a duty on employers to make reasonable adjustments to the workplace or working arrangements if a person with a disability is at a substantial disadvantage when compared with their non-disabled colleagues. This might result in the employer providing the disabled person with a handling aid or changing the size, weight and number of loads handled.

'Positive discrimination'

'Positive discrimination' can, and should, play a part in reducing the risks faced by a particular operator. Height and build are obvious factors which require such consideration. Quite often an operator will be working above head height as they reach to a rack or hopper simply because they are not very tall. Using a taller operator will reduce the risks of that particular handling operation and will not cost the organisation anything more than the time it takes to locate another operator.

The general rule, however, when considering the risks of a handling operation, should be that if a reasonably fit and healthy individual cannot do the job comfortably and safely then it is unacceptable.

Training and awareness programmes

Training and information programmes should be used as a means of protecting the individual once in a situation where they must manually handle loads. The programmes should provide operators with an understanding of good lifting techniques, as well as increasing their awareness of the need to develop a sensible approach to the whole working environment, not just the actual lifting of the load. Only an appropriately trained coach should present training sessions.

One of the most common statements made by operators is that they have been working in a particular manner for a long time and so far they have not experienced any problems. They assume that because they have remained relatively healthy to this point that nothing will happen to them in the future. Awareness programmes need to convince operators that most handling injuries result from the cumulative effect of years of abuse rather than from a one-off lifting situation. They need to be made aware of the fact that it is important to use proper lifting techniques each time they pick up an object – and not just at work.

Operators need to have an understanding of how to recognise the hazardous aspects of a handling situation so that they can take action to reduce the risks. They need to have a working knowledge of how to determine whether the load can be managed unaided. When faced with an unfamiliar load, operators should be advised to:
- rock the load from side to side to assess its likely weight before they attempt to lift it, so that they can decide whether they are able to pick it up
- rock the object on the edge of a work surface to find out whether the weight is evenly distributed

- test a box or barrel first to see whether it is empty
- lift the unfamiliar weight slowly from the surface, stopping before they clear the surface if it is apparent that the weight is too much for them to bear alone.

If operators are given any handling aids or protective equipment, they need to be trained in their use. Training programmes should also discuss the features of the workplace which have been put in place to increase safety. It should be made clear to operators that good housekeeping – which is within their control – has an effect on the level of risk in the workplace.

Those who work in environments that are not viewed as typical handling environments, such as an office, should be made aware of the fact that their ordinary clothes may not be suitable for the movement of loads. For example, a slim-fitting skirt may prevent the individual from adopting appropriate lifting postures. If there is a significant amount of lifting involved in a particular work area, the provision of protective shoes may be appropriate.

The operators should be made aware of how their individual characteristics and state of health can influence the level of risk of the handling operation (they should therefore act accordingly if they find that they are pregnant or unwell).

Finally, to ensure that operators lift objects safely it is essential that they receive training in good handling techniques – bearing in mind that good lifting techniques alone will not overcome the problems presented by a poor working environment.

If training is to be effective, operators should learn by doing, not watching. It is said that a person remembers:
- 10 per cent of what is read
- 20 per cent of what is heard
- 30 per cent of what is seen
- 50 per cent of what is seen and heard
- 70 per cent of what they do themselves.

At the start of the training programme, the operators should be made aware of the purpose of the exercise. Once they have received an explanation of lifting and handling in general, they should be asked whether they understand the basic principles before being asked to lift any object. Once operators start to lift and move objects they should receive feedback on their performance to enable them to correct any mistakes before bad habits are adopted.

Good handling techniques

The movement of the load should be thought of as the 'performance' aspect of good handling techniques. However, the operator should consider planning and preparation before starting to handle the load:

- **Planning** – before handling the load, the operator should decide whether the load actually needs to be lifted or moved. If so, they should not assume that only their hands will do the job. Instead, they should consider whether there is any equipment available which will help. If not, they should consider whether another person should help. They then need to determine whether there is enough room to move the load safely. Once they have planned how the load will be moved they should prepare for the lift.
- **Preparation** – the operator needs to ensure that they have suitable clothing and footwear which will not hinder them during the movement. They need to have an idea of the weight of the load and how the weight is distributed. They will also need to determine whether the edges are safe to hold and whether they can obtain a secure grip.

This procedure for planning and preparation may appear to be very time-consuming but an experienced operator will be able to run through the planning and preparation list mentally in a matter of seconds before they attempt to move an object. In most repeated lifting situations, all the planning and preparation will have been carried out during the job design phase so will not have to be done by the operator at all.

Before moving on to the action phase of moving a load, the operator needs to develop appropriate performance skills. These skills require practice so that they eventually become a natural part of the handling process. It is recommended that small, compact loads of approximately 5 kg are used for practice purposes in controlled manual handling training sessions.

Operators should be trained in the basics of a lifting operation, starting with a squat lift where the load is raised from the floor:

- The operator should stand close to the load with the feet hip-width apart.
- One foot should be placed slightly in front of the other and to the side of the load if possible (this will give a stable base from which to lift an object). The feet should adopt a 'ten to two' position: as the operator bends their knees they will follow the direction that their toes are pointing and as a result their thighs will not become an obstacle between the handler and the load – which would happen if the toes pointed forward. It is this element of good handling technique which is particularly difficult to implement if a female handler wears a skirt.

- The knees should be moderately bent and the back kept straight. The back does not have to be bolt upright – the operator can lean over the load slightly. However, the operator should not kneel on the floor or have a deep kneebend because this will make it more difficult to stand up.
- The load should be grasped firmly using the entire hand, not just the fingers.
- Having grasped the load the operator should look up, which not only lets them see where they are going but also helps to straighten the back.
- The load should be lifted smoothly using the leg muscles to stand up.
- The load should be kept close to the body. The heaviest side should be held closest to the body.
- Once standing upright, the feet should be used to turn around. Operators should not twist at the waist to deposit the load onto another surface.
- The load should be deposited slowly using the same sequence in reverse. Precise positioning of the load can be accomplished after it has been put down.

Once the squat lift has been learnt, operators can apply the same technique to moving an object from a raised surface. They will see that they follow the same principles, despite the fact that the load is being moved from a higher level.

If the operator is required to push or pull a load (eg a trolley or clothes rail), other considerations should be incorporated in the training session:
- The operator should keep the load's centre of gravity aligned with the body's own centre of gravity – directly in front of the body is best.
- Turning should be accomplished using the feet, not the upper body.
- All effort should be channelled through the legs. The operator should be encouraged to grip the load firmly and propel themselves forwards or backwards using their leg muscles.
- Sudden or jerky movements should be avoided.
- The operator should be as close to the load as possible when moving it. The arms should not be stretched out in front to apply pressure when pushing. Ideally, the elbows should be bent and close to the side of the body.

Once operators have become used to the movement of small, compact loads using the appropriate lifting techniques, they should progress to moving more difficult loads. At all times they should be aware that they must recognise their own limitations and stop if any load is too much for them to cope with.

Once operators have accomplished the movement of the heavier, more difficult loads, they should move on to the movement of loads they can expect to deal with in the real working situation (there is no point in only learning to move a 5 kg compact box when they are expected to move gas cylinders or sides of beef once back at work). The training programme should identify a range of loads the operators will be expected to move, and provide, if necessary, specific tuition on particular loads. Drums, barrels, cylinders, sacks and other problematic loads should be included in handling programmes for those operators who are expected to move such items by hand. A special lifting technique may need to be adopted for each item and operators will need to have the opportunity to practise under controlled conditions.

Training programmes should also provide an opportunity for operators to lift in teams so that they can come to terms with the additional problems associated with team lifting.

To ensure that training is effective there are a number of guiding principles. Before training even starts, there should be visible commitment from management, and managers (as well as team leaders and supervisors) should be familiar with the content of the training courses the employees are attending. The best way of achieving this is to require managers to attend the courses. The training should be viewed as only one part of an overall programme of risk management and it should be understood that one-off training is not sufficient. Refresher courses need to be provided at regular intervals.

Choosing the right trainer will go a long way to ensuring that the training will be effective. The trainer should be charismatic and credible, have in-depth experience and knowledge and should be able to engage the trainees. They should be fully aware of the trainees' level of awareness of the subject so that the material can be presented at the right level for the group. The trainer needs to be aware of the literacy and language skills of the group so they can take steps to include everyone in the course. The trainer should know what the fitness levels of the group are or whether they have any pre-existing injuries so that no-one is asked to perform a lifting task in the practical phase that might cause them harm.

It is essential that the trainer makes the course directly relevant to the handling performed by the trainees once they return to work. Practical sessions will be run most effectively if there are no more than 12 trainees per course. Trying to train more than 12 people at once can lead to boredom setting in as trainees wait their turn to lift the sample loads, and they are more likely to become distracted. Ideally, trainees should wear flat, comfortable shoes and trousers they can move in easily. However, the reality is that in office environments women typically wear skirts and shoes with heels and the trainer should be able to adapt the handling technique so that the women can get as close as possible to the most appropriate technique given the restrictions imposed by their clothing and footwear. This will involve them approaching the load with their feet closer together but still with one foot in front of the other, as far as their clothing will allow. They should bend their knees as far as their clothing permits and they should ensure that they keep their upper body and head upright. Because of limits imposed by clothing, assessors may need to conclude that women in certain working environments, such as an office, may need assistance when lifting or the amount they lift may need to be strictly limited.

A course of about three hours is probably enough to pass on the relevant information and allow the trainees to practise the lifts. At the end of the course it is useful to get immediate feedback from the trainees as well as to evaluate its effectiveness by monitoring how well the trainees apply their new skills in their own working environments after the course.

Problems preventing the introduction of good lifting techniques
On returning to the workplace following a training session, there is no guarantee that operators will continue to use their newly learnt lifting techniques. Managers and supervisors need to be aware of the reasons why people may revert to their old habits so that they can discourage them.

Some operators try to prove how strong and fit they are and develop foolhardy methods of work when trying to move twice as much as others. They should be made aware of the problems they could cause if they do not develop a more mature attitude. Other operators who are unable to cope with the movement of a heavy load may attempt to 'soldier on' rather than seek help because they do not want to draw attention to themselves. These individuals should be made aware that they are also putting themselves at risk and should be more confident about asking for assistance. To facilitate this attitude change, there will need to be a suitable response from others in the workplace when help is sought. Some operators will not use the proper handling techniques because they mistakenly believe that it is quicker the old way. Finally, the main reason why manual handling training may become virtually redundant once the operator returns to work is that it is very difficult to change long established habits. It is important to convince operators that although they may have avoided injury so far, long term abuse will probably catch up with them in the end.

If operators are to change their old habits they must be supported by appropriate supervision which encourages the use of proper handling methods and discourages inappropriate habits. Supervisors should lead by example. They should not ask someone to move something they would not move themselves, and if they do lift an object they should make sure that they use the relevant techniques.

Back belts

Some individuals believe that using a back belt while manually handling a load will reduce, if not eliminate, the problems associated with its movement. Other operators are under the impression that they cannot take a claim out against their employer in the event of an injury if they were not wearing such a belt.

The use of back belts should be considered very carefully. It should be understood that it is unlikely that operators will avoid injury through wearing a belt, and in fact, some operators may develop a false sense of security as a result of wearing one. If belts are provided, operators should be given training in their appropriate use and supervisors should ensure that they are worn properly when needed.

If back belts are already in use, it is not recommended that operators be prevented from wearing them. However, operators should not be required to wear a belt unless they wish to do so.

There are a number of guiding principles if back belts are to be worn during manual handling operations. In the first instance, handlers should select a belt of the appropriate size, and if they increase in girth over time they need to acknowledge this and ask for a larger belt. The belt needs to be positioned correctly and not slung off the hips casually. Reading the instruction leaflet that accompanies the belt before use will help in fitting it properly. Handlers need to be given information relating to what the belt actually does when they wear it. They need to understand that the belt is actually offering the body a form of artificial support and the muscles in the area where the belt is being worn may not offer as much support as they might have done if the belt had not been worn. In effect, these muscles are in a more relaxed state while the belt is being worn. The handlers frequently remove their belts suddenly at the end of the shift, almost shocking the inactive muscles by the abrupt and unexpected increase in workload focused on them as the belt is removed. To avoid this sudden transfer of workload, the handler should be made aware of the need to gradually loosen their belt, one hole at a time, as they work towards the end of their shift rather than whipping it off suddenly. This allows a gradual resumption of effort by the muscles.

Summary

- Direct delivery of loads, such as pumping to the area of use, will eliminate the need to handle the loads manually.
- Increasing the size of loads should reduce handling risks by making it impossible for the operator to move loads manually.
- Mechanical transportation of loads on rollerbeds and trolleys could be used as a means of reducing the stresses of the handling operation.
- If trolleys are used they should be maintained satisfactorily.
- Using trolleys does not eliminate all manual effort.
- When selecting a trolley, it is essential to consider the total load weight to be moved and the floor surface on which the trolley will be used.
- The correct style and size of trolley wheel, as well as the number of wheels and their location, should be selected on the basis of what the trolley will be used for during the normal course of the work.
- Trolleys should be fitted with brakes if they are frequently moved up and down slopes.
- Cylindrical trolley handles of 25–40 mm diameter, preferably covered in an insulating material, should be adequate.
- There should be sufficient clearance when pushing trolleys through doorways to avoid crushing the hands. Selecting a trolley of suitable width and with inset handles should allow for unhindered passage through doorways.
- Handlers should use both hands when pushing or pulling trolleys to enable them to adopt an upright, symmetrical posture and to share the workload out across the upper limbs.
- It is preferable for handlers to push a load in front of them.
- Limiting stacking heights of loads to no higher than 1,400 mm above floor level will permit all handlers to see over the top of a trolley.
- Assessors should use appropriate equipment to measure the forces involved in moving a trolley.
- During an assessment, measurements should be taken of the effort involved in starting the movement of the load and the effort involved in maintaining the movement. Measurements should be taken in typical areas, including on different floor surfaces, around corners, into or out of lifts and up slopes.
- Floor-based and ceiling-mounted hoists significantly reduce the stress of manually moving people.
- Ceiling-mounted hoists require less effort than floor-based hoists.

- Additional effort is required to turn a floor-based hoist, particularly in confined spaces and on rough wood or carpeted surfaces.
- Handling aids should only be introduced after careful consideration of their design and use.
- Reorganisation of the workplace may reduce the number of times individual loads are handled.
- The operator should adopt the correct posture before attempting to move an object.
- Loads should not be lifted or held at a distance from the body.
- Heavy objects that are difficult to handle should be stored between knuckle and shoulder height, with lighter objects that are easier to move stored above or below this range.
- Shelves or racking should indicate which objects are to be stored at which levels so as to accommodate the weight–shape consideration.
- Platforms, duckboards or steps should be made available if objects are to be moved at higher levels. None of these should pose a tripping hazard.
- Stacking heights should be controlled so that operators do not have to work at high levels.
- Lifting from floor level should be avoided. If possible, objects should be raised off floor level.
- If lifting from floor level, the load should not have to be raised above waist height in one move.
- Walking distances should be kept to a minimum by reorganising the layout of the work area.
- When pushing or pulling an object, the hands should not have to move outside the zone between knuckle and shoulder height.
- Unpredictable, sudden movements of the load should be controlled as far as possible.
- Additional care should be taken if the operator is handling a load while seated. The weights which are handled should be significantly reduced and the loads should not be placed on floor level or be at a distance from the operator.
- When two or more operators are involved in a team lift, they should be of equal size and ability, there should be sufficient space to move easily and care should be taken that each team member does not impede the view of the other(s).
- Rotation and regular rest breaks should be used to combat the stresses of handling.
- Reducing the size of the load will make it easier to move.
- A bulky item may be very difficult to pick up (even though it may be fairly light).
- A load may be so large that it impedes the operator's view when it is picked up or drags on the floor during movement. This will increase the risk of the handling operation.

- The distribution of the weight of the load is as important as the weight itself. If the weight is not evenly spread, the heaviest side should be held close to the body.
- Objects lacking rigidity should be moved inside a container wherever possible.
- Free-moving objects should be packed tightly within their container using materials such as polystyrene or bubble-wrap.
- Liquids and powders should be filled as close to the top of the container as possible to limit free movement during handling.
- Objects should be clearly marked to indicate their weight, distribution of weight and any additional handling guidance.
- Markings on loads should be in a form that is easy to understand – colour coding or symbols may be more appropriate than written instructions.
- Numerical guidelines, such as those provided by the HSE (2004), should be used in determining the level of risk associated with the movement of any object.
- Operators should have sufficient space around and above them to allow them to adopt suitable postures when moving loads.
- The floor should flat and smooth, with as few steps and slopes as possible.
- Temperature, humidity, ventilation and lighting levels should be assessed to ensure that they do not make the handling of loads more difficult.
- As a general rule, men have a greater lifting capacity than women. However, a degree of overlap exists and this will be influenced by health, strength, fitness, training and experience.
- Pregnancy influences a woman's ability to lift and move objects safely.
- Individuals are at their peak in terms of lifting and moving objects in their 20s and start their decline in their 40s. This should be viewed in parallel with the benefits of experience and maturity, which are usually lacking in younger operators.
- All those involved in moving loads should be given manual handling training. (This includes office personnel who sometimes are under the mistaken impression that they do not lift things at work.)
- Operators should learn that they have to plan and prepare for moving an object before they attempt to move it. This includes ensuring that they have enough room to move around, considering whether they need assistance and assessing the distribution of the load's weight. Operators should be advised to test all unknown objects before attempting to lift them.
- Training should be given in the use of handling aids and PPE, as well as manual handling techniques.

- On return to the working environment following a training programme, operators should be supported by appropriate supervision which encourages the continued use of safe handling techniques.

References and further reading

Ayoub M M and Mital A. *Manual materials handling.* Taylor & Francis, 2002.

Birnbaum R, Cockroft A and Richardson B. *Safer handling of loads at work – a practical ergonomic guide* (second edition). Institute of Ergonomics, 1993.

De Beeck R O and Hermans V. *Research on work-related low back disorders.* European Agency for Safety and Health at Work, 2000.

Health and Safety Executive. *Manual handling in drinks delivery,* HSG119. HSE Books, 1994.

Health and Safety Executive. *Manual Handling Operations Regulations 1992: guidance on Regulations,* L23. HSE Books, 2004.

Health and Safety Executive. *Manual handling: solutions you can handle,* HSG115. HSE Books, 1994.

Health and Safety Executive. *Manual handling training: investigation of current practices and development of guidelines,* RR583. HSE Books, 2007.

Health and Safety Executive. *The effects of thermal environments on the risks associated with manual handling,* RR337. HSE Books, 2005.

Jenkins D B. *Hollinshead's functional anatomy of the limbs and back* (7th edition). W B Saunders, 1998.

Kroemer K and Grandjean E. *Fitting the task to the human* (fifth edition). Taylor & Francis, 1997.

Marras W S, Knapik G G and Ferguson S. Lumbar spine forces during manoeuvring of ceiling-based and floor-based patient transfer devices. *Ergonomics* 2009; 52 (3): 384–397.

Mital A, Nicholson A S and Ayoub M M. *A guide to manual materials handling.* Taylor & Francis, 1997.

National Institute for Occupational Safety and Health. *Revised NIOSH lifting equation.* NIOSH, 1991.

Rice M S, Woolley S M and Waters T R. Comparison of required operating forces between floor-based and overhead-mounted patient lifting devices. *Ergonomics* 2009; 52 (1): 112–120.

7 Display screen equipment work

The office is probably the working environment that has changed the most over the last five to 10 years. Advances in computer technology have radically altered the way in which people do, or can, work. Wireless networking permits users to work almost anywhere at any time. But although technology has changed so much, users still face the same kinds of problem they encountered 10–20 years ago. Most of the problems stem from how people use their equipment and how they perform their work throughout the day. Users often experience upper limb pain, backache, headaches or sore eyes simply because they have not made minor adjustments to their equipment or they work for lengthy periods repeating the same type of work without much in the way of a break or change in activities.

Most of the common problems encountered in an office environment could be easily eliminated if the users were provided with the right type of workstation furniture, which does not necessarily mean the most expensive option. Being well designed and offering simple yet effective features is all that is needed in most equipment. In addition, if users are given a clear understanding of how they should use their furniture and equipment, and under what circumstances, they will be far less likely to report aches and pains.

Seating

The value of a well-designed chair should not be underestimated. Assuming that most people working in an office will be using a fixed-height desk, the majority will be able to sit at the right height relative to their desk and keyboard only if they have a chair that allows them to adopt a suitable working posture. To enable an individual to sit comfortably, the chair should meet several criteria which include height and backrest adjustability and a five-star base. No-one should be expected to perform a computer-based task sitting in a conference-style chair. This has particular relevance in hot-desking environments, where on core days more users often turn up than there are workstations in an office, resulting in some people sitting on chairs taken from meeting rooms or canteens.

Seat height adjustment
There are a number of standards available that give advice on the range of height adjustment that should be offered by a seat. There are few chairs that can meet the suggested ranges. However, most chairs on the market

will accommodate the majority of people who are likely to use them in an office. Those who will not be comfortably accommodated are likely to be at the extremes, such as very petite and extremely tall users, and in some cases users with special needs. The only way to determine whether a chair suits the intended users is to get one, or more, on trial before it is purchased. Suppliers are usually co-operative about lending chairs on a trial basis. If they are not, this may suggest that their products should be avoided.

Seat position adjustment
Some adjustable chairs offer the user the facility of either tilting the seat downwards or sliding the seat forwards, away from the backrest. This latter movement, in effect, increases the length of the seat and is particularly useful for taller users or users with long legs. Of course, to use this feature effectively the user needs to be aware that it is available. It should never be assumed that users will find features themselves – the majority will not.

Tilting the seat is not an essential feature, but it can suit some users who have specific conditions affecting their lower back or pelvis, as tilting the seat increases the angle at their hips. The drawbacks of sitting on a seat with a forward tilt is that the user is aware of the sensation of being tipped forward and will tend to 'brace' themselves with their feet. Sometimes women literally start to slide out of their skirts.

Backrest adjustment
The backrest should support the back once the user has adopted a comfortable working position. The most important point of contact is the lower back, which needs support if the person is to continue working without becoming uncomfortable. Given that people come in different shapes and sizes, it is important that the backrest can be moved or altered so that a good fit can be achieved between it and the user. To that end, the backrest either needs to adjust for height so that the lumbar support (the rounded section towards the bottom of the backrest) can be positioned correctly relative to the small of the back, or the lumbar roll within the backrest should be capable of being moved into the correct position, or the backrest should be constructed of a material that is designed to 'mould' to the shape of the back on contact. The seat should not be so long as to prevent the user sitting right back in their seat and making a firm contact between their back and the backrest of the chair. If smaller users are unable to sit back in the seat fully, they should be provided with an alternative chair that has a shorter seat. If they do not have a smaller chair, they are likely to perch on the front of their chair to avoid the leading edge sticking into the backs of their knees.

The backrest should be capable of tilting. Some seats will be designed to incorporate a rocking motion where tilting the backrest causes the seat to tilt by a corresponding amount. Users often want to move the back independently to the seat and it would be advisable to ensure that the backrest can be moved separately. It would also be advisable to ensure that the backrest has not been designed only with synchronised movement, which means it moves as the user moves. Users like to be able to lock the backrest off so that it offers a more rigid form of support (although most backrests will still flex slightly as the user moves).

Most chairs provide support to the lower and middle parts of the back. These are perfectly adequate. High backrests do not necessarily offer more support as the user often moves their shoulders out of contact with the top of a high-backed chair. Some users also find that larger, higher backrests interfere with the movement of their arms and shoulders.

The attachment of headrests to the backrest should be considered carefully. Normally a user's screen would be positioned so that their head is inclined forwards slightly. This would naturally move it away from and out of contact with any headrest attached to the chair. To be able to get the head in contact with the headrest, the user would have to maintain an erect, or backward-tilting, posture of the head and this would be fatiguing if they were involved in a screen-based task. Adopting this position would obviously be acceptable if the individual was simply resting.

Armrests
Armrests might be viewed by some as a trifling matter unworthy of much discussion. The fact of the matter is that armrests, more accurately unsuitable armrests, have created huge problems for users in the past and have caused many to experience discomfort in their upper limbs because of the impact they can have on posture. The worst offenders are non-adjustable armrests, particularly the large bulky type. These tend to come in contact with the leading edge of the desk preventing the user from sitting as close to it as they might wish. The user then leans forward in their seat to reach the keyboard or they perch on the leading edge of the seat to reach the keyboard. Other users will actually lower their chair to get the armrests under the desk so that they can get closer to the keyboard. However, by lowering the chair the user sits at a lower level relative to their keyboard, which causes them to raise their shoulders and arms to get their hands on the keys. This posture will be maintained by static muscle work, which is extremely fatiguing, throughout the period they sit and work at their desk – and this could be for several hours at a time.

Some chair manufacturers have developed armrests that allow the user freedom to sit wherever and however they want, which is ideal. The best armrests are those that are relatively short and are adjustable for both height and width so they can be lined up exactly with the user's elbows. If armrests are rather inflexible in terms of how the user can position them, then consideration should be given to removing them altogether. Most are added to the chair as an extra and can be removed easily. However, users are often very reluctant to give up their armrests if they are used to having them. Even so, there needs to be a logical evaluation of their worth. If they only contribute negatively to the user's sitting experience, they need to be removed. Users who resist the removal of armrests, or who object to getting a new chair without arms, should be encouraged to try working without the arms for a week. Typically, they will feel insecure in the chair for the first few hours – particularly if they tended to lean on the armrests when rising from the chair or when taking a telephone call. However, in almost all cases users appreciate the benefits of working without armrests by the end of their trial period.

It should be kept in mind that there are certain individuals who should only use chairs with armrests. These may include heavily overweight users who rely on the armrests for leverage to get into and out of the chair, or users who have mobility problems and rely on the armrests to help them stand up. Without question, these individuals should continue to use chairs with armrests, but only the type that do not compromise their sitting position.

Tension adjustment
One of the most underused features of a chair is the tension adjustment. It usually takes the form of a rotating knob and is found under the seat, close to the gas-lift column. The idea behind the tension adjustment is that the tension setting of the seat, such as when tilting the backrest backwards and forwards, can be changed. This ensures that when a petite user sits in the seat they can alter the tension setting so that they can easily tilt the seat backwards and will not get catapulted out of the seat when they release the backrest. At the same time, a large, heavy user can alter the setting so that it resists their weight more readily as they change the backrest position on the chair.

Adjustment mechanisms
The key to ensuring that users make the most out of the chair they have been given is to keep it simple in terms of the number and function of adjustments. All levers and knobs should also be easily reached from the seated position. It is also helpful if the levers and knobs carry simple diagrams that enable the controls to be used intuitively. If users have to

get the instruction manual out just to alter the backrest position that is not going to happen – assuming the manual has not simply been recycled to start with.

Alternatives to the task chair

Some uneducated users attempt to make themselves more comfortable when working by using alternatives to the standard office chair. Some sit in conference-style chairs, some even sit on pilates balls and others use backless chairs. Backless chairs provide a sloping seat and knee pads which take the weight of the body. The sloping seat generates the upright, S-shaped sitting position that some users feel is the ideal position. Unless they have a back condition that warrants the use of such a chair, they should be avoided. This is because the back never gets a chance to rest as there is no support for it, and the knees can get pressure points as they are not designed to support the weight of the upper body for long periods.

Users should not be permitted to just do their own thing. Most users do not appreciate that they need to sit in a properly designed chair; nor do many of them know what constitutes a suitable posture. Therefore, if they are to avoid back discomfort, they should be given suitable training. Some organisations spend substantial sums of money on seating for their employees. This is wasted if the chairs are not used effectively, as the impact on the user would be the same as sitting on something like a bar stool for long periods while trying to work.

Desks

Choosing a desk several years ago would have been an easy affair. There was really only the standard rectangular desk on offer or alternatively an L-shaped unit made up of two conjoined rectangular desks. Since then, manufacturers have increased the choice available, mainly with the intention of increasing the available workspace without increasing the footprint of the desk. Desks are now contoured and shaped and come in an almost endless range of possible combinations. Irrespective of the individual design qualities of any desk, there are certain characteristics it should incorporate if a user is to work comfortably.

Height

Most standard office desks are set at around 720 mm in height, measured from the floor to the upper surface. In the main, this height will be acceptable for most users, even very short people, as long as they use their chair to sit at the correct height relative to their keyboard and they use a footrest if needed. Taller users may find that the desk is not high enough for them to get their legs underneath comfortably and may feel that they want to lower their chair. These users should be provided with an alternative so that they can sit at a suitable height on their chair. Either they should be given a height-adjustable desk or their old desk should be elevated (safely) on blocks or by using a retro-fit kit for increasing height.

Height-adjustable desks should provide the perfect solution for users in an office environment, as each individual should be able to set the workstation up to suit themselves. However, height adjustment is not essential. A fixed-height desk is acceptable for most users as long as chairs and footrests are used properly.

The means by which height-adjustable desks are altered varies from model to model. Some have telescopic legs that can be lengthened or shortened to change the height of the desk. Others are suspended from partitions or frames at the rear of the desk. Although this form of adjustment is acceptable, it has to be kept in mind that it is more difficult to change once the desk has been set up and loaded with equipment. This is also the case if desks are being used in 'pods' or groups where they are inter-linked. Having a crank handle to change the setting is one of the easiest ways to change the desk height. Alternatively, electrically powered desk adjustment would also be effective and could prove useful in the case of a user with a disability who might not have the motor control or strength to use a crank handle. In a hot-desking environment, using electrically powered height adjustment increases the likelihood that users will change the setting of their desk, as it is an easy, effortless task. Additional thought needs to be given to the length of cables in situations where it is likely that the desk height will be changed regularly as well as possible damage to cables caused by pinching between desk surfaces and frames.

Surface features

One of the most important requirements of the desk is that the surface depth (from front to back) should allow the screen and keyboard to be aligned directly in front of the user with the screen being about fingertip distance away. This is easier to achieve with flat screens, as they do not require the same amount of space as bulkier CRT monitors. The only time a screen should be positioned to one side of the desk, and at an angle to the user, would be if the user was a copy typist who was reading a script positioned directly in front of them as they typed. However, they would still need to be able to pull the screen in front of them when editing the document, as this would require them to refer to the display. In situations such as this a monitor arm would be a useful addition to the workstation equipment.

In addition to supporting the screen and keyboard, the surface area should be big enough to accommodate other items such as a mouse, telephone, documents and copy stand; the user should also have some control over where they are positioned.

Some desks have split level surfaces with both sections being independently height-adjustable. This is a useful feature, as it allows the screen to be positioned at a suitable height for the user. The front section of the split level surfaces should be big enough to allow for comfortable positioning and operation of both the keyboard and mouse.

The leading edge of the desk should be curved rather than present a sharp or 90° angled edge. This is to avoid any discomfort that might occur if a user leans on it.

The styling of the desk surface should be reviewed when being used in conjunction with the task chair before any decisions are made about selecting a particular model of desk. The aim should be to allow the user to sit as close to the work area as they wish. If the contouring on the leading edge of the desk prevents them from sitting close then an alternative should be considered. For instance, in a situation where a user has an L-shaped desk and they are expected to sit across the corner of the desk, it is common for the armrests on the chair to come in contact with the edges of the V-shaped corner, keeping the user at a distance.

Undersurface features

It is uncommon for people responsible for making purchasing decisions relating to desks to actually crawl around on the floor under the desk. However, there are a lot of potential problems hiding under there and the only way to find them is to get under the desk and grovel around on the floor. Users should be able to sit at a desk at the appropriate height without worrying that they might bang their knees on a cross bar running under the surface or that brackets used to attach a computer cradle have been located close to their knees. Cable management should also function effectively so that the user does not get caught up on stray cables that cannot be contained by the cable management system. The system should also allow for the cables to be moved and repositioned easily such as when the equipment is changed over. The surface of the desk should be as thin as possible to allow the user to raise their chair unhindered to the desired height. Chunky leading edges limit how far the chair can be raised before the user's thighs come in contact with them, possibly forcing them to sit at too low a level.

The location of pedestal drawers under the surface should not limit the user's choice over where they sit when using the computer.

Worksurface layout

The aim should be to allow the user to sit upright in a forward-facing position when operating their keyboard and referring to the screen. To enable this, the screen should be directly in front of the user and the keyboard should be positioned between the screen and user. The keyboard should be about 10 cm away from the leading edge of the desk, thereby leaving a space for the user to rest their wrists when they are not using the keyboard. The screen should be presented at a height where the top of the viewable area of the screen is no higher than eye line. This will ensure that the user never has to look up or raise their head upwards when viewing the screen. If the screen does not have an adjustable stand, its height could be altered using a platform designed specifically for monitors. In the short term, a ream of copier paper could be used as long as the monitor is secure. It should be stressed that this screen positioning will not suit users who wear varifocal or bifocal glasses. They tend to look through the bottom of their lens when viewing the screen, and presenting it at the height suggested above would cause them to tilt their head upwards and backwards to be able to look through the bottom of their glasses. This is likely to result in neck discomfort. Their screen should be at a lower level so that their head is held in a relaxed position.

The desk surface should be divided into two zones: the primary work area and the secondary work area. The primary work area falls directly in front of the user and can be easily reached when the elbow is bent at 90° and the upper arm hangs naturally by the side of the body. The primary work area should be used to present any items used regularly or for long periods, such as the keyboard, mouse and possibly the telephone if using it is an integral feature of the work. The more distant areas of the desk are referred to as the secondary work zone and items used less frequently, such as reference manuals, should be stored in this area.

Trials

If an organisation is considering undergoing a programme of refurbishment where they will be replacing the desks and chairs, it is essential that they go through a proper selection and trial process. There are so many desks and chairs on the market that the organisation should first draw up a shortlist of what may be suitable for users. Shortlists in the early stages could be based on whether the equipment matches current criteria outlined in relevant standards and guidance. Once the shortlist has been drawn up, the only accurate way of identifying whether the furniture will be suitable is to use it under near-normal conditions. Furniture trials are a useful way of allowing users an opportunity of trying out possible furniture options before the organisation commits to spending a lot of money. The trials give users an opportunity to feed back their views on the furniture as they use it under normal conditions. Often the faults in workstation furniture only become apparent when they are being used in such circumstances. It is important that the trials are carefully managed by a trial manager and that user feedback is formally recorded using a set of pre-determined questions. Users can be asked to rate their preferences and this can assist the organisation in identifying what are the most suitable ranges of furniture for their workforce. So that bias does not alter a user's impression of any piece of furniture, they should be given detailed and accurate guidance on how to operate each item used. The trial manager should ensure that they are comfortably set up and every other item in the workstation arrangement, such as screen and keyboard, are in suitable positions so that they do not have a negative effect on the user's views.

Apart from helping an organisation to identify suitable workstation furniture, the trial phase also allows the employer to document the process that led them to make certain decisions and enables them to demonstrate how choices were made.

Accessories

Using the word 'accessories' should not give the impression that the items included under this category heading are of little importance and that users can live without them. Most of these 'extras' are the final pieces of equipment needed to ensure the user can work comfortably.

Footrests

If a user's feet do not touch the floor once they have raised their chair to an appropriate height relative to their keyboard, they should be provided with a footrest. If a user continues to work without a firm surface to support their feet they will find that the weight of their lower legs will cause the front edge of the seat to stick into the back of their thigh, making them uncomfortable. At the same time this can reduce the blood flow into the lower legs, again making the user uncomfortable, and they will start to fidget. It is also the case that the weight of the unsupported lower legs, which act like heavy pendulums, will cause the user to slide forward in their seat. This may only be by a small amount but it is sufficient enough to ensure that the lower back is no longer firmly in contact with the backrest of the seat. As a consequence, the user may experience some backache and blame the chair.

The footrest should, ideally, be adjustable for height and tilt. If a footrest is not height-adjustable it will be rather hit and miss whether it will accommodate the user's leg length. It should have a non-slip surface and should be large enough to support both feet easily. Well made footrests tend to be quite heavy and have rubber feet which prevent them from sliding across the floor if pressure is applied to them. Users should therefore be warned about the need to take care if repositioning footrests, especially if they do it with their feet when sitting down.

Document holders

Some users work under the misapprehension that only copy typists need to use a copy stand or document holder. What they do not realise is that any individual who refers to a document or any other source of printed information when carrying out a screen-based task should place it on a stand rather than lay it on the desk surface alongside the keyboard. If documents are placed on the desk surface the user has to repeatedly lower their head and turn to the side to look at the document. The head is then swung back up and forward as they refer to the screen again. This movement of the head will be repeated throughout the day and is extremely fatiguing for the muscles that control the position of the head and neck. Users should bear in mind that their head weighs in the region of 5 kg and in reality they are expecting their muscles to repeatedly swing the equivalent of 10 tins of soup around, unnecessarily, as they work. At the same time, the user has to refocus every time they look from the printed document to the screen as they are at different viewing distances. This increases the workload for the eyes and increases the rate at which they fatigue.

Users should use copy stands to present their document close to the screen at about the same height as the screen. Traditional copy stands, similar to an artist's easel, can be positioned alongside the screen so that they present the document at the same height as the screen. The drawback of these types of stand is that often they can support only A4-sized documents. Sometimes they are a little flimsy and fall over and they also take up space on the desk. Alternatives to these include document plinths, which can best be described as being similar in shape to a footrest. These are intended to be positioned between the keyboard and screen and they raise the document off the desk and tilt it. These stands also tend to be large enough to hold two A4 pages side by side and they are capable of 'bridging' a docking station if it is located in the area in front of the screen. Infrequently used items can also be stored underneath them thereby avoiding making large areas of the desk surface unusable.

People who use laptops in a variety of locations also need to consider how they can avoid placing documents on the desk surface. One of the options available is to use a particular document holder called a 'page-up'. This is similar in shape and size to an egg, but with a flat bottom so it stands up.

A curved slit has been cut into the side of the 'egg' and this allows several pages of A4 paper to be presented in an upright position. The curved nature of the slit ensures that the pages remain erect and do not flop. This document holder is extremely small and light and is easy to carry around in a laptop bag but at the same time it is extremely effective in terms of supporting printed material to be read while performing a screen-based task. These page-ups would also be useful for a user who has very limited space on their desk surface.

Wristrests
Wristrests are long sections of gel-filled fabric that sit in front of the keyboard. Unfortunately, many of the people who use these items are not aware of the fact that they should not be leaning on them when they are actually using the keyboard. To do so means that they anchor their wrist in place as they use the keyboard and the only way to reach the keys is to stretch their fingers and bend their hand at the wrist from side to side. If a user is sitting in the correct posture they should be 'hovering' over the keyboard which allows the larger muscles of the arm to reposition the hands. Users should only lean on a wristrest when they are not typing. It is important that an employer advises their employees how to use these items properly if they are provided.

Screen risers
Many flat screens are provided with height-adjustable stands, which is ideal for allowing an individual to present the screen at a suitable height. In those circumstances where there is no in-built flexibility over how the screen is positioned, some other means for adjusting the height should be provided. If users cannot adjust the height of their screen, they may have to work with their head lowered if the screen is too low or with their head raised above a comfortable point if it is too high – such as can occur if the screen is placed on top of the computer.

Screen risers enable the screen to be positioned at a height to suit the individual. Articulating arms offer the greatest flexibility and allow the screen height to be altered quickly and easily, which is what would be recommended in a hot-desking environment. However, other options can work just as well. For instance, platforms that can be increased in height layer by layer are also effective. The only drawback is that they are a little more cumbersome to alter and as such may be more suited to a desk that is used by the same person every day.

Telephone headsets
Users who are expected to make or take telephone calls regularly throughout the course of their work should be provided with headsets or

earpieces. Users should not be permitted to cradle a telephone handset between their shoulder and chin while performing a screen-based task, such as might occur if a caller asks the user for information stored on the computer system. Clamping the handset in such a manner causes the head and neck to be twisted to the side and static muscle work, where the muscles tense for an uninterrupted period of time, is required to fix the handset in place. This is particularly fatiguing for the muscles concerned and can, if performed frequently enough, lead to discomfort in the shoulders and neck.

Reading/writing slopes

Most individuals who spend long periods of time looking down at the desk surface will find that they start to experience neck ache and some will experience lower backache. This can happen if they have a lot of documents to read or if they are writing for long periods. If they start to experience discomfort as a result of the way in which they are working, they should be provided with a reading/writing slope. This will raise their source document off the desk and allow them to adopt a more upright position. Having good directional lighting, and possibly a magnification tool, will also prevent the user from leaning forward over the source document as a consequence of not being able to read the material easily.

Workstation use

Having been provided with suitable workstation equipment, it is important that users are given a thorough understanding of how they should use it. Many users are given a workstation and are left to sort it out for themselves. Unless they have been given an appreciation of how they adjust their chair and what they should do with it, they are highly unlikely to sit in an appropriate posture when working. Many users sit at their desks for more than six hours per day and it is not unusual for many of them to be sitting incorrectly. It is hardly surprising when these same users complain about feeling uncomfortable.

Assuming that users will be using fixed-height desks, the first thing they should do is alter the height of their chair. The chair should be set at a height where the user's elbow is level with the home row of the keyboard (ie the middle row of letters). One of the most effective exercises a user can carry out is to sit sideways to their desk and keyboard and to drop their hands into their lap. Once the arms are relaxed the user should compare the height of their elbow with the height of the keyboard. If the elbow is lower than the keyboard when the user is sitting in this relaxed position they will clearly see how much they have to raise their arms and shoulders in order to use the keyboard. The muscles responsible for raising the shoulders and arms will be required to keep them in that position all of the time the user sits at their desk and they will probably only get an opportunity to relax when the user stands up and walks away from their desk. This might not be for several hours at a time.

Once the user sits at the correct height relative to their keyboard, their upper arm will hang naturally by the side of their trunk and their forearm will be parallel with the floor, allowing their hands to 'hover' over the keyboard (see the figure below). If the user adopts a position where they have a straight line running through their forearm and wrist and into their hand, they are less likely to experience discomfort in their wrists when working. If the keyboard is positioned about 10 cm away from the leading edge of the desk, the user will not have to reach forward and the upper arm will be able to remain in a neutral position along the side of the trunk, which is the least tiring position for it.

Once the chair has been altered for height, a decision should be made about whether a footrest is required. Users should only be given a footrest if their feet are not firmly on the floor. If a user is given a footrest when their feet already touch the floor, this can create problems they did not

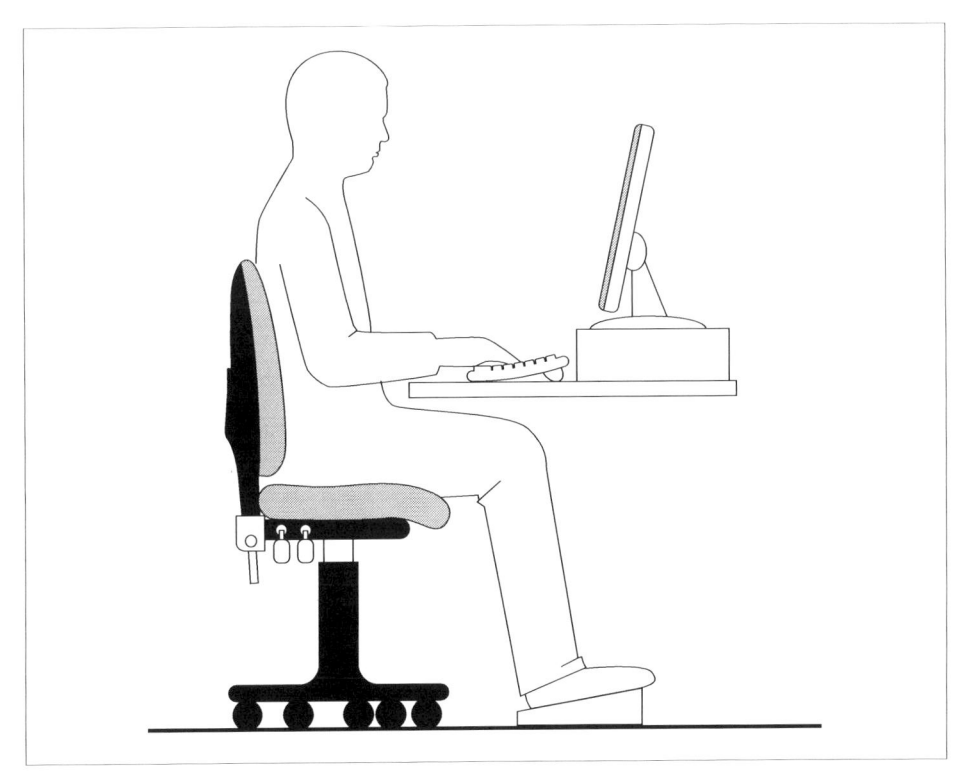

The seated posture
Reproduced from Work with display screen equipment: Health and Safety (Display Screen Equipment) Regulations 1992 as amended by the Health and Safety (Miscellaneous Amendments) Regulations 2002 *(HSE 2003)*

have previously. In this example, as they lift their foot onto the surface of the footrest they will start to raise the back of their thigh off the seat. As a consequence, a smaller surface area is supporting the weight of their upper body and they can start to experience pressure points which will make them uncomfortable and cause them to fidget. Most users will be unaware of the real source of their discomfort and will blame their chair.

The backrest on the chair is the next item to be adjusted. The inclination should be altered first as this will affect the positioning of the lumbar support. The user should sit reasonably upright, but not rigidly so. They should avoid leaning too far back in their seat as this will cause them to reach further forward with their arms when using the keyboard or mouse. Once the inclination has been set the user should reposition the lumbar support so that it falls in line with the small of their back – assuming they are not using a chair that 'moulds' to the shape of the back. This posture can be varied within a suitable range throughout the day.

Input devices

Although the keyboard and mouse are still the main means of entering and extracting information from a computer system, there are many alternatives available. These alternatives come in a variety of shapes, forms and mode of operation. Even one type of input device, such as a mouse, can come in many different guises and, as is the case with most work equipment, some designs are less likely to cause discomfort to users than others.

When selecting what type of input device is going to be used, questions need to be asked about who is going to operate the device and whether they have any special requirements such as a result of injury, illness or disability. Questions also need to be asked about whether the device will be used to simply point at an object on the screen, whether it will be used to track movement, whether items will be dragged from one area to another, whether the objects will be repositioned or reorientated, and whether information will be edited, inputted or extracted.

Keyboards

Standard QWERTY keyboards have been in use for a long time in offices. It is almost taken for granted that they must be an acceptable means of interacting with the computer system. However, it is clear that standard keyboards are designed in such a way that they have the potential to cause problems for the user if not used under the right circumstances. For instance, the way in which the keys are laid out in horizontal rows causes the user to position their hands so they have to have their palms facing down (pronation) and they bend their hand at the wrist in the direction of the little finger (ulnar deviation) – see the figure below. This posture is considered to be quite stressful for the arms if the user works for long periods at the keyboard without interruption. It has been suggested that smaller keyboards cause even greater deviation (Pheasant & Haslegrave 2006). This has quite serious implications for the use of laptops and notebooks and underlines the importance of limiting extended, uninterrupted use. 'Ergonomically designed' keyboards have been developed with the intention of allowing the user to adopt a more neutral position of the hands and wrists when pressing the keys, which in turn makes it less likely that they will experience discomfort. Such keyboards are worth considering if a user has reported ongoing hand or wrist pain that does not seem to settle.

Ulnar deviation during keyboard use. *Reproduced from Introduction to ergonomics (Bridger 2009, Figure 5.12, page 200)*

The force with which keys are depressed is an important issue. Unfortunately, as many users have not received any form of typing training, they use excessive force when hitting the keys and this is usually combined with using only one or two fingers of each hand. In addition, if users are provided with 'stiff' keyboards they tend to use more force to press the keys. It has been suggested (Rempel & Gerson 1991) that users can apply 2.2 to 4.7 times more force than the minimum amount needed to successfully press a key. When standard desktop keyboards are compared with notebooks it would appear that users tend to apply greater overstrike force (ie hitting the key harder than is necessary) on the notebook (Bufton *et al.* 2006). This could be improved by selecting notebooks with greater tactile feedback built into the keys and increasing travel distance in the keys. It would be helpful for users to have an understanding of the need to use their keyboards properly and to minimise the force they use when pressing keys.

It is standard practice in most offices to provide a keyboard with an integral numberpad. This has an impact on the positioning of the mouse relative to the user's seated position. Inclusion of the numberpad causes the mouse to be positioned further out to the side, which in turn causes the user to reach further – see the figure below. Unless users are inputting numbers for a major proportion of the day, it would probably make more sense to provide them with a keyboard that does not have an integral numberpad. This will enable them to keep the mouse closer, as shown below. Even users who input numbers for significant proportions of the day might benefit from a separate numberpad that can be used independently of the keyboard. This would allow them to move the keyboard to the side and position the numberpad directly in front of the hand being used to input the numbers.

Differences in reach caused by keyboards with and without a numberpad. *Reproduced from Office ergonomics: practical applications (McKeown 2008, Figures 6.2 and 6.3, page 84)*

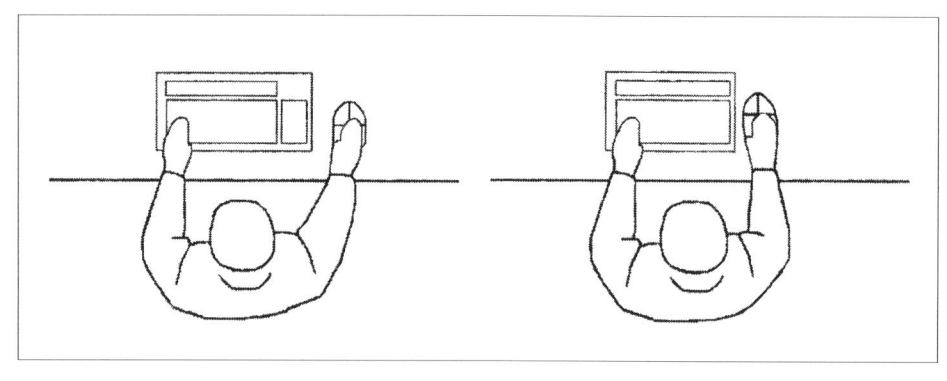

The positioning of the keyboard on the desk is important. Users should avoid the temptation of placing documents on the desk surface directly in front of the keyboard. This causes the keyboard to be positioned further away from the user and they have to compensate by reaching forward with their arms and possibly leaning forward also. This will increase the likelihood of them experiencing discomfort.

If users are experiencing discomfort when using their mouse they could consider, as an alternative, using keyboard shortcuts to reduce the extent of their mouse use. Users do not, as a rule, get much in the way of training in keyboard shortcuts and they are very much underused.

The use of PDAs ('personal digital assistants', for example the BlackBerry) should be mentioned at this point, because their keys are so small. Most users depress BlackBerry-style keys with the tip of their thumb. This causes them to overflex their thumb, and extensive use of it in this way can lead to discomfort. Although devices in the BlackBerry category are proving to be very valuable from a business perspective, it needs to be recognised that extensive, extended use of the keys should be avoided as this is likely to lead to problems of pain and discomfort for the user.

Mice
The mouse is probably the most common non-keyboard input device and many users use it for significant proportions of their working day. This is a little unfortunate as many mice are poorly designed and have not incorporated even the most basic principles of hand tool design – for that is what the mouse is, a tool to be used by the hand in the completion of work activities.

Typically, mice are not adequately formed to the size or shape of the hand. The most commonly employed types are rectangular lumps, possibly with some token contouring where the thumb might rest. Given how much time users spend gripping and moving the mouse, it is important that due care and attention is paid to the selection of this piece of equipment.

The most basic design of mouse requires the user to work with the palm of their hand facing down. The hand does not naturally fall into this position; the hand and arm have to co-operate in order to get the hand into an appropriate orientation to grip the mouse. Once the mouse is gripped it is not uncommon for the user to rest their hand on the mouse and their forearm on the desk. This causes them to extend their wrist – ie bend the hand upwards at the wrist. The extension is more pronounced if the mouse has greater depth and particularly if the user has rather small hands. Although using a mousemat with integral wrist support does support the wrist in a more neutral position, using such a mat anchors the arm in place and the only way to reposition the mouse is to move the hand from side to side at the wrist, which is not an ideal method. If a user finds that they are experiencing discomfort in their wrist when using the mouse and it is determined that they need some wrist support, the user could try a 'puc'. This is similar in size and shape to an ice hockey puck and it supports the wrist as the user grips the mouse. As its base is nylon, the puc glides across the desk as the user moves their arm when changing the position of the mouse. Care should be taken to ensure that the height of the puc is compatible with the height of the mouse so that a straight line runs through the wrist and into the hand.

If a mouse has been 'contoured' to accommodate the thumb or the fingers, it should be offered in a left- and right-handed version.

It is recommended that laptops be used with a separate 'standard' mouse. Unfortunately, as a means to cut down on weight and bulk, many laptops users are provided with 'mini-mice' – in other words, extremely small mice. To put it in perspective, mini-mice are dimensioned in such a way that they suit the hand size of very young children. Mini-mice are acceptable for occasional use only. They are so small that it is not possible for the hand to adopt anything resembling a neutral or comfortable posture. If users are working with laptops for long periods, such as more than an hour a day, they should be given a standard-sized mouse.

There are many mouse designs on the market and the only way to identify whether they can be used successfully is to take them on a trial basis. The starting point when assessing the suitability of a mouse is to look at the neutral position of the hand, when it is resting on the surface of the table and relaxed, and observe how that position has to be altered when gripping the mouse. The mouse should almost 'fit' into the relaxed resting position of the hand.

Some mice have been designed to offer a range of adjustment, either by lengthening and shortening them or by changing the angle at which the hand is supported. These increase the likelihood of the mouse being a good fit for the hand.

Although mice appear to be such an insignificant feature on a desk, they have quite serious implications for the user, given their likely intensity of use. No-one should use a mouse for extended, uninterrupted periods. This is likely to result in them experiencing discomfort.

Touchpads
Touchpads are a common feature of laptop computers. They are positioned centrally towards the front of the keyboard. This location causes the user to work with a hand position which is probably as extreme as that which is adopted when using the keyboard. The location of touchpads at the front of the keyboard also increases the reaching distance to the keys. In addition, users tend to use the tip of one finger when interacting with the touchpad to avoid sending out the confusing messages that might occur if several fingers were touching its surface. This focuses the workload on a single finger. Using the touchpad for long periods should be avoided and it is advisable to use a standard mouse instead.

Joysticks

Joysticks are a more common feature of desk-based work than might be expected. For example, they are used frequently in control rooms where users have to monitor environments with CCTV and use joysticks to reposition the cameras. The type of joystick employed depends on the precision required in the work. If the user needs to make small precise movements, a small stick gripped by the fingertips is probably the most effective design. Some joystick designs require the operator to press buttons regularly with their thumb. Using the thumb in such a manner repeatedly over long periods is not advisable, particularly if the joystick design is such that the thumb is held at a great distance from the main body of the hand.

Trackballs

Trackballs can be separate from the keyboard and used to the side like a mouse, or they can be embedded in the centre of keyboard in a similar position to a touchpad. Usually a trackball can be activated by the hand, fingers or thumb, so increasing the user's choice over how they work. The main drawback of trackballs is that they are usually supplied with a surrounding hand support which is elevated above the desk surface. Once the hand is on the trackball, the user tends to rest their forearm on the desk, which results in extension of the wrist.

Touchscreens

Touchscreens are operated easily by users reaching and touching various parts of the screen. This type of operation is being used more frequently, particularly in environments where laptops are being used away from offices, such as by employees of utilities companies or police officers working in vehicles. Locating the screen is not straightforward because two conflicting requirements have to be met: the screen needs to be far enough away to be read easily, yet it should not be so far away that it causes over-reaching.

The display has to be thought about carefully. Each icon needs to be of a suitable size so that it can be easily recognised and can be activated by the hands of both large and small users. They also need to be positioned far enough apart to avoid inadvertent activation. Priority information should be displayed in the upper areas of the screen as information displayed in the lower points can be obscured by the outstretched hand.

If a touchscreen is presented vertically and is intended to be operated by a standing user, they should not have to reach above shoulder height when touching the screen. Screens that are presented in the horizontal plane should be no higher than elbow height.

Tablets and pens

Graphics tablets and pens are commonly used by users working with computer-aided design systems. They are also used successfully by people who have experienced a degree of discomfort when working with a mouse. Although they can offer the user greater precision when performing their work, it should be kept in mind that the pinch grip used to hold the pen is particularly tiring for the hand and users should be encouraged to put the pen down and carry out alternative tasks at regular intervals.

Voice recognition software (VRS)

Users who have experienced difficulties in the past when using keyboards or mice, and people with learning disabilities, have used VRS successfully in place of more traditional equipment. Using VRS takes some planning and dedication on the part of the user. This is because the system has to learn to interpret what they are saying. The starting point is 'training' the system to recognise the user's voice and this is usually achieved by having the user read aloud a standard predetermined text for about 30 minutes. If the user wants the system to work effectively, they need to learn to talk fluently, clearly and consistently. If words need to be corrected, the user does not necessarily have to edit the text with the keyboard. Depending on how the system has been set up, they should be able to use voice commands to rectify text.

The practicalities of using such a system need to be considered. Confidential material would not normally be read out aloud and this may prove problematic in some environments. Users employing VRS may be distracting to other users who can hear them talking to their system. Very noisy workplaces, such as areas where there are several printers, may cause interference with the system – however, this can usually be dealt with by providing a good quality microphone that can filter out background noise.

Although VRS reduces the workload for the hands, it does increase the workload for the voice and it is not uncommon for people who talk a lot as part of their work, such as in call centres, to encounter problems with overuse of the voice.

Laptops

Laptops have added a whole new dimension to the issue of working with computers. They allow people to work from the office, from home, in a vehicle, when travelling and when staying in hotels. They have added great value in terms of where and how people work. However, they are also responsible for introducing a whole host of problems not encountered previously. Most of these problems are simply down to how the equipment is used as opposed to being inherent and unavoidable drawbacks of using laptops. If people had continued to use their laptops as they were originally intended, for short periods only, it is unlikely that users would have experienced the range of problems that are typical of laptop users.

Many of the problems with a laptop stem from the low-level screen. When a user looks at the screen they may have to lower their head by about 45°. The situation is compounded by the fact that the screen has to be pulled closer than a user might wish as they need to be able to reach the keyboard. Pulling the screen closer makes the user look downwards at an even greater angle. The impact of adopting such a posture is heightened by the fact that most laptop screens can only be viewed clearly within a narrow range of viewing angles and moving the head even by a small amount can make the display more difficult to read. This discourages users from changing their head position; maintaining the unchanging posture can be fatiguing for the muscles involved in positioning and supporting the head.

Some laptops have a deep surface directly in front of the keys to accommodate the touch pad. The depth of this surface increases the user's reaching distance to the keys. Using the touchpad causes the user to alter the position of their hand and wrist, and ultimately they end up working with the hand bent in the direction of their little finger (ie ulnar deviation) as they line their fingers up with the pad. Using the point stick embedded in the centre of the keys causes similar awkward postures, and it can only be activated by the tip of one finger, which focuses the workload on a single digit.

Most of the problems associated with laptop use can be eliminated by using them in conjunction with other equipment if they are to be used for long periods rather than briefly and intermittently. Ideally, docking stations should be made available to users employing laptops in the office or at home. A docking station allows the user to work with a standard screen, keyboard and mouse and lets them work more comfortably. Heasman *et al.* (2000) have found that docking stations lead to a reduction in complaints of discomfort among laptop users.

It is accepted that docking stations are an expensive option. However, organisations can still ensure that users can work comfortably simply by providing a standard keyboard and mouse which can be plugged into the laptop, and by raising the laptop on a surface so that the screen is presented at a better height. Separate mice are always recommended so that users do not have to adopt an awkward hand or wrist position to use the touchpad or point stick.

One of the other big problems associated with laptop use is their weight and the manual handling issues surrounding their movement. In contrast to industrial environments, very few office workers are given manual handling training. Yet, laptop computers can easily weigh up to 8 kg even without the added weight of the bag, the transformer and any documents the user decides to place in the laptop bag. Laptops are also handled in a range of awkward places, resulting in users becoming vulnerable to injury. For instance, users often sit in the driver's seat of a car and pull their laptop across from the passenger footwell or from the back of the vehicle through the gap between the front seats. Handling loads typically weighing over 8 kg in poor postures will increase the likelihood of the user being injured. Anyone who transports a laptop should be given training on manual handling techniques and this should focus specifically on the movement of laptops. Laptops should be stored in the boot during transport in a vehicle so that they do not become a missile if the car is involved in a collision. It also reduces the likelihood of the laptop being stolen at times when the car is stationary, such as at traffic lights.

Consideration should also be given to how the laptop is transported. Standard laptop bags may not be the most appropriate option. Wheelie bags or rucksacks may be better options. In the case of wheelie bags, it must be remembered that in certain circumstances they will have to be picked up and carried, such as when crossing gravel, walking up steps or using escalators. If rucksacks are being used, advice needs to be given on the correct way to use the rucksack. Slinging it off one shoulder is not acceptable as this focuses the load on one side of the body; the user leans to one side and the rucksack can move around as the person walks. Rucksacks should be worn over both shoulders and ideally the buckles should be fastened to make them more secure and less likely to move around. Getting the rucksack onto the shoulder has to be done carefully, and not by casually swinging it up from the floor and onto the shoulder in one sweep, which is the typical move employed by rucksack users. If possible, users should raise the rucksack onto a halfway point, such as their desk, using standard manual handling techniques, then slip one arm through a strap so that it rests on their shoulder before gradually standing upright and raising the load off the desk and locating their other arm through the remaining strap. Any straps on rucksacks or standard bags should be broad and well padded to spread the weight out over a larger area rather than focus it on a small area which will lead to local discomfort.

Anyone involved in buying laptops should be aware of the need to reduce load weight as far as possible. Heasman *et al.* (2000) have established that users found the weight of laptops was their most undesirable feature and also the aspect they would most like to change.

Manual handling risk assessments should also be carried out in situations where laptops are regularly handled. During these assessments, assessors should be aware of the need to consider all the extras carried by the user, such as documents and reference materials, and they should consider how the total weight handled could be reduced.

Working outside the office

Wireless technology has increased the opportunities open to people in terms of where they can work. Many people now work from home, while others use laptops in their vehicles.

Home workers

It is hard to understand sometimes why some employers only give due consideration to workers they can see every day sitting in an office directly in front of them and forget that their home workers are facing the same kinds of issue. It is uncommon for companies to have a strict policy on what home workers should use at home and many of these employees are 'allowed' to use whatever furniture they happen to have available. As a result, many home workers sit at the kitchen table or at a breakfast bar on a stool when working. Others might have a desk but use it in conjunction with a rattan chair from their conservatory. As a result, it is not possible for them to adopt a comfortable working posture. If they were only working for an hour or so, once or twice a week, they could probably cope with these less than satisfactory conditions. However, many home workers put in as many hours as their colleagues who work in the company's office. If that is the case, they either need to be given similar workstation furniture to their office-based colleagues, or they need to be given guidance on what to purchase for use at home. They also need to be reminded that they need to take regular breaks throughout the day. One of the problems associated with working from home is that there are fewer natural interruptions caused by meetings, telephone calls or chatting with colleagues. Home workers may also work for more concentrated periods because they have to make up for lost time, perhaps after dropping children to school or collecting them.

If it proves to be the case that the user is working without a suitable workstation, they should be given furniture advice so that they can make the best use of what they already have in place until new equipment can be provided. For instance, if they are sitting on a kitchen chair, they should roll a towel up into a long sausage shape and place this in the small of their back for support. Using a cushion is unlikely to suffice as it will be too large and will probably reduce the perceived depth of the seat. If the table is too high and is causing them to work with their arms raised, they should sit on a cushion to raise themselves up. Smaller users should support their feet on a briefcase, cushion or telephone directory. Screens should be propped up on telephone directories or a large book. Anyone working from a hotel room should take similar steps to make themselves comfortable.

Laptops in vehicles
Laptops are being used in many forms in vehicles. Some individuals use laptops in their standard format and simply support them on their knee as they work in a car, such as a sales representative may do after having visited a customer. Other users employ laptop systems that are partially embedded in the body of the vehicle. For instance, some organisations have permanently sited screens in the sun visor or roof liner and use a separate keyboard which they position on their lap as they input information or interrogate the system. Other organisations have mounted touchscreens within the vehicle, some on the dashboard, others at higher levels such as in the roof liner.

It has to be accepted that working in a vehicle imposes quite severe limitations on how the equipment can be positioned and used. It is just not possible to position the screen and keyboard in the ideal location that would be suggested for an office environment. As a consequence, there are potential negative implications for users working in a vehicle. However, that is not to say they will definitely encounter problems. By following some basic guidelines even people working in a vehicle can do so more comfortably.

Typically, the length of time a user will be expected to work in their vehicle will be limited and unlikely to match that of their counterparts in an office. This is a major positive feature which will help to counteract the effects of working in a cramped space.

The two different ways in which laptops are used in a vehicle need to be tackled differently. Users who have their laptop in the standard hinged screen and keyboard format should be advised to sit in the passenger seat when working – assuming they feel secure enough to do so. If they are working in an area that is known to be a security concern, they may wish to remain in the driver's seat so that they can drive off quickly if they feel threatened in any way. This underlines the importance of users being given driver safety training in addition to standard training in the use of their office equipment. Otherwise, users should sit in the passenger seat because this gives them more room to position their legs comfortably and to position their laptop at a more suitable viewing distance. Sitting in the driver's seat limits this choice because of the location of the steering wheel. In addition, there is a possibility that the airbag might be deployed should another vehicle collide with the user's car. This would propel the laptop towards the user, as would repositioning of the steering wheel, which could also occur following an impact. If the user sits in the front passenger seat, they should switch off the airbag on that side if one is fitted.

The backrest of the passenger seat should be altered so that the user is supported in an upright position. If needed, they should place a small support in the small of their back, such as a rolled-up towel or specifically designed lumbar roll of an acceptable size and shape. The location of the laptop on the thighs results in the screen being positioned lower than is ideal and will cause the user to work with their head lowered, so this should be limited to only short bursts of work. The positive aspect of working in this position is that the user is able to work with the laptop directly in front of them, avoiding the need to twist.

For users who have their equipment permanently embedded in the structure of the vehicle, there are other considerations. If the screen is located in the sun visor, the user will flip it down into position when needed. The difficulty is that the screen will be presented at a height that causes them to raise their head and eyes as they work. If they are required to work for long periods in this position, they are likely to experience fatigue, if not discomfort. If a separate keyboard is being used in conjunction with the visor-mounted screen, it is necessary to consider where the keyboard will be stowed when not in use. Some organisations stow it in the glove box or under the passenger seat. However, both locations could cause the user to reach, twist and lean to the side; if repeated regularly throughout the day, this may result in the user experiencing lower back discomfort.

Some users will work with a visor-mounted touchscreen instead of using a separate keyboard, and this will result in them raising their hands above shoulder height. Holding the arm in such a raised position will be extremely fatiguing, particularly if performed for a long time.

Other locations for the positioning of screens include the roof liner, around the interior light, and centrally on the dashboard. Attaching the screen to the roof causes the user to work with their head raised as they look at the display and they have to raise their hands above shoulder height if using a touchscreen. In addition, they will also have to twist towards the centre of the vehicle, which will increase the likelihood of lower backache. Positioning the computer system on the dashboard, around the heater vents, allows for a less extreme head position. Although the user has to turn their head to the side, they do not have to turn it beyond a comfortable range and they do not have to raise their head to a high level. Dashboard-mounted screens tend to result in viewing heights that are similar to those presented in offices. They also allow for less demanding arm positions when touching the screen. The only issue that needs to be considered is that right-handed users sitting in the driver's seat will have to reach across their body midline when touching the screen, which may cause them to twist. In addition, their hand may get in the way of portions of the screen as they reach across. Careful design of the display can limit the impact of this issue.

Users working in vehicles should be given the chance to perform lengthy screen-based work back in their office, where they can use standard office equipment and adopt more regular postures.

Environmental features

Lighting

When reviewing lighting in an office environment, both the location and level of light need to be considered. The level of light should be determined by the demands of the task. If a user is reading documents, they need a bright light of about 700 lux. If they are involved in a screen-based task, they need a lighting level of about 500 lux if they are to be able to see the display clearly. The best compromise is setting the room lights to a level that suits the computer-based task and providing individual directional desk lighting so that a user can illuminate any documents that need to be read. However, many offices want to avoid having extra clutter on the desk and will not give users desk lamps. Despite this, it is possible to create a lighting environment that suits combined screen and paper-based tasks. That is not to say that users will necessarily like the lighting levels or sources of light they are given. Lighting is such a personal issue that it is virtually impossible to please every user. What an employer has to confirm is that they have created an environment that allows users to get on with their work easily without causing them discomfort.

Glare is a common complaint of users. This can either be direct or indirect glare. Direct glare is emitted directly by a source, such as when an artificial light is directly in a user's eye line. Indirect glare is reflected off a surface, such as when a light source is reflected off a computer screen. Disability glare occurs when a source of light which is brighter than that of the task itself causes interference, making it difficult to complete the task. This is different to discomfort glare, which relates to having a bright source on the periphery of the visual field that does not interfere with the completion of the task.

The best way of avoiding glare is to ensure that users sit in between banks of lights where possible, rather than in line with rows of lights. If users have to sit in line with rows of lights, facing the ends of the light sources may be preferable to facing their sides, which can cause greater problems with glare. For that reason, some planning needs to go into the positioning of lights on the ceiling so that users are not presented with glaring open sides. Rotating the lights within their mounting points in the ceiling by 90° may be less distracting or disruptive to the user. If the light sources cannot be moved or presented in a different orientation, but continue to be a source of glare, consideration should be given to repositioning the screen on the desk or repositioning the desk within the office. Fitting different shields to the lights is another option. Using up-lighters in place of ceiling-mounted lights is likely to avoid most of the problems associated with glare. This kind of indirect lighting provides a more even distribution of light and reduces the shadowing that occurs with direct lighting. The effect is even better if a larger number of lower-powered sources of light are used rather than a few high-powered sources.

Artificial lights are not the only source of glare. Natural light coming through windows can also cause problems. This can be controlled by using suitable blinds or curtains. The area around the window should not be designed so that it presents a very dark frame to the window, as this only intensifies the glare problems. Ideally, users should sit sideways on to a window rather than facing it, where they will be aware of the glare. Sitting with the back to the window can result in indirect glare as the light bounces off the computer screen. Although most users would prefer to work in an office filled with natural light, having many large windows makes it much more difficult to control the temperature in the office as well as the lighting levels.

Apart from dealing with glare issues, the lighting experience in an office can often be improved through a series of very simple steps. Regular cleaning of lights and their covers is often overlooked. Providing lighter surfaces when selecting desks, filing cabinets and cupboards and avoiding dark heavy woods increases the furniture's reflective values. Assessing the light levels in an office will indicate whether the space is uniformly lit and if it is not, this can be addressed by moving lights closer together, adding more, removing obstructions from around them and cleaning them. Alternatively, the workstations can be repositioned to make the most out of the lighting that is already present.

As may be expected, people prefer to work in environments where they have windows and are able to see the outside world, rather than in a windowless environment with no view.

Temperature

At the same time as looking at the temperature in which a user works, thought also has to be given to the humidity and air velocity (or draughts). As is the case with lighting, it is particularly difficult to create a thermal environment that most users are consistently happy with. Many things can influence their level of satisfaction with the temperature, such as what they are wearing, the time of year, their age, sex, what food they have eaten that day, their weight and so on. It is also difficult for users to have much of an impact on their environment if they feel too hot or too cold, because most modern offices have sealed windows and the heating and ventilation is driven by a remote computer system.

When setting the temperature for an office, some thought has to be given to whether the individuals in that area typically sit at a desk as they work or whether they are active, such as workers in a mail room. Temperatures between 20 and 26° C are thought to be a suitable range for sedentary workers, with temperatures of around 21.5–22° C being most acceptable. Workers who are more physically active when working prefer temperature ranges of about 18–19° C.

Even if the temperature has been set at a level that might normally be considered acceptable, it is possible for the user to perceive the environment to be colder if they are subject to draughts. Draughts coming from behind them or that are felt around the feet or neck are the most likely to have a negative impact. Users who remain at their desks for longer without getting up and moving around are more susceptible to the effects of draughts.

If humidity levels are low, users will be aware of the drying effects of the air. They will experience irritation of the nose and eyes and contact lens wearers will experience the most extreme eye irritation. A relative humidity of about 40–50 per cent is considered satisfactory for most sedentary occupations if combined with a moderate range of temperatures.

The only way to confirm that the thermal environment is satisfactory is to take measurements. These should be taken in a variety of locations in the office, but alongside users, so that they provide a true overview of the temperature levels at the points where people are actually working. They should be taken at ankle, chest and head height and should be taken at different points through the day.

Organisational features

The importance of organisational features should not be underplayed. Even if an individual is asked to perform what might be considered a potentially hazardous operation, such as repetitive use of a keyboard or continuous use of the mouse, the likelihood of them developing a problem could be significantly reduced by ensuring they take proper breaks and/or get an opportunity to do other things.

The current accepted thinking is that continuous interaction with a computer system, whether using the keyboard, mouse or simply looking at the screen, should be interrupted at least once an hour for five to ten minutes. Despite this view, many office managers allow their staff to remain at their workstations without a change in activities for many hours at a time. Few offices have a regimented break system in place any more, whereby staff take a 15-minute break at 11.00, a 30–60-minute lunch break and a 15-minute break at 15.00. Most offices have a less formal approach to breaks and work on the basis that users can leave their workstations whenever they want to get a drink, to visit the washrooms or to attend a meeting. The reality is, however, that users working in these conditions tend to spend long periods sitting at their desks without getting up. It is not uncommon for users to work for two to three hours without any form of interruption. There are many reasons for this. Some users feel under too much pressure with deadlines and workloads to take breaks. Other users get absorbed in their work and do not realise how long they have been working without a break. Others are conscious of being monitored by their manager or team leader and do not want to be seen leaving their desk. Some users do not appreciate that they should be taking breaks because they have never been told by their employer that they should do this.

The problem is that users who spend long periods sitting at their desk performing a screen-based operation without interruption or a change in activities are likely to experience discomfort. Some users may eventually develop symptoms of an upper limb disorder. Unfortunately, many office jobs are such that there is little opportunity to carry out any other type of work apart from screen-based work. Everything a user may need is usually found online, so there is no need to use reference manuals or phone directories, or even to read letters or documents, since most material of this type is scanned and accessed through the computer system. If the user's work cannot be restructured in such a way that they get brief breaks from their screen-based work, they should be given regular rest breaks. Users should also be made aware of the need to manage their own work more carefully. They need to understand the importance of using additional tasks, even seemingly simple tasks such as filing or photocopying, as a means to break up their screen work regularly. Users should also be advised to leave their workstations to have their lunch rather than remaining at their desks. Employers should provide suitable facilities for lunch breaks that are attractive enough to encourage users to want to use them.

If assessors are reviewing how work is being performed, it is important that they get an accurate view of how the user works. Although the assessor should investigate whether the user is missing out on breaks, they should not necessarily accept unquestioningly the user's reports that they spend 80–90 per cent of their time at the desk using the computer because this may not actually be the case. Sometimes users do not recognise that they do, in fact, get a lot more breaks than they realise. They may overlook the fact that they have to collect documents to complete their work, or that they have team briefings every morning or perhaps they take a series of smoke breaks throughout the day. Although these may not be official breaks, they do offer a brief break away from screen work, which is beneficial.

Once someone has become used to the demands of their work (ie work hardening), it is important that they work consistently throughout the day and from day to day. They are less likely to experience discomfort if they work at the same rate consistently. Unfortunately, there are some workplaces where peaks and troughs in workload are considered to be unavoidable. For instance, accounts departments often have month ends and year ends that result in a temporary increase in workload. Because such increases in workload are intermittent, the user never has an opportunity to become fully accustomed to the change in demands and cannot become fit enough fast enough to cope easily with the increased demands. As a consequence, it is common for users subject to peaks and troughs to experience discomfort.

Health concerns

Many users are concerned that long term work with computers is likely to damage their health in some way. Typical complaints include backache, eye fatigue, headaches and upper limb disorders. In the main, it has been established that the commonest aches and pains experienced by users when working with computers are caused by unsuitable workstation equipment and furniture and/or by using it incorrectly and working for long periods without task variety or regular rest breaks.

Backache
Backache is often caused by using an adjustable chair incorrectly. Few users have been given any instruction in how to use and adjust their chair and, as a consequence, they rarely set the chair at the correct height for their work. Few of them manage to give suitable support to their back. Some organisations assume that because their users have worked through online training packages that discuss posture, they will have adjusted their own chairs correctly. It is not unusual for users to find it hard to transfer online training to their own workstation. One-to-one instruction at the user's workstation is the most effective way of ensuring that the furniture and equipment is set up correctly for the user and that they avoid discomfort as they work. Having set the workstation up correctly, users need to be told that they must take regular breaks and move away from their desk.

Manual handling tasks should also be considered a possible contributor to the onset of backache. Few office workers are offered formal manual handling training but significant numbers are involved in handling boxes of copier paper, archive boxes, laptops, desks and even bottles of water that are lifted into water dispensers. Anyone required to handle loads should be provided with suitable practical training – and that does not mean sitting passively watching a training DVD.

Visual fatigue
Visual fatigue is a far more accurate description of what most users experience than the common term 'eye strain'. Many users work to the point where their eyes are tired and as a consequence they experience a range of symptoms, such as irritation and reddening of the eyes, blurred vision and headaches. These are unlikely to be permanent symptoms and should be resolved if the user changes the way they work. The eye, like any other part of the body, also benefits from a change in activities, regular rest breaks and looking at different viewing distances rather than simply focusing on a screen for long periods.

Upper limb disorders
Some users experience pain or discomfort in their upper limbs when using a keyboard or mouse. The symptoms they experience can include aching, pins and needles, numbness, tingling or general weakness. These are symptoms of upper limb disorders (ULDs), which are covered in detail in

Chapter 8. In brief, a user can be diagnosed as suffering from a ULD anywhere from the fingers, across the hand and wrist, into the arm, up to the shoulder and into the back of the neck.

One of the common cases of ULDs is poor posture. Once a user sits at a desk, the height of the chair relative to the keyboard will dictate the posture of the arm. If their sitting height is not correct they will adopt, and maintain, unnatural arm positions as they use the keyboard and mouse.

The way in which someone uses a keyboard and mouse has an impact on the likelihood of them experiencing upper limb discomfort. Reaching to the keyboard or mouse increases the workload for the arms and makes them more susceptible to fatigue and possible injury over time. Hitting the keys with more force than is necessary is also a possible contributory factor. Some users work at extremely high speeds as they enter data onto the computer system. Data-entry operators are known to be more likely to encounter problems because of the speed at which they press the keys.

The most important factor in reducing the likelihood that a user will develop a ULD when using a computer system is to ensure that they take regular breaks. Working for long periods performing the same type of work without interruption increases the likelihood that they will encounter problems.

Summary

- To enable a person to sit comfortably, an office chair should be adjustable for height, have backrest adjustment and should have a five-star base.
- Armrests on a chair are not essential and can create problems for the user. If they do, they should be removed.
- Fixed-height desks are acceptable as long as the chair is used properly to adopt a suitable sitting height.
- Height adjustment in a desk offers greater flexibility to users, especially in hot-desking environments.
- The undersurface of the desk should be free of obstructions that might restrict where the user sits.
- The screen should be located directly in front of the user with the keyboard in alignment between the user and the screen.
- The top of the viewable area of the screen should not pass above the user's eye line.

- Bifocal wearers may need their screen lower than other users to avoid exaggerated head positions.
- All workstation furniture should be trialled before full introduction into the workplace.
- Footrests should only be provided if the user's feet do not touch the floor when their chair is at a suitable height relative to the desk.
- Users referring to documents while operating DSE should use a copy stand rather than place their source document on the desk surface.
- Wrist rests should not be used to anchor the wrists in place while the keyboard is in use.
- If screens are not height-adjustable they should be placed on screen risers to modify their height for taller users.
- Reading/writing slopes should be considered for people who spend long periods leaning towards the surface of their desk when reading or writing.
- Users should adopt a sitting position where their elbows are level with the home row of the keyboard, their elbows should be bent at 90° and they should be facing forward in a reasonably upright position.
- Mouse designs, and input devices generally, vary significantly and trials should be run to identify the most suitable for users.
- Mini-mice should be avoided.
- Home workers and people who work away from the main office need as much consideration as DSE users who work in the office in terms of the equipment they use and the work they perform.
- Laptop use should be limited either by using docking stations or by using add-ons such as external screens, keyboards and mice.
- Careful thought needs to be given to the manual handling implications of using laptops.
- Laptop use in vehicles should be avoided or at least performed under strict guidelines.
- Lighting levels should suit the combined DSE and paper-based tasks.
- Glare should be avoided by following basic guidelines such as sitting between banks of lights, using natural light where possible and using up-lighters.
- Temperature, humidity and draughts can have a negative impact and need to be assessed to ensure they fall within suitable parameters.
- Regular breaks away from DSE work and the workstation are the most effective means of reducing the likelihood of users experiencing ill health as a result of their work.
- Backache, visual fatigue and ULDs are common complaints in offices and much of the discomfort is caused by unsuitable working conditions and a lack of regular breaks. Often, simple changes significantly reduce the problems.

References and further reading

British Standards Institution. *Ergonomic requirements for office work with visual display terminals (VDTs) – Part 5: Workstation layout and postural requirements*, BS EN ISO 9241-5. BSI, 1999.

British Standards Institution. *Ergonomic requirements for office work with visual display terminals (VDTs) – Part 6: Guidance on the work environment*, BS EN ISO 9241-6. BSI, 2000.

Bufton M J, Marklin R W, Nagurka M L and Simoneau G G. Effect of key-switch design of desktop and notebook keyboards related to key stiffness and typing force. *Ergonomics* 2006; 49 (10): 996–1012.

Grandjean E. *Ergonomics in computerized offices*. Taylor & Francis, 1994.

Health and Safety Executive. *How to deal with sick building syndrome: guidance for employers, building owners and building managers*, HS(G)132. HSE Books, 1995.

Health and Safety Executive. *Seating at work*, HS(G)57. HSE Books, 1997.

Health and Safety Executive. *Work with display screen equipment: Health and Safety (Display Screen Equipment) Regulations 1992 as amended by the Health and Safety (Miscellaneous Amendments) Regulations 2002*, L26. HSE Books, 2003.

Health and Safety Executive. *The law on VDUs: an easy guide – making sure your office complies with the Health and Safety (Display Screen Equipment) Regulations 1992 (as amended in 2002)*, HSG90. HSE Books, 2003.

Heasman T, Brooks A and Stewart T. *Health and safety of portable display screen equipment*, CRR3004. HSE Books, 2000.

Kerr J, Griffiths A and Cox T (eds). *Workplace health, employee fitness and exercise*. Taylor & Francis, 1996.

Kirby M A R, Dix A J and Finlay A E (eds). *People and computers*. Cambridge University Press, 1995.

Leuder R and Noro K. *Hard facts about soft machines: the ergonomics of seating*. Taylor & Francis, 1994.

McKeown C. *Office ergonomics*. CRC Press, 2008.

Moon S D and Sauter S L (eds). *Beyond biomechanics: psychosocial aspects of musculoskeletal disorders in office work*. Taylor & Francis, 2007.

Morris A and Dyer H. *Human aspects of library automation* (second edition). Gower, 1998.

Pheasant S and Haslegrave C M. *Bodyspace, anthropometry, ergonomics and the design of work* (second edition). Taylor & Francis, 2006.

Rempel D and Gerson J. Fingertip force while using three different keyboards. In: *Proceedings of the Human Factors Society 35th Annual Meeting*, San Francisco, 1991: 253–255.

Sauter S L, Dainoff M and Smith M. *Promoting health and productivity in the computerized office.* Taylor & Francis, 1990.

8 Upper limb disorders

Introduction

As long ago as 1713 Bernardino Ramazzini identified a condition in scribes which has since become known as repetitive strain injury. Over time it became evident that it was not just repetitive work that was responsible for the range of symptoms and disorders experienced by people in their hands, arms, shoulders and neck, and the condition was renamed upper limb disorder (ULD). This term offers a more acceptable description of what the affected person may experience.

Despite the fact that in the UK the term ULD is used fairly widely, many people still debate the accuracy of a term that is not universally accepted. For example, in Japan the same condition is referred to as occupational cerviobrachial disorder (OCD) and in the US the term cumulative trauma disorder (CTD) is used. Sometimes the argument is put forward that if there is not even agreement on the name that should be used, how can the causes of the condition in the workplace be tackled? Others argue that it does not really matter what the condition is called – as long as it is recognised that the person has been injured in some way by a process or arrangement at work and that steps should be taken to tackle the issue.

Although some dispute that there are such things as work-related ULDs, this chapter takes the stance that ULDs do exist and that they may be caused, or exacerbated, by elements in the workplace.

Having drawn attention to the work-related causes of ULDs, it should be understood that these are by no means the only causes of these conditions. It is now generally accepted that certain hobbies, domestic activities and medical conditions can play a part in the development of a ULD. Therefore, when an individual reports pain or discomfort in the upper limbs, a holistic approach should be taken to identify the possible cause(s). It should not be assumed that work alone is to blame.

Postures of the upper limbs

Before considering ULDs in any detail, it is advisable to explore the postures adopted by the upper limbs during the course of a day. An appreciation of the range of postures used will assist in understanding why certain wrist or arm positions are more likely to be stressful for the limbs than others. Each major joint in the upper limbs can display a wide range of movements. However, any movement that pushes the joint away from a neutral or natural position can be harmful, particularly if carried out repeatedly or for extended periods.

When describing the work being carried out by the limb, it is important that an accurate description is given of its position or direction of movement. For example, is the palm facing up or down? Is the arm alongside the body or stretched out to the side? Because of the importance of describing limb positions accurately, a specific vocabulary has been developed which describes the positions adopted by the whole arm or just part of it. Some of the more commonly adopted limb positions are shown opposite and a description of the terms used in the illustration follows.

- **Abduction** – moving the arm outwards and away from the side of the body.
- **Adduction** – moving the arm across the front of the body.
- **Pronation** – rotation of the forearm which results in the palm of the hand facing down.
- **Supination** – rotation of the forearm which results in the palm of the hand facing up.
- **Radial deviation** – bending the hand at the wrist in the direction of the thumb.
- **Ulnar deviation** – bending the hand at the wrist in the direction of the little finger.
- **Wrist flexion** – bending the hand down at the wrist.
- **Wrist extension** – bending the hand up at the wrist.

Types of ULD

It is generally accepted that ULDs can affect any area of the upper limbs from the fingertips to the neck. Specifically named disorders usually identify which part of the body is affected and what type of symptoms the person is suffering. The following section outlines some of the more common disorders that can be experienced.

Hand and wrist area

Tenosynovitis
This term has probably been used more often and more inaccurately than any other condition identified as a ULD. It was regularly used in the late 1980s and early 1990s as an umbrella term to denote that a work-related ULD had occurred. Tenosynovitis is, in fact, a specific ULD. It arises from inflammation in the lining of the synovial sheath of the tendons, most commonly in the hand and wrist. The tendons and their sheaths are shown on page 184.

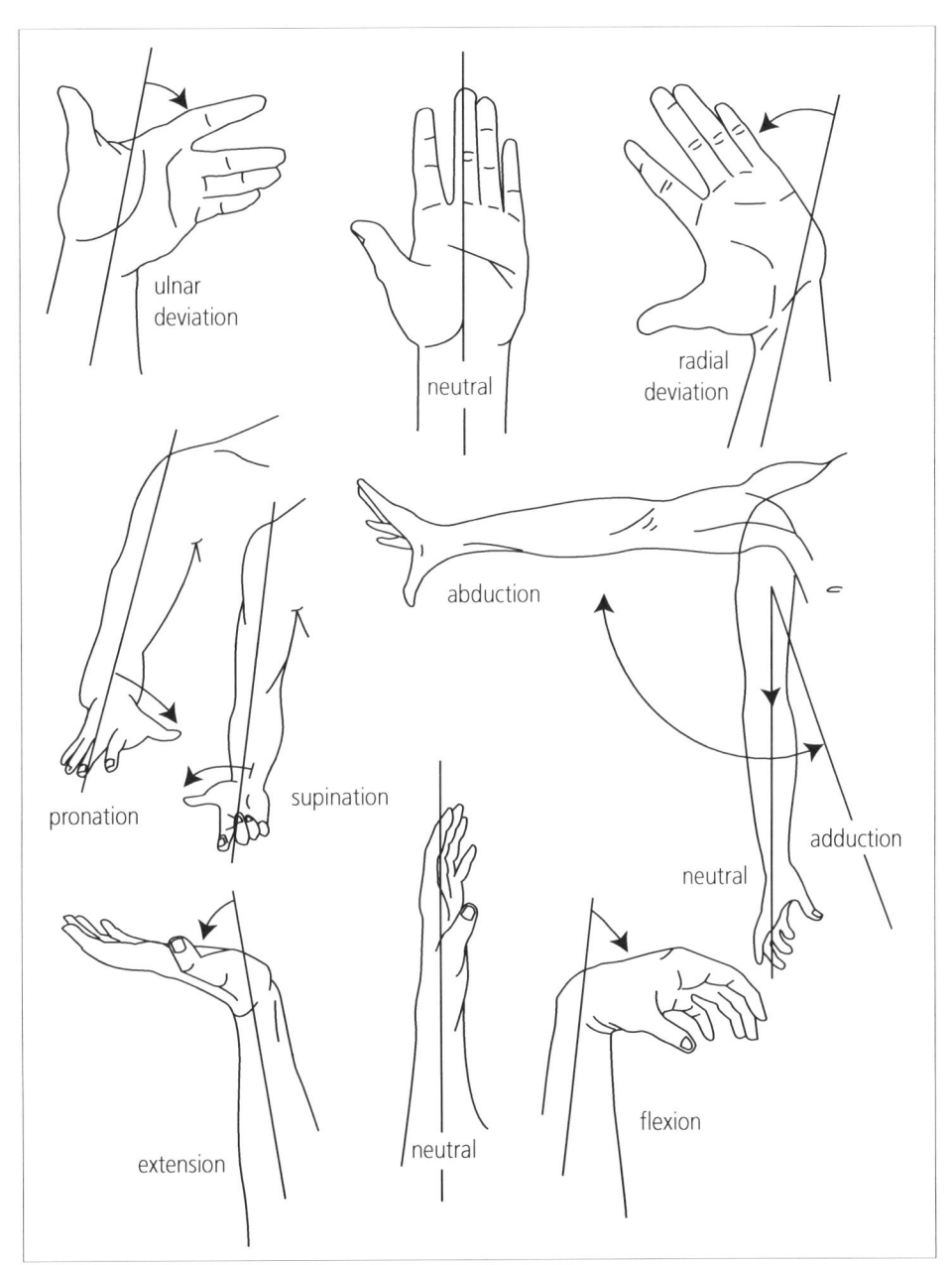

Commonly adopted upper limb positions *Reproduced from Cumulative trauma disorders: a manual for musculoskeletal diseases of the upper limbs (Putz-Anderson 1988, Figure A1, page 116)*

The tendons normally move freely inside the sheath, which is lubricated and offers protection as the tendon passes under ligaments or around corners, such as when the wrist is bent. Repetitive work is often cited as a cause of tenosynovitis. However, it is generally accepted that a traumatic injury, such as a heavy fall or blow to the wrist, may predispose an individual to developing tenosynovitis, particularly if they

Tendons and sheaths in the hand
Reproduced from Cumulative trauma disorders: a manual for musculoskeletal diseases of the upper limbs (Putz-Anderson 1988, Figure 3, page 11)

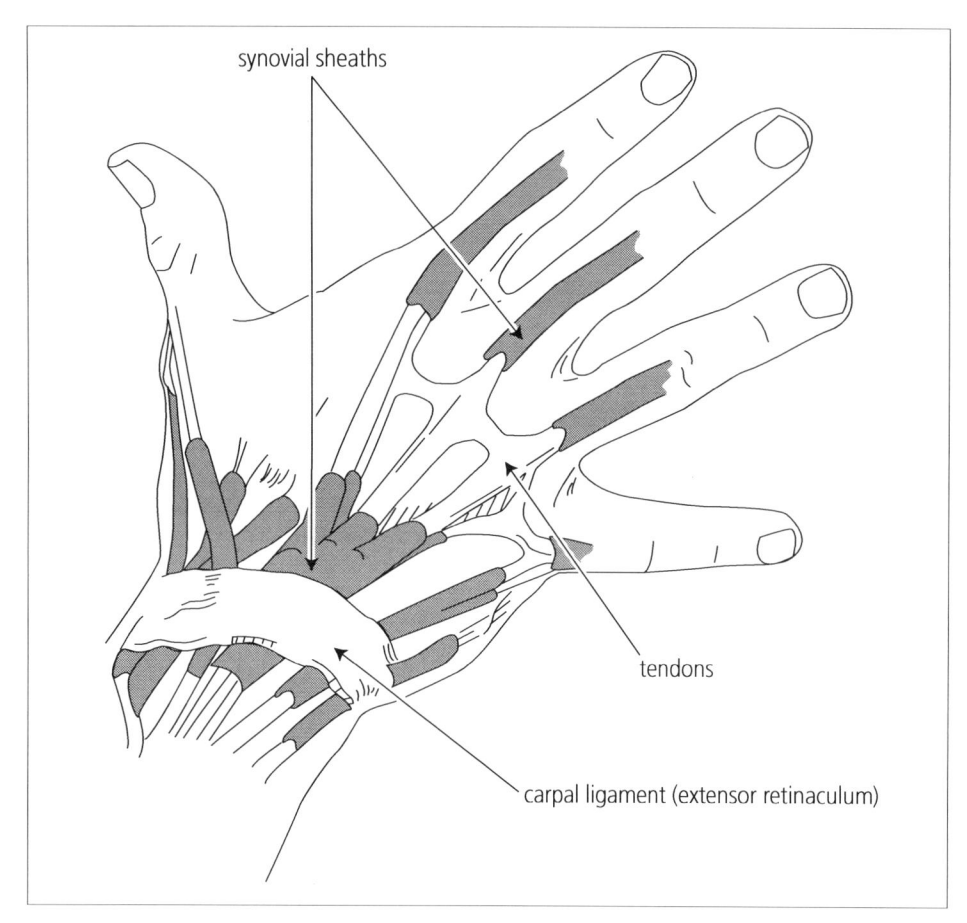

are employed to carry out an activity where the work is manually intensive. Other work-related factors which are closely associated with the development of this condition are forceful gripping, usually when carried out repetitively, and working with the hands away from the neutral position (illustrated on page 183). Those suffering from tenosynovitis may experience symptoms such as an aching in the wrist, a weakness of grip, swelling (or even just the sensation of swelling) and sometimes crepitus, a crackling sound similar to the noise made when someone walks over dry snow.

A slightly different condition called stenosing tenosynovitis is caused if the movement of the tendon inside the sheath is impaired. If the abductor pollicis longus and extensor pollicis brevis tendons are involved the condition is referred to as De Quervain's disease. These tendons can be easily seen on the hand at the base of the thumb. They form the outer wall of the 'anatomical snuffbox' – the small indent in the surface of the hand just above the wrist area on the side of the thumb. Prolonged exertion, repeated strain or unaccustomed work have been implicated as precipitating factors in this particular condition. Operations which involve deviation of the wrist combined with forceful grasping, particularly of larger objects where the thumb is moved outwards away from the hand to wrap around the side of the object, are also considered to be more likely to contribute to the development of this condition.

If the tendons of the finger flexors are affected, the individual will be diagnosed as suffering from trigger finger. The flexors are the tendons which allow the fingers to be pulled in towards the palm, such as when making a fist. This condition usually results from overuse of the fingers and is often associated with the repeated or extended use of tools, particularly when the handle or trigger has hard or sharp edges. Sufferers may find that they can only make jerky movements of their fingers.

Carpal tunnel syndrome

The tendons responsible for flexing the fingers, as well as the median nerve and blood vessels, pass from the forearm into the hand through the carpal tunnel under the carpal ligament (illustrated on the previous page). The median nerve, which is shown on page 186, is responsible for the sensation in the thumb, the majority of the palm, the index finger, middle finger and part of the ring finger.

Carpal tunnel syndrome is caused by compression of the median nerve. This compression can result from irritation and swelling within the confines of the carpal tunnel, such as occurs in tenosynovitis. It can also result from the repeated deviation of the wrist, repeated forceful gripping and the vibration connected to tool use. The syndrome has also been associated with pregnancy, the menopause, a local trauma such as a fracture, diabetes and rheumatoid arthritis.

Typical symptoms of carpal tunnel syndrome are numbness and tingling, usually in the areas of the hand connected to the median nerve. Symptoms are known to be so severe at night that they can wake the sufferer. There may be a loss of sensation in the hand, which can make it difficult for the sufferer to pick up small objects, giving the hand a rather clumsy feel.

Dupuytren's contracture

This condition is caused by a shortening and thickening of the fibrous fan on the palm of the hand known as the palmar fascia. The shortening and thickening causes a gradual and permanent bending of the fingers unless surgical treatment is sought. The most common digits to bend are the little and ring fingers.

Cross-section of the wrist *Reproduced from Cumulative trauma disorders: a manual for musculoskeletal diseases of the upper limbs (Putz-Anderson 1988, Figures 5a and 5b, page 13)*

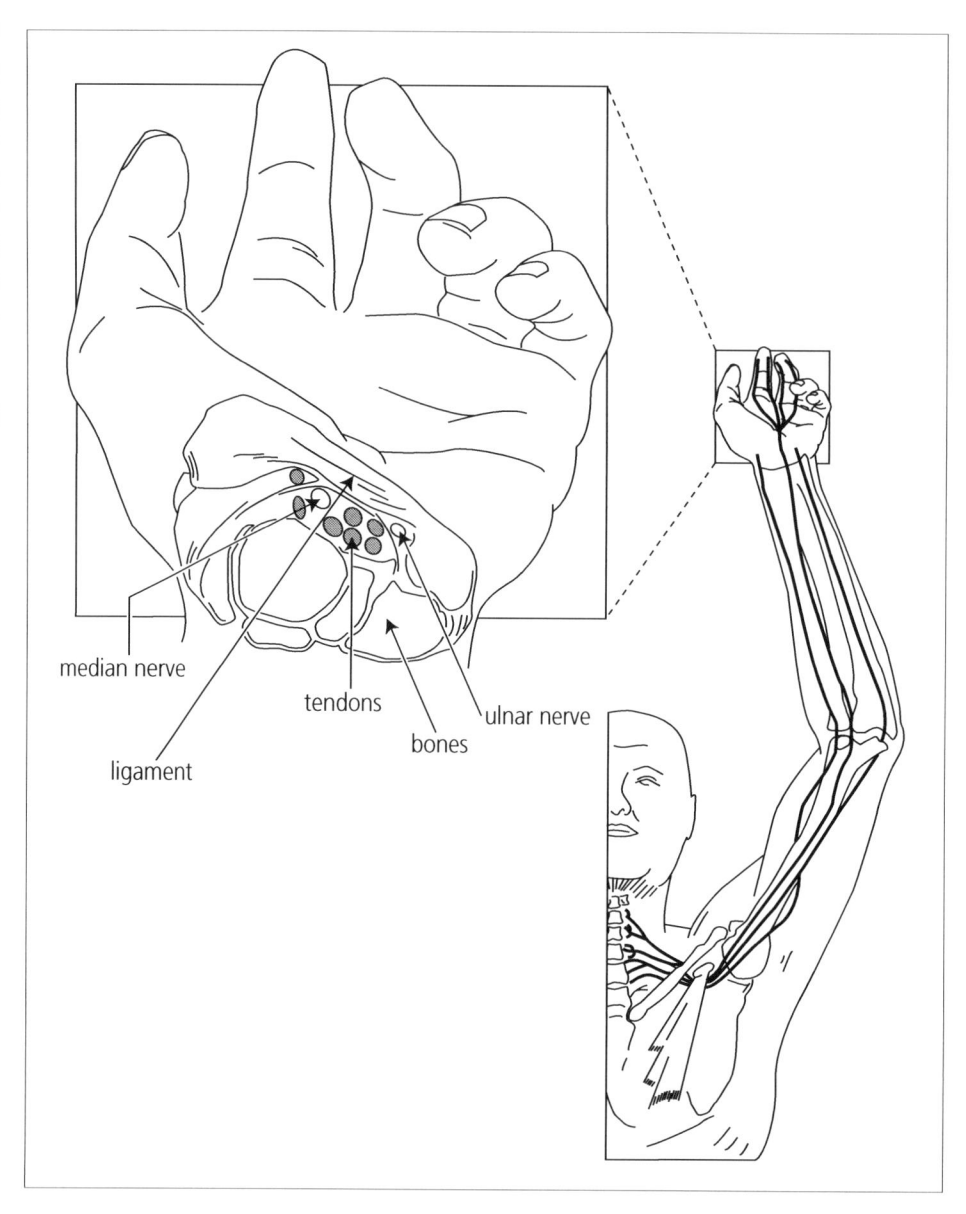

Repeated minor trauma to the palm of the hand (such as occurs when a carpenter hits a chisel end with the palm) and the use of vibratory tools may cause the condition. Specific injury, such as a laceration to the hand, may also contribute.

Dupuytren's contracture has been shown to be congenital and may not therefore have a work-related component in some sufferers.

Ganglion

A ganglion is a fluid-filled swelling, usually found on the back of the wrist or hand. It is generally about the size of a large pea but can be bigger. Although ganglia are not painful, and some would suggest that they are not work-related, it is usually considered that a high incidence in a particular workplace is often a sign that the operators are exposed to inappropriate working conditions (eg an excessive work rate) or that they are adopting irregular upper limb postures while working.

Lower and upper arm

Epicondylitis

There are two types of epicondylitis – commonly known as tennis elbow and golfer's elbow. Tennis elbow is more accurately referred to as lateral epicondylitis and affects the side of the elbow which is in line with the thumb when the arm is held out in front of the body with the palm facing upwards. Golfer's elbow affects the opposite side of the elbow.

Lateral epicondylitis means that the area around the epicondyle – the bony bump on the outside of the elbow – is inflamed. The epicondyle is the point where the muscles responsible for extending the wrist and fingers originate. Overuse of these muscles can cause pain as the epicondyle becomes tender and swollen.

Forceful movements that bring the hand upwards at the wrist (eg when throwing an object) or repeated rotation of the forearm (eg when using a screwdriver) are considered to be likely to contribute to the development of lateral epicondylitis. Heavy lifting, particularly when the back of the hand is facing upward (eg when lifting a brick), is also considered to be associated with the development of this condition.

Golfer's elbow, or medial epicondylitis, is very similar to lateral epicondylitis but is not as common. It is an irritation at the point of origin of the flexor muscles on the inside of the elbow and is usually caused by repeated flexion of the wrist, ie where the hand is bent downwards at the wrist, and rotation of the forearm.

Tendinitis

Tendinitis is a condition which can affect any tendon in the body. Humeral tendinitis, or rotator cuff tendinitis, is an inflammatory condition which affects the tendons of the muscles responsible for the rotation of the arm at the shoulder and the movement of the arm away from the body. Other surrounding soft tissue, such as the subacromial bursa, is also affected. The subacromial bursa is a cushion which protects the tendons from the bony ridge that overhangs them during movement. This bony ridge is the acromian.

Shoulder problems, such as humeral tendinitis, are generally found in operators who work with their arms raised for extended periods, or those who raise their arms repeatedly.

Frozen shoulder
Continued overhead work, where the arms are repeatedly raised or held in this position for an extended period, can lead to thickening of both the tendons and bursa. This results in the condition known as frozen shoulder, which causes the sufferer to experience pain and impaired function. However, many cases of frozen shoulder have been shown to have no connection with work activities.

Thoracic outlet syndrome
The condition involving the nerves and adjacent blood vessels in the shoulder and upper arm is known as thoracic outlet syndrome. It is a general term used to indicate that the nerves and blood vessels between the neck and shoulder have been compressed. The individual will experience similar symptoms to those of carpal tunnel syndrome, such as numbness in the fingers.

Work involving frequent reaching above the shoulder or activities which require the shoulders to be pulled backwards and downwards (eg when carrying a stretcher) are known to contribute to the development of this condition. People who repeatedly carry weights directly on their shoulders (eg bricklayers supporting a hod) or who suspend weights from their shoulders (eg postal workers) are more likely to experience this condition.

Other conditions

Cervical spondylosis
Cervical spondylosis is a common condition of the neck and spine. It is an inflammation of the synovial joints of the neck and is often associated with age. It has also been associated with those who habitually carry heavy loads on their shoulders (eg bricklayers using hods).

Osteoarthritis
Osteoarthritis is a degenerative condition more accurately known as osteoarthrosis. It is caused by general wear and tear which affects the articular cartilages of the synovial joints. Localised osteoarthritis can occur when a particular joint has been subjected to long term stress (eg the elbow joints of slaughterhouse workers involved in pulling skins off animals).

Causes of ULDs

It is widely accepted that most ULDs are caused by easily identified aspects of the workplace. Numerous sectors (commercial, service and industrial) and occupations are closely associated with high rates of ULDs among the workforce. In most instances where an individual develops a ULD, it is a result of a combination of factors rather than exposure to one single factor.

There are various main causes of ULDs and certain additional aggravating factors. More often than not, these act together to the detriment of the individual.

Main causes of ULDs

The main causes of ULDs include repetition, poor posture, force and static work. However, it should always be borne in mind that just because an activity includes one or more of these elements and therefore has the potential to cause harm, it is not inevitable that an operator will develop a ULD. The outcome is mediated to an extent by contributory or aggravating factors – discussed later in this chapter.

Repetition
Any job that requires an operator to carry out the same operation or sequence of operations repeatedly within a short timescale should be considered to put them at risk. Muscles that have to work rapidly develop less tension than muscles that can work more slowly. As a consequence, more effort is required to complete an operation carried out at a fast rate. As a result of applying more effort, the operator requires a longer period of time for recovery, which work–rest schedules rarely take into account. It was thought at one time that repetitive work would cause a ULD only if it was combined with excessive force. However, it has since been accepted that high rates of repetition are sufficiently stressful to promote the development of a ULD without excessive force being present. People who work in manufacturing and assembly facilities are often involved in activities that could be described as short cycle and highly repetitive. The tasks are considered to be short cycle because the sequence of movements is of a limited duration and the sequence is repeated at the end of each cycle.

Putz-Anderson (1988) classified tasks on the basis of the cycle time and the percentage of cycle time performing the same fundamental cycle. Jobs can be categorised as low repetitive if the cycle time is more than 30 seconds, or if under 50 per cent of the cycle time involves performing the same kind of fundamental cycle. Jobs can be categorised as high repetitive if the cycle time is less than 30 seconds, or if more than 50 per cent of the cycle time involves performing the same kind of fundamental cycle. An example of where the same fundamental cycle is repeated can be seen where operators remove food products from conveyor belts and pack them into outer cases. It may take operators 40 seconds to fill one outer case which might suggest that the task is not highly repetitive. However, they place 20 products in the outer case at a rate of one product every two seconds (ie the fundamental cycle is repeated every two seconds) which means that the task would be classified as high repetitive. Operators who carry out a task that falls within the high repetitive category are considered to be at a greater risk of developing a ULD.

Other factors in a facility, apart from the speed of the line or general production rate, may influence the repetitiveness of the operation. For example, a piece-rate system of pay or a productivity target may encourage operators to work at a rate that could move them out of the low repetitive bracket into high repetitive. It is also possible that an operator might unintentionally make their own task high repetitive. For example, an operator may be given freedom over how an assembly operation is completed. The operator may be required to make a number of products within a specified time. The product could be made up of several individual parts, each of which is attached in a different way using a variety of tools and manual effort. In a bid to speed up the rate of production, the operator may decide to abandon the method of work where one complete unit at a time is assembled and opt instead to repeat the same operation on a number of units, adding the same part repeatedly to each successive unit. The operator would then move on to attach the second part in the same way, resulting in a second highly repetitive operation, and so on. This redesign of the operation results in a series of highly repetitive sub-routines which are likely to accelerate upper limb fatigue and enhance the development of a ULD.

There are various means available to combat the repetitiveness of an operation; the most obvious is a reduction of the speed at which the operator works. Alternatively, more regular breaks in activity could be provided – as formal rest breaks or job rotation. If rest breaks are to be effective, they should be taken at regular intervals distributed evenly throughout the shift. The success of rest breaks lies in their timing, not in their length. The intention should be to allow operators to rest before they reach a point where they are tired. Once an operator reaches this point, a rest break becomes a recovery period only. Short, frequent breaks are better than long, infrequent ones.

If job rotation is to be effective, each successive task should be qualitatively different from the preceding one. Simply moving an operator to a different location to carry out a second similar task will not provide the intended relief. This form of rotation is commonly found in manufacturing and assembly operations where the programme of rotation dictates that the operators follow the same production path as the product, which often results in them moving through a series of similar tasks. For rotation to work properly, an analysis of the activities available to the operator should be assessed and an appropriate rotation programme developed. During the analysis, consideration should be given to the degree of repetition, the postures adopted and the movements involved. One of the most effective methods of collecting detailed information relating to the demands of an activity is through a task analysis. Details on how to carry out such an analysis, along with a suggested form for use, can be found in the chapter on risk assessment. In assembly and manufacturing operations, it may be necessary for operators to follow a path where they miss out one or two tasks in the production sequence and then double back to these at a later point in the rotation schedule.

Posture
The posture adopted by the upper limbs while the operator is working plays a significant part in the development of ULDs. If an operator is required to overextend a joint (such as when reaching forwards to pick an object off a conveyor belt) or reach upwards (such as when applying plaster to a ceiling), they may experience problems if the action is carried out repeatedly or for a sustained period. Movements of the wrist from side to side or up and down – which shift the wrist away from the neutral position – are also considered likely to cause a ULD if carried out rapidly or repeatedly or sustained for extended periods. Poor posture is a regularly occurring feature in many workplaces. For example, it is not uncommon to observe a keyboard operator, who has not adjusted their chair properly, working with their hands bent upwards or downwards at the wrist, depending on their sitting height in relation to the height of the keyboard. The sustained deviation of the wrist could lead to the development of discomfort in this area, particularly if regular breaks away from the workstation are not taken.

Ideally, people should be able to carry out their work with their upper arm hanging naturally at the side of the body with the forearm bent no higher than where it forms a 90° angle at the elbow. A straight line should run from the elbow, through the wrist and into the hand. This allows the person to work within their normal working area (the concept is discussed in Chapter 3 and relevant data are offered in Chapter 2). Deviation from this position increases the stresses placed on the upper limb and if such deviations are carried out repeatedly, or are sustained for an extended period, they can cause problems.

Particular postures of the upper limb that have been identified as being stressful (shown on page 183) include ulnar deviation, radial deviation, extension, flexion and pinching (where the tip of the thumb and the tip of the index finger are brought together to hold something). The pinch grip is five times more stressful than the power grasp, where the hand can be closed firmly around an object.

The posture of the whole arm is usually dictated by the workstation design and layout. If the working heights and reaching distances have not been designed to fall within the anthropometric parameters of the working population, then the operators have to overcome the shortfall by raising their shoulders and arms or reaching forwards with their arms. Operators working in these positions for any length of time may start to experience difficulties.

The deviations of the hand and wrist are usually dictated by the activity being carried out by the operator (eg tightening a screw, assembling a printer, sprinkling broccoli on top of a pizza). The hand is considered to be at its most powerful when it is in the neutral position or slightly extended. Grip strength may be reduced by up to 25 per cent if the hand is used when it is bent towards the little finger. If the hand is bent towards the thumb there may be a loss of grip strength of up to 20 per cent. This loss of strength emphasises the importance of allowing the operator to adopt a neutral posture while working. Working with irregular upper limb postures will ultimately be fatiguing for the operator and more likely to result in the development of a ULD. Consideration should therefore be given to finding a mechanical alternative to manual effort. For example, it is common to find the non-dominant hand being used as a clamp while the dominant hand uses a tool to tighten a nut or to cut through a material. Using a clamp would release the hand from the stressful task of gripping the item.

Workstations should be designed in a manner which reduces the need for the operator to work with their arms raised or outstretched. Chapters 2 and 3 should provide sufficient guidelines for the development of appropriate workstations. Tools should also be redesigned or replaced in an attempt to eliminate deviation of the wrist. Chapter 4 will assist with this issue. The task and the product being handled should be assessed to determine whether the task can be completed, or the product assembled, in an alternative way that eliminates the need to adopt highly irregular postures.

Force
The degree of force used when carrying out a task is another factor associated with the development of ULDs. The amount of force that is

used is determined, in part, by the tool being used or the objects with which the operator is working. For example, the weight, size and shape will influence how easy an object is to take hold of and this will dictate the degree of force required to grip it. In assembly operations, the ease with which parts fit together and whether they are off-specification will determine how much force an operator has to apply when completing the task. The pliable nature of some products influences the level of force required to complete a task. For example, a sewing machine operator may have to match up a number of individual pieces of fabric. If the fabric is tough and resists attempts to stretch it, the operator will have to pull forcefully to make the separate parts match up appropriately while being stitched.

Applying undesirable forces in a repetitive manner or for a prolonged period is likely to contribute to the development of ULDs. The level of force required for an operation should therefore be controlled as far as possible. This can be achieved through a number of measures:

- the effort required to close two independent units of a tool or a piece of equipment should be reduced (eg when using spring-opening grips, the tension level of the spring should not require the operator to press firmly each time the grips are closed)
- triggers on tools should offer the least amount of resistance possible while remaining at a level which is compatible with the avoidance of accidental activation
- cutting edges of tools such as shears, scissors and knives should be inspected regularly and kept sharp
- where possible, other sources of power should be applied to eliminate the need for manual effort (eg jigs and clamps should be used instead of requiring the operator to use a hand to clamp a part in place)
- the length of tool handles should be compatible with the degree of effort required to complete an operation. In some instances, a longer tool handle will afford greater leverage, which will reduce the degree of effort required of the operator
- quality control measures should be put in place to ensure that only parts of appropriate specification are used in assembly areas
- operators should be trained not only in the method of completing a task but also in the amount of force appropriate to the operation (operators may consider that if they use more effort they will do a better job – however, they are simply more likely to tire at a faster rate)
- all equipment, tooling and mechanical aids should be included in a maintenance programme which schedules regular services (equipment that resists easy use by the operator will require an increase in applied effort).

Static work
Static muscle work occurs when muscles are tensed in a fixed position for an extended period. Discomfort and fatigue are typical features of static work. It can be observed in postures where the arm is held away from the body such as above the head or out sideways as the operator carries out an activity. During assessment of a task it is not uncommon for the observer to focus on the dynamic aspect of the operation (eg the hand rotating or polishing an object) and to overlook the non-movement involved where the arm is held in an inappropriate fixed position as the hand completes the work.

Muscles involved in static work need more than 12 times the length of the actual task duration to recover from the fatigue. Few work–rest schedules take this into account. Dynamic work, where the muscles contract and relax rhythmically, is less likely to result in fatigue and possible injury.

Alternative means should be developed to replace the need for the limb to be held in a fixed position. For example, instead of requiring the operator to fit an exhaust to the underbody of a car located overhead, the car could be rotated and presented on its side to the operator. This would mean that the operator could work in an area located directly in front of their body, which would significantly reduce the extent of the static muscle work involved.

Other contributory factors

Temperature
Exposure to colder temperatures can increase the likelihood of an operator developing a ULD. Lower temperatures can be evident in an entire area (eg a chilled food storage area) or can be transferred to the operator through a point of contact (eg when holding a tool with a stainless steel handle – such handles are often resistant to warming up during a shift). Operators should be protected from the effects of working in a cold environment. In particular, the hands should be protected – for example, gloves may be needed by operators who handle cold products such as chilled foods, or who work with air tools that produce a cold air stream during use. If the wrist and forearm area needs protection, gauntlets may need to be provided.

However, gloves or gauntlets should only be provided where it is not possible or practical to make a work area warmer through the use of heaters and so on. Before providing gloves, consideration should be given to the possible reduction in tactile capability and the increase in grip strength requirements that may result from their introduction.

Other controls include fitting air tools with a take-away hose which reroutes the stream of cold air, and covering tools with cold handles in a compliant material (eg rubber).

Various (perhaps less obvious) situations can involve the operator routinely coming into contact with cold surfaces. For example, an operator may lean on the side casing of equipment for support during a quality control task involving watching products passing by on a line. If the operator's bare skin, particularly the wrist and forearm, comes into contact with the cold surface, a degree of heat exchange may occur.

Operators may not necessarily work in very cold environments but may be exposed to a sudden reduction in temperature at intervals throughout the shift. For example, operators working in a factory site may be located close to external doors that are left open for long periods, which can result in the internal temperature falling sharply. Others may work alongside chillers, which may result in the room temperature falling each time the doors are opened. Protective steps may include:
- screening off the area to protect it from draughts
- providing operators with thermal clothing and waterproofs
- issuing gloves
- providing heated pads to warm the hands
- supplying tools with heated handles.

Vibration
Vibration is known to be a possible cause of a number of hand injuries, including impaired blood circulation and damage to muscles and nerves. Operators who are exposed to vibration, such as when holding vibrating tools or workpieces, are at risk of developing a ULD. The level of risk is dependent on the vibration magnitude and how long the operator is exposed to it (ie the vibration dose). The level of risk is affected by a number of other factors:
- **The degree of force employed** as the item held in the hand is gripped and pushed forwards – a tighter grip results in more vibration energy being transferred to the hand. This has implications for the design of the tool handle, which will influence the degree of effort required to hold and use the tool. It also has implications for the use of gloves with vibrating tools and workpieces, as this sometimes impairs the dexterity of the hand, making it more difficult to hold the object and causing the operator to grip it even more firmly.
- **The exposure pattern of the individual** – this takes into account the frequency with which the operator carries out the task involving the vibrating items and the duration of the activity. It also takes account of any rest periods that interrupt the work.

- **The area of exposure** – the vibration may be transferred to the whole hand or part of it. The area of exposure should be accurately identified so that the level of risk can be determined.
- **Individual issues** – some operators may be more susceptible to the effects of vibration than others (eg smokers may be more susceptible, given the effect of smoking on blood circulation).
- **Environmental conditions** – working in colder temperatures increases susceptibility.

If the risk of an operator developing a ULD is to be reduced, the level of vibration should be controlled. Options include:
- automating or mechanising the process so that vibrating tools do not need to be used
- eliminating the need for the operator to hold vibrating workpieces by providing clamps and jigs
- providing tools with handles that have been designed in a way which makes them easy to hold and reduces the forces required to hold them during use
- ensuring that the operator has suitable training in the use of tools (how to hold and operate them correctly, including the required degree of force)
- using tools that are appropriate for the task
- using tools that have been designed specifically for low vibration (eg fitted with antivibration mountings or vibration-isolation handles)
- maintaining tools and equipment so that they function properly and do not cause excessive, unnecessary vibration
- ensuring that the operator's hands and body are kept warm
- providing gloves that fit properly and which do not hinder the use of tools
- limiting the operator's exposure time to the task involving the use of vibrating tools
- developing a programme for job rotation which limits the operator's exposure time to tasks involving vibration.

'Antivibration' gloves are not usually considered to be effective in reducing the amount of vibration reaching the hands. If such gloves are not an appropriate fit, they may even increase vibration transmission.

It may be beneficial to encourage operators who use vibrating tools to exercise and massage their fingers during rest periods, as this will help blood circulation.

Organisational factors
As discussed above, the frequency with which an operator can take breaks away from work, whether through a rest break or job rotation schedule,

will play a part in determining the likelihood of the development of a ULD. Clearly, overtime can play a contributory part in the development of an injury as it extends the length of time the operator is exposed to the injurious agents and reduces the overall amount of recovery time available in any one day. It may not be appropriate to extend the working day for those involved in high risk activities. It may be more appropriate for the overtime to be shared out between operators on an intermittent basis. (It is also worth noting that where excessive overtime is worked by any single operator, a reduction in their hourly productivity rates across the shift may result.) Generally speaking, excessive overtime may lead to increased absenteeism and accidents. Of course, an operator diagnosed as a ULD sufferer should not be permitted to work overtime unless it is specifically sanctioned by an appropriately qualified medical adviser.

Effective training and supervision play an important role in the control of the development of ULDs. It is not uncommon for on-the-job training to amount to little more than standing alongside an experienced operator and copying what they do (including any poor working practices).

It is important that all operators learn from the outset the safest and most efficient methods of work. Once they have learnt the techniques, they should be supported by appropriate supervision in the workplace. Managers, supervisors or team leaders may turn a blind eye and take the attitude that as long as the job is done they do not care how it is done. Supervisors should actively encourage workers to adopt appropriate working practices and discourage poor practices.

Peaks in workload are also associated with the development of ULDs. It is considered that all operators require a period of time in which to become accustomed to the demands of their tasks. During this period they build up a level of stamina or 'task fitness' which matches their task requirements – this is known as 'work hardening'. Sometimes the workload can increase suddenly and the operator does not have a period in which to adjust. As a consequence, their level of task fitness does not match the increased demands and the operator may find that they become overloaded. Working in an environment where operators have to deal with a workload with peaks and troughs may result in them being more susceptible to injury. Work rates should be kept as consistent as possible and the workload should be spread out evenly across a shift.

Operators returning to work after an absence (eg holiday, sickness or maternity leave) also need a period of adjustment. During the absence their body will not retain the same level of task fitness and they therefore require a gradual build-up period to become reaccustomed to the work demands without overloading themselves. The same principle should be applied to new starters.

Sudden changes to the work routine or environment can have similar effects. The body will have become accustomed to working in a particular way and will have developed a level of fitness for that procedure. However, if the task or environment is abruptly changed – even though the underlying process may remain basically the same – the body is suddenly required to carry out a different task. As a consequence, there is a mismatch between the body's task fitness and the demands of the new procedure. Unless an acclimatisation period is allowed, the operator may become susceptible to injury.

Personal factors
Certain hobbies and activities and some medical conditions may predispose the operator to developing a disorder. However, it is not uncommon for the ULD sufferer to find it hard to accept that a factor outside the workplace is the source of their condition.

Playing certain musical instruments involves movements and postures which are likely to enhance the development of a ULD. The type of instrument will influence the site of the disorder. For example, pianists frequently suffer symptoms of pain in their hands and wrists similar to those experienced by keyboard operators. Violinists typically complain of neck pain from having to clamp the violin under their chin while holding their head at an irregular angle. Trumpeters and trombonists sometimes complain of shoulder problems from gripping the instrument and supporting its weight away from the body.

Other activities such as knitting, crocheting, bell-ringing, playing on games consoles and texting are also associated with the development of ULDs. Certain sports have also been closely associated. Racquet sports in particular – squash and tennis top the list – have been highlighted as a likely cause of ULDs. However, as is the case with work-related causes, sufferers need to be involved in these activities frequently and for extended periods for them to have a bearing on the development of a condition. Clearly, few people spend as much time indulging in their hobbies as they do carrying out their work, and opportunities for rest during the practice of a hobby are greater. It is often the case that hobbies 'add insult to injury' as the operator uses their limbs more extensively than colleagues who may use their non-work time to rest.

A knock or blow to a vulnerable area such as the wrist may make it more susceptible to developing an injury. Certain conditions, such as pregnancy, the menopause and diabetes, have also been associated with ULDs. Although not necessarily indicated as a precipitating factor, psoriasis has been shown to be a common condition of ULD sufferers.

There is a higher incidence of ULDs among female than male workers. However, this is likely to be a result of the fact that in many instances women outnumber men carrying out highly repetitive operations.

Responding to ULDs

ULDs can be permanently disabling. They normally become progressively worse unless action is taken to identify the source of the problem and deal with it. Obviously, the most effective action is one which prevents the onset of the condition in the first place. However, this does not assist those organisations which are already faced with operator injury and which need to take appropriate action in response.

In the first instance it is important that a clear diagnosis is made by someone with a thorough understanding of the condition and who will not be swayed by subjective reports regarding the working conditions or task demands. An accurate diagnosis is necessary so that the individual can be given the appropriate treatment and so that the organisation knows exactly what it is dealing with. In some cases the organisation can be satisfied from the outset that the condition is not work-related.

Treatment

It is common for a ULD sufferer to be signed off work for a period of time to rest. Alternatively, the employee may be advised to return to work on light duties. If this is the case, the organisation should ensure that these duties do not incorporate activities which are likely to aggravate the condition further. When an operator returns to work after an absence, they should be given an acclimatisation period in which to become used to the demands of the task again. They should be closely monitored during this phase. Of course, if factors within the workplace have been identified as being the cause of the injury, they should be addressed before the individual's return. Consideration should be given to whether other individuals are experiencing similar problems.

Sufferers may be prescribed painkillers and be advised to attend physiotherapy sessions. In some cases the affected limb will be immobilised in a splint or plaster cast. Injections into the limb are also offered for certain conditions – these are painful for some time after the injection has been administered. Surgery is an option in more severe cases.

Irrespective of the treatment, ULD sufferers need to be reminded that certain medical interventions will suppress their symptoms and make them think that they can return to work before they should. They should be guided by their GP or consultant.

Reporting symptoms
As most ULDs are progressive, it is essential that the organisation responds appropriately to cases of injury as soon as possible. The longer the operator is exposed to the conditions which have been identified as harmful, the more severe their condition will become and the less likely it is that they will return to their original health. To facilitate the response process, organisations should have a facility in place whereby operators can report symptoms at the earliest opportunity. Operators should be advised of the symptoms they may experience as a result of the task they are carrying out.

Operators should feel comfortable about reporting symptoms. It is in the organisation's own interests to find out as soon as possible that the operator is experiencing difficulties. Without treatment and action on behalf of the employer, the operator's condition will probably worsen, eventually resulting in their absence. This will have implications for the remaining workforce – and ultimately the sufferer may decide to make a claim against their employer.

Assessing risks
Organisations will have in place a mechanism for assessing risk and this should be used as a means of identifying areas where ULDs may occur. This will enable the organisation to take steps to reduce the risk. When reviewing the workplace to identify the potential causes of ULDs, the organisation should consider the workstation design, task demands, organisational factors, environmental conditions, tool and equipment design, and the contribution made by the operator. It is only by looking at the workplace as a whole that an accurate profile of the likely causes of ULDs can be developed.

On a positive note, most ULDs are caused by relatively simple aspects of the workplace and therefore, in most instances, addressing problem areas should be fairly straightforward. It is unlikely that ULDs will be eliminated completely but it is possible to reduce them significantly. Employers should undertake systematic risk assessments of their activities to reduce the risk of onset. Chapter 9 contains a number of sample checklists that will help to identify factors likely to contribute to the development of a ULD. Consideration of the factors discussed here will go a long way towards ensuring that the workforce remains free of musculoskeletal problems – providing appropriate action is taken.

Summary

- ULDs can affect any area of the upper limbs from the fingertips to the neck.
- The main causes of ULDs are repetition, poor posture, force and static work.
- Other contributory factors include exposure to vibration or reduced temperatures, lack of appropriate rest and/or rotation, overtime, poor training and changing work demands without an acclimatisation period.
- Personal factors such as hobbies and certain medical conditions may predispose an individual to develop a ULD.
- Appropriate action should be taken once an individual reports symptoms of a ULD to prevent any further deterioration in the condition – and its possible onset in others.
- The assessment process should be used as a means of identifying the potential for ULDs in the workplace and appropriate action should follow.

References and further reading

Buckle P and Devereux J. *Work-related neck and upper limb musculoskeletal disorders.* European Agency for Safety and Health at Work, 1999.

Health and Safety Executive *A pain in your workplace?*, HSG121. HSE Books, 1994.

Health and Safety Executive. *Musculoskeletal disorders in supermarket cashiers.* HSE Books, 1998.

Health and Safety Executive. *Upper limb disorders in the workplace*, HSG60(rev). HSE Books, 2002.

Kuorinka I and Forcier L (eds). *Work-related musculoskeletal disorders (WMSDs): a reference book for prevention.* Taylor & Francis, 1995.

Moon S D and Sauter S L (eds). *Beyond biomechanics: psychosocial aspects of musculoskeletal disorders in office work.* Taylor & Francis, 2007.

Pheasant S. *Ergonomics, work and health.* Macmillan Press, 1991.

Putz-Anderson V. *Cumulative trauma disorders: a manual for musculoskeletal diseases of the upper limbs.* Taylor & Francis, 1988.

Tindall A. *Tenosynovitis: a case of mistaken identity.* Iron Trades Insurance Company Limited, 1993.

9 Risk assessment

These days, risk assessments are an integral part of any organisation's functioning. They form a core part of a company's health and safety management system. Some organisations view assessments as a burden that they would prefer to avoid. These organisations are not looking at the whole process from the right perspective. Assessments allow them to identify the potential for harm in their workplace and to take avoidance action before harm occurs. This would seem, logically, to put the business on a more productive footing, whereby it can continue functioning without having to deal with injury, ill health, rehabilitation, inspections, form-filling, recruiting, inducting, training and so on, all of which are part of the domino effect of someone being injured in the workplace. Assessments allow businesses to see where they stand with regard to health and safety and put them in a position where they can develop effective control strategies.

When discussing the issue of risk assessments, it is helpful to distinguish between safety risks and health risks. Safety risks can lead to immediate danger or injury, such as touching a live cable. Health risks may not be apparent for a long time and symptoms may only present themselves after long term exposure to the unsuitable working conditions.

The first part of the assessment process is the identification of hazards in the workplace. Some people use the terms 'hazard' and 'risk' interchangeably as if they mean the same thing. They do not. A hazard is something with the potential to cause harm. Risk is an indicator of how likely it is that harm will occur as a result of exposure to that hazard. The risk assessor not only has to be able to identify what could injure or harm the worker but they also have to evaluate how likely it is that the person will come to harm if the environment remains unchanged. Having done that, the assessor needs to consider the range of risk reduction measures that could be introduced and determine whether they would be considered reasonably practicable solutions in that particular situation.

In many working environments where assessors are very familiar with the work, they will quickly and easily identify the main hazards. They will probably also find that there are known solutions to those problems; for example, operators working at a conveyor belt that is too high can be given a platform to stand on when working. Occasionally, assessors will be faced with unfamiliar operations or problem situations for which they have no experience or specialist knowledge. There are many sources of useful advisory information that should be used. For instance, just reading the standard operating procedures relating to a task provides a grounding in what should be happening and in what order. There is a lot of downloadable guidance and advisory information available on the internet; trade association information often details similar problems and how they were dealt with; and networking with other companies is often an effective method of confirming that other organisations have similar problems and offers an opportunity to see how they deal with them. In addition, assessors can either attend a training course which gives them a suitable knowledge base or enlist the help of a specialist. Sometimes using outside consultants is preferable simply because the workforce views them as independent and they may be likely to accept their input more readily than would be the case with in-house assessors.

Once the assessor has identified the hazards they need to evaluate the risk. This is necessary when a number of assessments are being completed because it provides an instant indication of how likely it is that any individual or group of people will be harmed and it helps to prioritise tasks. Companies have limited finances and will need to have a clear list of what is critical and what can wait. One of the most effective ways of prioritising is to identify whether a task is high, medium or low risk. Some assessors are not comfortable relying on their judgment to identify where the risk rating falls. If that is the case, they can use a risk matrix to identify the level of risk. This is a simple procedure that most assessors learn about when they attend a risk assessment or health and safety training course. To use the matrix the assessor thinks about what the possible outcomes might be for someone if they are exposed to a particular hazard – eg a minor injury, moderate injury or a serious injury. They assign the numbers 1 to 3 to each of these outcomes. The next step is for the assessor to think about how likely it is that the individual will come to harm and decide whether it is unlikely, likely or very likely. Again, they assign the numbers 1 to 3 to these variables. Having picked their 'consequence' and 'likelihood' variables, the assessor multiplies them. For example, if they are watching a manual handling operation where a single handler is lifting a 50 kg load every four minutes out of a high-sided container standing on the floor, they will probably conclude that the handler could have a serious injury (3) and it is very likely to happen (3). Their risk rating is therefore $3 \times 3 = 9$. The assessor knows that values 1 and 2 are low risk, values 3 and 4 are medium risk and values 6 and 9 are high risk. On that basis, they can state that the operation they are assessing is rated as a high risk activity as it was rated 9. Using the risk matrix is a very simple process, but it is also very effective and gives many assessors confidence in their decision-making.

Quite often the easy bit of the assessment process is finding the problems. The difficult bit is coming up with an effective solution. Clearly, avoiding the hazardous situation is the most effective risk reduction strategy. For instance, if an assessor establishes that transferring 25 kg bags of flour from a pallet located on the floor up to a shoulder-high hopper is a high risk activity, the company could consider direct feed from a silo, thereby eliminating the manual effort. If the activity cannot be avoided and cannot be changed, at the very least the assessor should ensure that the operator's exposure time to the hazardous situation is limited or interrupted regularly through rest breaks, job rotation or job enlargement.

Assessment checklists should not only record the problems and possible solutions. It is also important that they record the control measures that are already in place. Consideration needs to be given to whether they are still effective or whether alternatives need to be introduced. If the assessors believe that new interventions are required, they should detail on their form the timescales involved so that those responsible for making the changes know what timetable they are working to when they start their programme of risk reduction. Often a number of people from different sections of the organisation will have to co-operate to ensure that the risk reduction strategies are introduced successfully. For that reason the whole organisation needs to have an understanding of what the risk assessment process is all about and what it is trying to achieve. This should mean that when the health and safety manager approaches directors or the accounts department for some investment, they will not have to start with an overview of the process of risk assessment and the employer's responsibilities while at the same time trying to convince the budget holder that they have a valid reason to request additional funding.

Once the checklist has been completed and the strategies for risk reduction have been identified, the organisation needs to ensure that the process does not grind to a halt at that point. There needs to be an impetus to see things through, not only in terms of introducing changes, but ensuring that they achieve what they are supposed to achieve – which is the reduction of risk.

Having completed the process, the organisation needs to carry out periodic reviews to ensure that the findings of the assessment are still valid and the control measures are still working effectively. Changes in the working environment should prompt the start of the process all over again.

Task analysis

Although not a form of risk assessment, one of the most effective methods of collecting detailed information relating to the demands of an activity is through a task analysis. Sometimes it can be helpful to get a complete picture of what the task involves before trying to assess it. A task analysis is a formal means of describing the demands of the task and analysing those demands.

During a task analysis a complete job is broken down into components and subcomponents. This is achieved by observation of an experienced, skilled operator over a long time and recording each separate movement or action. Once the analysis is complete there will be a profile of the job that shows the requirements of the task, the environment in which it is carried out and the behaviours required of the operator to complete it. It should be kept in mind that the recorded behaviours are heavily influenced by training and experience as well as psychological and physiological factors.

The task analysis provides an insight into how much time is needed to complete each element of the overall task and what percentage of the overall task each element represents. This part of the analysis allows the assessor to identify what the priorities are in the task, as it highlights those aspects that are repeated most frequently or for the longest periods of time. By developing a methodical sequence of task demands, the assessor can match this against what they understand about human capability. This not only helps the assessor to pick out any inefficiencies in the work system from a simple business perspective; it also helps them to identify inefficient use of the musculoskeletal system.

The information that is generated during the task analysis is extremely useful as it assists the assessor to decide whether the layout of the workplace suits the priorities of the task and whether new equipment or workstations are needed. For instance, the task analysis may highlight that a significant feature of the work is the transfer of trays of meat from a conveyor to the shelves of a blast freezer. If the operator has not been provided with a trolley, they will repeatedly walk backwards and forwards throughout the shift carrying trays of meat. Another benefit of task analysis is that it can help to identify the skills needed by operators if they are to complete their work successfully.

At the start of the process there needs to be agreement on what the analysis is intended to achieve. This helps the assessor to make decisions about how many individuals they are going to observe. Making the decision about who will be observed is not necessarily straightforward. They need to be representative of the site's working population but at the same time it needs to be recognised that each worker will have different levels of training and experience, which may affect how they complete a task. The influence of personal work practices must also not be overlooked. The task area may need to be observed at different times if the jobs vary depending on the time of day or week, or if different groups of operators make different comments or complaints about the same type of work. For instance, it is not uncommon for managers to draw attention to the fact that they get a lot of complaints about workload from the night shift yet they get no complaints from the day shift who do the same amount and type of work. If work cannot be observed for some reason, perhaps because a line is not functioning on the day of the analysis, discussions need to be held with relevant parties in the area to ensure that this does not adversely influence the findings of the overall analyses.

Before the analysis starts, the assessor needs to have decided whether they will interrupt the operator as they observe them to ask for clarity on certain issues or whether they will wait until the end of the operation and have a debriefing session. If the operation is timed the question needs to wait until the end of the period of observation – an untimed run-through is always recommended before the timing starts so the assessor knows what to expect during completion of the task. If the assessor interrupts as the work is being performed this offers a 'real time' view of what is being done by the operator. If a debrief is used, this needs to be done as soon as possible after the end of the task so that there is no decay in the quality of the operator's recall. It should be kept in mind that some operators perform movements or carry out actions that they are not even aware of; often it is difficult for them to recall these after the task has been completed. Operators could be asked to give a commentary as they work so that they offer an explanation of what they are doing and why. They need a full explanation of the purpose of the analysis to be able to assist with this aspect fully. If the operator is reluctant to offer a commentary they quite often gain the confidence to provide comments if they are part of a group discussion after the analysis. However, care needs to be taken that more dominant members of the group do not monopolise the discussions.

Taking video footage will avoid the need for an operator to repeat a particularly difficult or arduous task. However, some operators may be on their best behaviour when they are being videoed and may not complete their tasks as they normally would when not being observed. Other operators may feel self-conscious, which may affect their performance. To avoid any adverse influence resulting from using a video, operators should be videoed over a period of time so that they start to feel more relaxed about the process. They may even forget about the camera and start to behave in a more representative manner.

Some assessors will attempt to draw up a likely sequence of actions before their analysis on the basis of reading training manuals or job descriptions. These documents are unlikely to record every incidental element of the task and will not be sufficiently detailed. The original writer of these documents might also use ambiguous language or have based their record on erroneous assumptions, making it difficult for the assessor to determine exactly what is done during execution of the task. The documents themselves may also be out of date and no longer directly relevant to the task.

As a means to ensure that the task components and subcomponents are accurately recorded, some cross-referencing between different individuals analysing the same jobs is recommended. The assessors should also record in detail exactly what was observed, in what environment, with what equipment and who performed the tasks. All of this information is important as it may be relied on in the future as part of an audit trail that identifies why certain purchasing or engineering decisions were made.

Once the assessor has a full understanding of the task demands, they will break it down into a series of parts or subtasks. Once they have done this they can assign other information to the subtasks, such as the frequency with which the task occurred and how long that aspect of the task lasted. Page 210 shows a simple example of a task analysis sheet completed during the observation of a checkout operator. The sheet records how often each subtask is performed and the duration of each.

Checklists, questionnaires and ratings scales

There are many checklists that have been produced by a range of different people. Some have been created by ergonomists, some by physiotherapists, and there are a number of useful checklists provided by the Health and Safety Executive. Depending on the subject of the assessment, a variety of checklists could be used to identify hazardous working conditions. For instance, if a company has a concern about upper limb disorders, they could use RULA (Rapid Upper Limb Assessment), QEC (Quick Exposure Checklist) or REBA (Rapid Entire Body Assessment).

In some circumstances, before carrying out a full-blown investigation of whether factors exist in the workplace that could cause ill health, an organisation may feel the need to establish on a simple level whether its workforce are encountering discomfort as a result of their work. Carrying out a discomfort survey is easy and provides an accurate indicator of how the workers feel as they work throughout a day. Page 211 illustrates a body parts discomfort questionnaire that has evolved from original work by Corlett and Bishop (1976). The worker shades the area of the body where they feel the discomfort. This questionnaire allows an organisation to correlate specific symptoms in specific regions of the body with particular tasks demands or sections of a working environment.

As it is common for the workforce to experience an increase in symptoms as their shift progresses, it is useful to have operators complete the form at different points during the shift – this gives a more accurate overview of how the symptoms develop and at what rate. The form on page 212 is an alternative version of the body parts discomfort questionnaire that can be filled in throughout a shift. Workers should be reminded at intervals about the need to complete it. Employees can be asked to add additional information to the form by describing the type of discomfort they are experiencing such as pins and needles, aching and so on. They can also rate the extent of the discomfort on a scale of 1 to 5 by writing the appropriate number alongside the shaded area. This form is particularly helpful because it does not rely on the same levels of literacy skills as normal written questionnaires.

On pages 213–232 there is a series of specific risk assessments or checklists that can be used to identify hazardous elements in the workplace, to record control measures already in place and to record further recommendations for change:
- DSE assessment checklist (pages 213–219)
- ULD risk assessment record (pages 220–223)
- Manual handling assessment checklist (pages 224–227)
- Pushing and pulling assessment checklist (pages 228–231)
- Quick reference guide – elements to consider (page 232).

Each checklist includes some practical tips for carrying out the assessment efficiently and accurately.

Reference

Corlett E N and Bishop R P. A technique for assessing postural discomfort. *Ergonomics* 1976; 19: 175–182.

A simple example of a task analysis sheet completed during the observation of a checkout task

Activity	Remove item from belt on right	Scan item	Place item on belt to left	Place item on scales	Use credit card machine	Remove receipt	Place cash in drawer	Remove item from belt on right	Use keyboard	End of task
Task started at (seconds from start of cycle)	0									
		2								
			3.5							
	5.25									
		7.25								
			8.75							
	10.5									
		12.5								
			14							
	15.75									
				17.75						
			21.25							
									22.5	
							25.75			
						29.5				
										31.25
Total time on activity	8	4.5	6.5	3.5	0	1.75	3.75	0	3.25	
% of overall cycle	25.6	14.4	20.8	11.2	0	5.6	12.0	0	10.4	100.0
Frequency	4	3	4	1	0	1	1	0	1	

Body parts discomfort questionnaire

Name	Date
Department	Time

Please mark on the body outlines below where you've felt discomfort while carrying out your work tasks.

Body parts discomfort questionnaire for completion at intervals throughout the working day

Name	Date
Department	

Please mark on the body outlines below where you've felt discomfort while carrying out your work tasks at the times stated.

Time:

Time:

Time:

Time:

Time:

Time:

Display screen equipment assessment checklist

Assessor	
Employee	
Job title	Department
Site	Date of assessment
Shift length	Rest breaks
No. hours using DSE per day	No. days using DSE per week

Type of equipment used	Hours of use per day	Days of use per week	Comments
Single desktop PC Multiple displays Laptop BlackBerry/PDA Other (specify)			

Remedial action required	Completed on (date)	Completed by (name)	Outcome

Date for review of assessment	

Desk	Yes	No	Comments	Action taken
Is there enough space on the desk to set the equipment up correctly and carry out the work?				
Can any item used be reached easily by the user when seated?				
Can the user move their feet/legs freely under the desk without coming into contact with an obstacle?				
Are the user's feet/legs unlikely to come into contact with trailing cables?				
Is the desk in good condition?				
Is the desk surface free of glare or reflections?				

Chair	Yes	No	Comments	Action taken
Has the chair got castors or glides and a five-star base?				
Does the chair swivel?				
Can the chair be adjusted for height?				
Is the user sitting at the correct height for their desk and keyboard?				
Is the user's overall posture suitable?				
Can the backrest be altered for height?				
Does the backrest tilt?				

Chair *continued*	Yes	No	Comments	Action taken
Do all the adjustments work properly?				
Does the user know how to adjust the chair properly?				
Can the user sit how and where they want even if the chair has armrests?				
Can the user easily touch the floor with their feet, or do they have a footrest?				

Screen	Yes	No	Comments	Action taken
Can the screen be swivelled and tilted?				
Can the user work without glare or reflections?				
Is the screen free of dirt, fingerprints or other marks?				
Can the brightness and contrast be controlled?				
Does the user know how to adjust the brightness and contrast?				
Is the screen positioned in front of the user?				
Is the screen set at a height and distance that suit the user?				
Can the user read the displayed characters easily?				

Screen *continued*	Yes	No	Comments	Action taken
Can the user attach a laptop to a docking station or plug in a separate keyboard and mouse?				
Does the user place source documents on a copy stand alongside the screen?				
Is it acceptable for the user to work without a copy stand?				

Input devices	Yes	No	Comments	Action taken
Is the keyboard separate from the screen?				
Does the keyboard have feet to change the angle of the keys?				
Does the keyboard work properly?				
Is the keyboard directly in front of the user when in use?				
Has the user positioned the keyboard so that they can rest their wrists on the surface directly in front of it?				
Does the user press the keys with minimal force?				
Does the user keep the mouse close when in use?				
Does the user know how to adjust the speed setting on the mouse?				

Input devices *continued*	Yes	No	Comments	Action taken
Does the user maintain a natural hand position when using the mouse?				
Does the user remove their hand from the mouse when not using it?				
Is the user using a mousemat if needed?				

Software	Yes	No	Comments	Action taken
Is the software designed so that the user can work at their own speed?				
Does the user find the software easy to use?				
Has the user been trained to use the software?				

Environment	Yes	No	Comments	Action taken
Are lighting levels sufficient to allow the user to do their job effectively?				
Can the user work without problems caused by overhead lighting?				
Can the user work without problems caused by light from windows?				
Are curtains or blinds available?				
If so, are they effective?				

Environment *continued*	Yes	No	Comments	Action taken
Can the user work without problems caused by temperature or ventilation?				
Is the user satisfied with the level of moisture in the air?				
Can the user work without being distracted by noise?				

Organisational factors	Yes	No	Comments	Action taken
Has the user been trained to use their workstation correctly?				
Has the user been trained in the health and safety aspects of their working environment?				
Does the user know who to tell if they have symptoms of ill health?				
Does the user stop their DSE work at least once an hour to do something else or have a rest break?				

Record any additional information about the user or their workstation here

Hints when completing a DSE assessment

1. Observe the user's sitting position as you approach them, or as you complete other assessments in the area. This will give you a better impression of how they really sit and work when they are not aware of being observed.
2. Use a digital camera to take before and after photographs of the user in their 'at work' position. The before photograph can be shown to the user to illustrate how they are using their workstation and to highlight possible problems.
3. Always check screen height by stepping back from the workstation and lowering yourself to the user's head height.
4. Familiarise yourself with the range of adjustments available on the chair before you carry out the assessment, so changes can be made quickly. The same is recommended for screen adjustments, such as for height, brightness and contrast.
5. If the user is reluctant to accept changes to their workstation set-up, ask them to try it for a few days and then review it. If they refuse to change the way they work and you believe this is likely to cause them problems in the future, record your concerns on the assessment and pass it on to a relevant person to address.
6. Take an illustration along to the assessment showing an 'ideal' user sitting position, so you can use it to refer to aspects of the posture that are relevant to the user and so they can see what they are aiming to achieve.
7. Be aware of any manual handling performed in the work area. Although the main focus of the DSE assessment is the DSE workstation and work performed there, the assessment often provides the opportunity to note other tasks being carried out in the area. If manual handling tasks are part of the user's work, check that they do perform them and that they have received manual handling training.

Upper limb disorder risk assessment record

Assessor	
Employee	
Job title		Department	
Site		Date of assessment	
Shift length		Rest breaks	

Brief description of task being performed:

Control measures already in place

Is this employee considered to be at risk?   Yes ☐   No ☐

Remedial action required	Completed on (date)	Completed by (name)	Outcome

Posture – Does the operator...	Yes	No	Comments
Work with their arms held out in front of them for long periods, or move them out repetitively?			
Work with their elbows away from the side of the body for long periods, or move them outwards repetitively?			
Work with their hands above elbow height with an angle of less than 90° at the elbow?			
Move their wrists from side to side repeatedly over long periods?			
Work with their wrist bent to one side for long periods?			
Move their wrist up and down repeatedly?			
Repeatedly rotate their forearm so that their palm faces up/down?			
Adopt hand or finger positions that are not natural?			
Grip with significant force repeatedly or for long periods?			
Tilt their head forward?			
Turn their head from side to side repeatedly or work for long periods with their head turned to one side?			

Task activity – Does the operator...	Yes	No	Comments
Apply force repeatedly or for long periods?			
Apply force with their arms towards the extreme limit of their reach?			
Use static effort to support something or hold it in place while completing a task?			
Perform a task rapidly?			
Work without a break or a change of activity for long periods?			
Have peaks and troughs in their workload?			
Make sudden, abrupt movements to complete their task?			

Equipment characteristics	Yes	No	Comments
Does the design of a tool or other equipment cause the operator to adopt unnatural hand, wrist or arm postures?			
Does the design of the workstation make it difficult for the operator to adopt a natural, comfortable posture?			
If the operator uses a chair, does it prevent them from adopting a comfortable working posture?			
If the operator has to view a monitor or other display, can they adopt a natural, comfortable head position?			
Does the operator support their wrists or forearms on any sharp (90° angle) edges?			

Environmental conditions	Yes	No	Comments
Can the operator see clearly while working?			
Does the operator change their posture because of poor lighting, shadows, glare and so on?			
Does the operator work in extremes of temperature?			
Are noise levels within acceptable limits?			

Personal factors – Is the operator...	Yes	No	Comments
Reporting symptoms such as tingling, pins and needles, pain, aching or swelling?			
Using any products such as wrist splints, supporting bandages or heat sprays?			
Working more quickly than necessary?			
Working without taking available breaks?			
Regularly working extra hours?			
Having to meet consistently short deadlines?			
Using work techniques that could be considered jerky or hurried?			
Lacking training to eliminate poor practices?			

Personal factors – Is the operator... *continued*	Yes	No	Comments
Unhappy or dissatisfied at work?			
At a disadvantage because of their sex, given the demands of their work?			
At a disadvantage because of their stature, given the demands of their work?			
At a disadvantage because of their ability, given the demands of their work?			
At a disadvantage because of an injury or ill health, given the demands of their work?			
Performing a manual handling task? (If yes, complete a separate manual handling checklist)			

Hints when completing an upper limb disorder assessment

1. Video the whole operation. You can use the recording to time the whole cycle and elements within it. It is also useful to watch it in slow motion, when subtle or rapid hand/wrist movements can be detected.
2. Confirm whether what you are observing is typical of everyday work, or whether different activities are performed on different days or across different shifts.
3. Find out about unofficial breaks as well as formal ones. Unofficial breaks may occur as a result of line stoppages, product changes, shift changeovers or smoking breaks.
4. Compare the techniques used by different operators, as individuals may adopt unique postures or movements that are the source of their problems.
5. Never assume or accept that as the job has always been done that way, it will continue to be done that way. There are always different ways of ending up with the same result, and they are often better than the original.
6. No matter how diligent you are, once you are very familiar with a site, you stop noticing all the problems. A fresh pair of eyes is always useful, so ask someone who is less familiar with the site or task to have a look at it and confirm that your conclusions are accurate.

Manual handling assessment checklist

Assessor	
Employee	
Job title	Department
Site	Date of assessment
Shift length	Rest breaks

Brief description of task being performed:

Weight of loads [ ] Handling rate [ ] Carrying distance [ ]

Control measures already in place

Is this employee considered to be at risk?   Yes [ ]   No [ ]

Remedial action required	Completed on (date)	Completed by (name)	Outcome

Indicate whether an element is present by ticking Yes or No. If yes, identify the level of risk by noting whether it is high (H), medium (M) or low (L) in the Risk column. Use the comments column to record any other useful information.

The task	Yes	No	Risk	Comments
Is the load held at a distance from the body?				
Does the handler twist at the waist?				
Does the handler stoop when lifting a load?				
Does the handler reach upwards when picking up or putting down a load?				
Does the handler move the load from a high point to a low point or vice versa?				
Does the handler carry the load for more than 10 metres?				
Does the task involve strenuous pushing or pulling? (If so, complete a separate checklist)				
Do loads move unpredictably when handled?				
Are loads handled repetitively?				
Can the handler stop moving loads at regular intervals to rest?				
Does the handler work to keep up with a production line?				

The load	Yes	No	Risk	Comments
Is it heavy?				
Is it difficult to get hold of because it is bulky?				
Is it difficult to grasp because of its shape or packaging?				
Is it unstable or unpredictable?				
Is it capable of injuring the handler because it is hot, sharp or corrosive?				

The working environment	Yes	No	Risk	Comments
Can the handler adopt an upright, forward-facing posture when lifting?				
Is the floor surface likely to interfere with the manual handling task?				
Does the handler walk up or down steps or slopes?				
Is the handler exposed to strong winds?				
Is the task made more difficult by the lighting levels?				

Individual capability	Yes	No	Risk	Comments
Does the job require unusual strength or ability?				
Would the job be considered problematic for a handler with a health problem?				
Would the job be considered problematic for a handler with a learning difficulty?				
Would the job be considered problematic for a handler who is pregnant?				
Does the handler need special training?				

Protective clothing	Yes	No	Comments
Does clothing or PPE interfere with the manual handling task?			
Does the handler need additional PPE to complete the task safely?			

Hints when completing a manual handling assessment

1. Photograph important moments in the lifting sequence.
2. Take video footage of the whole task.
3. Measure heights of work surfaces and stacking heights, and record height ranges where necessary.
4. Sketch the area and mark the direction of movement of loads.
5. Look out for and record additional handling on the periphery of the main task. For example, if an operator is packing products into cases from a conveyor, this will be the main focus of the assessment. However, the operator may also remove waste from the line and throw it into a skip – this is also manual handling.
6. Check whether what is occurring is typical of every day and every shift. You may find, for example, the night shift works slightly differently.
7. Find out about and record any unofficial breaks resulting from line breakdowns, changeovers, product changes and so on. You need to build an accurate profile of how the work is performed and over what periods.
8. Be aware of handlers relying on assistance from back belts or other forms of support.

Pushing and pulling assessment checklist

Assessor	
Employee	
Job title	Department
Site	Date of assessment
Shift length	Rest breaks

Brief description of task being performed:

Frequency of operation   Distance

Control measures already in place

Is this employee considered to be at risk?   Yes ☐   No ☐

Remedial action required	Completed on (date)	Completed by (name)	Outcome

Indicate whether an element is present by ticking Yes or No. If yes, identify the level of risk by noting whether it is high (H), medium (M) or low (L) in the Risk column. Use the comments column to record any other useful information.

The task	Yes	No	Risk	Comments
Are high levels of force needed to start the load moving?				
Are high levels of force needed to keep the load moving?				
Does the handler use jerky actions to control the load?				
Does the handler have to navigate around obstructions or manoeuvre/park the load precisely?				
Does the handler use one hand to move the load?				
Does the handler work with their hands below waist height or above shoulder height when pushing or pulling?				
Does the handler move the load quickly?				
Does the handler push or pull the load for more than 20 metres?				
Does the handler perform repetitive pushing or pulling actions or push or pull for a long time?				

The load	Yes	No	Risk	Comments
Can the handler grip it properly?				
Is the load stable while being moved?				
Can the handler see over and around the load?				
Can the handler easily stop the load moving?				
Is the trolley, or other handling aid, suitable for the load being moved?				
Are the wheels suitable for the flooring?				
Is the trolley, or other handling aid, easy to steer?				

The load *continued*	Yes	No	Risk	Comments
Are the wheels damaged or unco-operative?				
Do the brakes work effectively, if present?				
Are the trolleys inspected and maintained regularly?				

The working environment	Yes	No	Risk	Comments
Is the handler able to adopt an upright, forward-facing posture when moving the load?				
Does the handler have to work in narrow aisles or confined spaces?				
Does the condition of the floor make moving the load more difficult?				
Is the load moved across uneven floors or up/down slopes or ramps?				
Are there any trip hazards in the walkway?				
Do the lighting conditions make the task more difficult?				
Does the temperature make the task more difficult?				
Do strong winds make the task more difficult?				

Individual capability	Yes	No	Risk	Comments
Does the job require unusual strength or ability?				
Is the job problematic for someone with a health problem?				
Is the job problematic for someone with a learning difficulty?				
Is the job problematic for someone who is pregnant?				
Does the handler need special training?				

Protective clothing	Yes	No	Comments
Does clothing or PPE interfere with the manual handling task?			
Does the handler need additional PPE to complete the task safely?			

Hints when completing a pushing and pulling assessment

1. Unless the forces involved are obviously trivial, always measure the effort needed to move the load. It may be easier to work with someone else when you take the measurements, so one person can apply the effort and the other can take and record the reading.
2. Have some rope available to attach the measuring device to the load if it does not have any handles.
3. Measure the effort involved in a range of likely situations, such as over different floor surfaces, round corners, into/out of lifts, with the wheels pointing in the wrong direction and so on. Take several sample measurements in each situation. Remember to record the force needed to start the load moving as well as that required to keep it moving.
4. Make sure you verify which side of the trolley you are supposed to steer it from – this will vary with the wheels used.
5. Always include a measurement that covers the worst case scenario, so that you cover all possible outcomes.
6. Consider the impact of the handler's footwear while they are pushing or pulling the load.
7. Check whether what is occurring is typical of every day and every shift. You may find, for example, the night shift works slightly differently.
8. Find out about and record any unofficial breaks resulting from line breakdowns, changeovers, product changes and so on. You need to build an accurate profile of how the work is performed and over what periods.
9. Be aware of handlers relying on assistance from back belts or other forms of support.

Quick reference guide – elements to consider during an assessment

Workstation design
- Height
- Reach
- Sitting or standing
- Controls
- Additional influences:
  - guarding
  - anti-fatigue matting
  - foot supports

Work equipment
- Tools and implements
- Gloves
- Other PPE
- Hoists and assistors
- Storage units and racking
- Waste bins and skips
- Trolleys and carts

Task design
- Nature of task, eg:
  - repetitive
  - prolonged
  - varied
  - manual handling
  - heavy or light
  - hand–eye co-ordination
- Force
- Self- or system-paced
- Postures
- Static or dynamic muscle work

Work organisation
- Speed of operation
- Duration
- Rest breaks:
  - timing
  - length
  - flexibility
- Task rotation
- Autonomy
- Bonus system
- Overtime
- Training
- Supervision

Working environment
- Temperature:
  - air temperature
  - surface temperature
  - air movement
  - humidity
  - air quality
- Lighting:
  - levels
  - location
- Noise
- Vibration
- Floors:
  - condition
  - levels
- Space:
  - overhead clearance
  - foot clearance
  - knee clearance
  - surrounding area

The worker
- Bad habits
- Training and skill base
- Age
- Sex
- Experience and maturity
- Health, disability and psychological issues

Other
- Products
- Packaging
- Quality control
- Process failure
- Seasonal demands

10 Case studies

Ergonomics can be applied in many situations and the following case studies demonstrate how the application of sound principles of ergonomics can assist in the development and introduction of effective designs.

Sewing machinists in a car assembly plant

A sewing machine area in a car assembly plant had a steadily increasing number of ULD cases among the machinists who made up seat covers. As the company in question did not have in-house ergonomists, it decided to enlist outside assistance to deal with the problem.

A thorough task analysis was carried out to evaluate the task demands. During this process, machinists undertaking a range of varied machining tasks were videoed. In addition, they were observed and their activities recorded on a data sheet, which provided a breakdown of task components and duration of each subcomponent. The machinists were interviewed individually so that they could relay any information on particular activities they completed on specific days and which had not been observed to date. The individual interviews also acted as a means of highlighting any personal styles of work.

At the end of this task analysis, the machinists' work rate, the order in which sections of fabric were stitched together, the number and weight of fabrics being handled, and the postures required to complete the operations were clearly defined. It became apparent from the task analysis and operator interviews that the particular fabrics used to construct the seat covers had certain inherent characteristics which made the sewing operation more difficult.

The workstation design was assessed by comparing its dimensions and layout with the anthropometric data of the user population and with the requirements of the task identified during the task analysis. It was determined that the poor postures adopted by the operators during their machining activities were a direct result of the unsuitable design and dimensions of the workstation.

The work organisational issues, such as rest breaks and rotation, were discussed with managers, supervisors and operators to ensure that there were no serious gaps between the work routine detailed at management level and that which was active at shop floor level. As a result of this exercise it became apparent that certain slower machinists were working through their breaks in an attempt to meet their daily targets. This practice had gone unchecked by the company.

The machinists completed comfort questionnaires that were intended to highlight specific areas – such as wrists, fingers and forearms – which were a source of discomfort. The questionnaire was also designed to help to develop an accurate profile of exactly how many operators were suffering from symptoms of a ULD. It could not be assumed that every operator who had developed symptoms had reported this to their supervisors.

At the time when the ULD problem surfaced, there were rumours that the sewing machine area of this plant was to be closed down and some of the operators were to be made redundant. Therefore, operators did not want to draw unnecessary attention to themselves. Using a confidential questionnaire enabled them to be honest about their condition.
Although it was recognised that other factors had contributed to the development of ULDs among the machinists, the workstation design was of greatest concern.

Workstation design
The operators were required to use sewing machines which were attached to the surfaces of workbenches. Each workbench was made of wood and structured so that it had five sides – left and right panels, a back panel, an upper surface and a floor panel which mirrored the upper surface in length, width and depth. In effect, the workstation took the form of a box with the front panel missing. The workstation was of a fixed height, with a Formica-type surface and angled edges. Each sewing machine was located centrally on the work surface.

Two pedals were in use. One was shaped like the sole of a foot and was intended to be used by the right foot to raise and lower the machining foot. The second pedal, which operated the machine, was located to the left of the first and was large enough to be used by both feet. The pedals were attached to the floor panel, at a distance from its leading edge. The right-hand pedal was fixed slightly in front of the left and was at a different angle. Neither pedal was adjustable for height, inclination or distance from the operator.

The operators were provided with very basic seating for use at their machines. Many of them were using stools. Some of these stools were identical to those which would typically be found in a bar, while others were the original cast iron Singer stools. None of the chairs or stools was adjustable in any way; most of them had no seat padding; and the stools obviously had no form of back support. In addition, the location of the chairs and stools in relation to the work surface was restricted by the floor panel, which was approximately 80 mm in height. This prevented the chairs and stools being moved forwards, thereby stopping the operators from positioning their knees and legs under the work surface.

As a result of the workstation design, all operators:
- sat at a distance from the focal point of the sewing machine, ie the needle, because the floor panel prevented them from moving their chairs or stools closer
- leaned to the left when using the machine because it had been lined up centrally on the work surface, despite the fact that the needle is located on the left side of the machine
- had to sit at heights dictated by the particular chair or stool they had been given, which typically forced their arms upwards towards the work surface
- had no back support as a result of either using a stool or having to lean forwards to reach the work surface
- had to place their feet at heights, distances and in orientations dictated by the pedal positions
- spent long periods leaning on the sharp edge of the work surface as they fed each piece of material past the needle
- struggled to pull the largest pieces of fabric back towards them having fed them past the needle (this was because as each large piece was stitched, it would move over the work surface and fall over the rear edge – and as the rear edge was sharply angled like the front, this caused the material to become snagged, making its retrieval more difficult).

Workstation redesign
The work surface was redesigned completely. Its new form was dictated by the needs of the operator and the requirements of the task. The new work surface was designed to be adjustable in height. The means of adjustment were based on a modified, standard adjustable office desk. The adjustment was achieved by pulling a crank handle out from beneath the work surface and turning it until the surface approached the desired level. The degree of adjustment available had been determined by evaluating anthropometric data and calculating ranges of dimensions which would be representative of the user population. Once the handle was pushed back into position under the work surface, the workstation was locked in position and was incapable of being moved unintentionally.

The work surface was fabricated like a standard office desk and was contoured so that it took the shape of a horseshoe, which effectively enveloped the operator. This shape enabled the operator to move closer to the needle and provided support for the arms where necessary. The work surface was extended in length on the left side to support the weight of large pieces of fabric as they were fed towards the needle. The sewing machine was located so that the needle was positioned centrally on the work surface, thereby eliminating the need for the operator to lean to the left. The edges of the work surface were rounded to minimise compression of the wrist. A roll-bar was fitted to the rear of the workstation to help with retrieving large pieces of fabric which had fallen over the rear section. It was designed to rotate as the fabric was pulled across it.

The pedals were redesigned so that both were located side by side at the same height, angle and distance from the operator. The pedals were adjustable for height, inclination and distance from the leading edge of the workstation. The degree of movement had been determined by evaluating the appropriate anthropometric data and calculating ranges of dimensions which would be representative of the user population.

Operators were given inexpensive standard office chairs (without castors for safety reasons). Each chair was adjustable for height and the backrest was adjustable for height and inclination and incorporated a distinct lumbar support.

Operators were also given new trolleys, which had a dual function. Previously, the operators remained at their workstations throughout the course of a shift, except for breaks. Their material and threads were brought to them by another operator who was solely responsible for the replenishment of materials. Therefore, the machinists had no reason to leave their workstations at regular intervals. The trolleys were provided so that operators could collect their own batches of work materials and wheel them back alongside their workstation. The collection of materials provided operators with an opportunity to have a short break from their main task and workstation. The trolley's secondary function was to act as an additional work surface for storing materials alongside the workstation.

Trial period
Before the full introduction of new workstations for all the machinists, a prototype was built. It was adjustable but on a more basic level than the final design. This prototype was used by as many of the operators as possible under normal working conditions during their shifts. Each operator was given a full briefing on the use of the workstation, and all were encouraged to adjust the pedal and work surface positions through a wide range of settings. The management made allowances for decreases in operator output during these trials.

Operators were videoed during the trials and each of them filled in questionnaires at regular intervals during the use of the prototype. Any verbal, throw-away comments were recorded.

As a result of the trials, which lasted several weeks, ranges of movement were standardised and any teething problems dealt with before the design reached its final form.

Introduction of the new design
Before the new workstations were delivered, the operators were fully briefed. Once the workstations were installed, every operator was given one-to-one tuition in their use. Production targets were reduced for a period of time to allow the operators to become accustomed to the new way of working. Targets were increased gradually until they reached their original level. This was an essential aspect of making the exercise work – the operators needed to become accustomed to the new postures and efforts required. If such an acclimatisation period had not been provided, operators may have suffered further symptoms of ULDs.

Operators were monitored regularly after the introduction of the new workstations to ensure that they did not encounter problems at a later date.

As a direct result of the alteration in workstation design, the incidence of ULDs was immediately capped and gradually reduced to a minimum. In addition, the level of absenteeism was reduced to an all-time low for that particular work area. This had an obvious positive effect on productivity. Another positive outcome was an increase in the quality of the seat covers being assembled. As a result of the operators being able to sit comfortably when working and being able to reach the appropriate areas of their workstation easily, they were able to stitch the covers properly at the first attempt. This meant a significant reduction in rework time.

Designing an on-board service trolley

A train operating company decided that as part of their programme for increasing passenger comfort they would introduce an on-board trolley service in place of the buffet car. By doing so, the refreshments were brought to the passengers and the buffet car could be replaced with a passenger carriage, allowing more passengers to be carried. It was intended that the new trolley should enable passenger 'hosts' – ie train staff – to offer hot and cold drinks, alcohol, sandwiches and snacks. It was also intended that the trolley should be operated by a single passenger host while the train was in motion.

A list of likely passenger host behaviours was prepared so that reference could be made to various design characteristics, such as reaching distances and working heights. In brief, it was concluded that, in addition to being able to steer and control the trolley, the passenger host also needed to be able to reach the tea and coffee dispensers located on top of the trolley, as well as other items such as milk, sugar and stirrers. In addition, they needed to gain access to sandwiches and snacks from the main body of the trolley. They also needed to be able to store money, and transport and use a credit card machine.

Initial drawings for the new trolley were prepared and a mock-up of the basic design was constructed. It was established from these that the proposed handle height would fall between knuckle and elbow height for all female and male operators, which would enable them to stand upright while steering the trolley. It was noted that the prototype positioned the handle so that an overly large gap existed between the trolley and the handle. There had been no particular rationale for this positioning and spacing. The consequence of this was that the reaching distance to the main body of the trolley was increased. Reference was made to anthropometric data to establish what clearance was required to pass the fingers through the gap between the handle and the trolley. As a guide, the anthropometric data enabled the designers to recognise that the knuckle depth of the 95th percentile male was 58 mm and if an additional distance was added to allow for the hand to move unhindered within the gap, there would be sufficient space.

It was suggested that the handle diameter would be in the region of 25 mm. Given that the hand would be grasping the handle in a similar manner to the way in which a tool would be gripped, the same general principles were applied. It was recommended that the handle should be in the region of 30–38 mm in diameter, thereby allowing the 5th percentile female to grip it without having to reach their own maximum diameter. Staying within this dimensional range would ensure that the handle could be gripped easily and the trolley controlled. If a large or very narrow handle was employed, it would make it more difficult to hold and increase the effort required when manoeuvring it. Although the task of gripping the handle would have been made easier by covering it in a rubber material, this was discounted for hygiene reasons.

As it was intended that hosts would use hot water flasks with lever-style pump dispensers, consideration was given to reaching distances. It was recommended that the distance from the handle of the trolley, where the host would be standing, to the point of depression on the hot water flasks should be no more than 400 mm. This was equivalent to the elbow–fingertip length of the 5th percentile female, ie the smallest female who was likely to work with the trolley. If this dimension was incorporated into the positioning of the hot water flasks, then the train operating company could be sure that no-one would have to repeatedly over-reach during the course of their work – it was known that dispensing tea and coffee would be the most frequent task of the host. The same guiding principle was applied to the location of other frequently used items such as the EPOS (credit card) unit.

Having identified the ideal reaching distances, working heights were then considered. Although it would generally be recommended that employees should be able to work with their hands at or slightly below elbow height, this would not have been realistic with a food trolley, as it would have severely limited the size of the trolley and the amount that could be carried on it. Although it was accepted that passenger hosts would have to work above elbow height, it was agreed that they should not have to work with their hands above shoulder height. This was an important issue given the height of hot water flasks and the height operators would have to reach to once the flasks were placed on the top shelf of a trolley. On that basis, a maximum working height was agreed of 1,240 mm, which is equivalent to the shoulder height of the 5th percentile female.

Apart from the design considerations relating to when the trolley was in use, thought had to be given to what would be done with the trolley when not in use. As it would be transported on a moving train, it would have to be securely stowed. It was initially planned that the trolley would be located in a recess in a storage area and aligned with securing points attached to the wall. However, the trolley had to be 'driven' into the recess front end first; because of the tight fit, the back end of the trolley had to be lifted into position in the recess, as shown in the figure on page 240.

It was evident that this intended form of storage resulted in one end of the trolley being raised off the floor by the operator. The total weight of the trolley once loaded with refreshments would be excessive. The passenger host would have to handle this load at a distance from their body as it was not possible to move with the trolley into the recess. The passenger host would have to extend their arms as they loaded the trolley into the recess and they would have to twist their upper body. It was clear that this storage method would present a high risk to passenger hosts. Ultimately, the decision was made to design a more basic method of 'drive-in, drive-out' storage that did not involve the need for the trolley to be raised off the floor nor handled to one side of the body. However, it did transpire during trials that one end of the trolley was being lifted at times when it was being moved between adjoining carriages and they were set at different heights. If the trolley got stuck the passenger hosts tended to lift the end of the trolley to get it over the difference in floor levels. This was addressed by changing the styling and arrangement of the wheels.

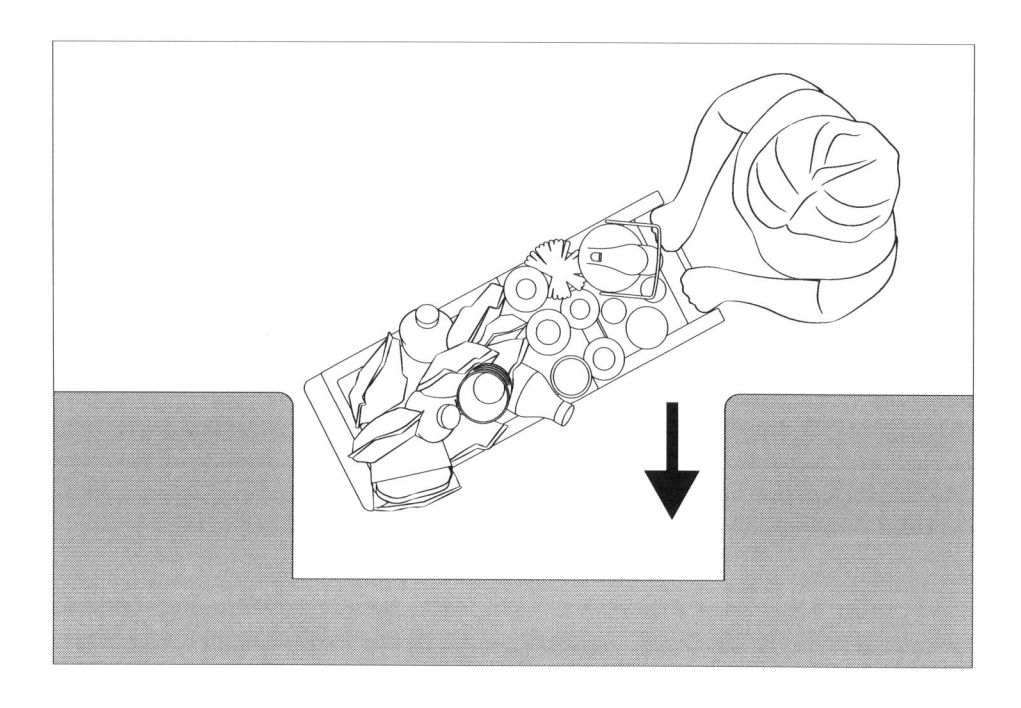

Trials for the new trolley design were run on passenger services and a range of male and female passenger hosts used the trolleys under normal circumstances. During the trial the manner in which they interacted with the trolley was recorded and they were asked for feedback at the end of their shift. Any comments they made regarding the performance of the trolley were recorded during the trial itself. As a result of their feedback and observations in the field, final changes were made to the trolley so that the most important items – ie the hot water flasks, cups, milk and sugar – were all in accessible positions and the passenger host did not have to reach or work with their arms raised. They could also see the smaller items, such as sugar packs, easily without having to bend down to locate them.

Control room redesign

A large utilities business planned to refurbish one of its main control centres. Previously, controllers had been provided with curved workstations in a horseshoe shape. They were viewing between eight and

10 screens simultaneously and these were located in two rows, one on top of the other, in an arc around the perimeter of the desk. The lowest level of screens was positioned directly on the desk surface. All of the screens were located behind a solid glass 'wall', thereby making it impossible for the controller to change the screen position in terms of distance, angle or height. The screens were spread over such a large area that the controllers had to move their chairs around constantly to line themselves up with the appropriate screens. Because of the number of screens in use, the controllers also had to operate numerous keyboards and mice, and as a consequence it was not unknown for a controller to use the wrong piece of equipment and change a setting unintentionally.

Controllers worked shifts of either seven or 12 hours and workstations were manned 24 hours a day. There were no formal breaks and whether a controller got a break or not depended on what was happening in the control room. Because of the implications of their work, controllers were not compelled to leave their workstations in case something happened in their absence.

Having spent time identifying the important elements in terms of task demands and workstation needs, and having recorded feedback from users, a prototype workstation was developed. The desk, which was quite long and slightly curved, was designed to offer two separate sections. The front section was intended to house the keyboard, mouse and any documents used during the course of the work. It had a leading edge depth of 25 mm, which would allow controllers freedom to raise their chairs to a suitable height. The rear section of the desk was dedicated to supporting the screens. By adjusting the rear portion of the desk, the controller would be able to present the screens at a height that suited them. Both sections of the desk were height adjustable and the settings could be changed by pushing a button located to the side of the desk. A digital display recorded the height of both sections of the desk, making it quicker for controllers to alter the height setting to suit them after they had been used by someone else. The range of adjustment built into the desk was intended to offer flexibility to the controller over whether they wished to sit or stand as they worked, thereby allowing for a change of posture.

The rear section of the desk housed four 30-inch screens in place of the eight to 10 smaller screens. The screens were chosen on the basis that they offered a better quality of display and as they were larger more information could be displayed simultaneously. In addition, the screens could be split, allowing for a range of information to be displayed at one time. Using fewer screens also meant that the number of keyboards and mice in use was also reduced. Ultimately, it was possible to reduce this to one keyboard and one mouse on the desk surface that could be used to interact with all four screens.

Given the reduction in screen numbers and the contouring of the desk, it was established that the controller could sit centrally at the desk and move their head within a comfortable zone from left to right when viewing the screens. The controller was briefed that the most important screens and information had to be displayed centrally, with less important screens and information being located at the edges.

The mouse was replaced with one that had been designed with a user's hand in mind. It was dimensioned and contoured in such a way that the hand could rest in a more natural position during operation and this would increase comfort levels.

Each user was given a thorough briefing on how to set up their workstation once it was provided and reminded that it needed to be altered at the start of each shift. They were encouraged to leave their workstation as frequently as possible and they introduced a 'buddy' system, whereby one controller would cover for another if they left their workstation. As a consequence the controllers felt more comfortable about not manning their workstation 100 per cent of the time.

Redesign of an assembly workstation

A large manufacturing facility employed about 60 operators to assemble computer equipment. They were provided with a workbench on which they assembled the equipment using a series of small tools. They were provided with handheld mirrors, like dental mirrors, to help them see the interior of the equipment as it was being assembled, particularly when small screws were being put in place. At the end of the assembly phase, the equipment had to be tested and it was attached to the power supply and a computer testing unit. The power cable was plugged into the rear of the equipment and the USB ports were also located at the back of the equipment. The computer test was run by inputting details relating to the assembled equipment using a keyboard and by making selections displayed on a screen using a mouse. Once the equipment passed the test satisfactorily it was carried to a trolley. The operator then moved onto the next assembly unit. Operators tended to work on the same type of unit for the whole of a shift.

A number of operators had reported lower backache and discomfort in their upper limbs. Analysis of the workstation design and task demands established a number of problematic features. Although the workbench was set at a height which was suitable for the assembly of the outer casing of the unit, once the operator had to add subcomponents to the interior of the casing, they had to raise their arms and shoulders as they worked. In addition, the operator also had to work around the outside of the casing at low levels, which caused them to bend forward as they worked. The mouse and keyboard had been removed from the surface of the bench to create space, and had been placed on a shelf above the workstation. This resulted in operators having to raise their hands to around shoulder height each time they used the keyboard or mouse. The screen was located on a bracket above the keyboard and mouse and was at such a height that everyone had to look upwards to view it. When attaching the power and USB cables, the operator leaned over the top of the unit to reach the back of it. The units could weigh anything between 8 and 14 kg depending on the model. When the unit had been assembled and was moved onto the trolley, it was raised to above shoulder height when placed on the top shelf. This resulted in the heavier loads being considered excessive when placed on the upper shelf. By working on the same type of unit throughout the shift, the operator performed the same sequence of tasks repeatedly.

As a result of a series of recommendations for improvement, operators were provided with height-adjustable workbenches. These could be raised and lowered by pressing a pedal found under the workbench. This enabled the operator to alter the height of the bench so that the unit was presented at a suitable height for them and for the area of the unit being addressed. The unit was placed on a turntable which was flush with the surface of the bench. This enabled the operator to rotate the unit when plugging the power and USB cables into the rear. The keyboard and mouse were located on a pull-out tray positioned directly under the leading edge of the workbench. A wireless mouse and keyboard were provided to avoid entrapment of cables as the bench was adjusted and as the keyboard tray was stowed. The screen was placed on an articulating arm that allowed it to be positioned within a range, so that the top of the screen could be presented at a height where no operator had to look up. A directional, articulating light was provided to make assembly within the interior of the unit more straightforward. A limit was set on the weights that could be loaded onto any particular shelf of the trolley. All of these changes were tested during a strictly managed trial during which operators were asked to offer feedback. As a result of the trial phase, a number of modifications were made to improve the final designs. The allocation of work was also managed differently so that operators had an opportunity to assemble different types of unit throughout a shift, thereby allowing them to work through a different sequence of steps at different times rather than repeating the same sequence throughout the shift.

New DSE workstations

A firm employing 500 staff was in the process of arranging to move to a new building. As part of the relocation to the newly refurbished offices, the firm decided to provide each user with a new workstation. The workstations in use before the move were very old, traditional wooden office desks and a selection of malfunctioning chairs was available.

Before the move it was decided that a formal trial would be run to identify the chair that would be most suited to the users. An ergonomist was employed not only to run the chair trial but also to generate the shortlist of chairs to be included in the trial. The ergonomist was also responsible for selecting the appropriate desk arrangement on the basis of the work that the users would be doing. This involved observation and analysis of the work performed in each department by each person at different levels in the organisation.

Having developed a profile of the work performed and user needs, several office furniture suppliers were contacted on the basis that their products appeared to offer the range of facilities needed by the workforce. Eight different desk arrangements were delivered to the site and set up in an area removed from the actual work area. The ergonomist assessed each of the desk arrangements for their stand-alone characteristics and how these features would interact with the user. The designs and dimensions were compared against current standards and guidance and some desks were eliminated for failing to meet basic standards, such as clearance beneath the worksurface or surface depth. One desk system was identified as offering all of the features needed to accommodate the workforce and the tasks they performed. The majority of users would be provided with a fixed-height cockpit-style desk in a 'pod' arrangement, where four or six desks were located back to back. Height-adjustable desks would be made available to very tall users and those who were identified as having other special needs.

A selection of six chairs was identified for inclusion on the shortlist. Each of these chairs offered the minimum ranges of adjustment and design features recommended in relevant standards and guidance. All logos and other identifying marks were removed from the chairs and they were assigned a letter from A to F. Volunteers from within the organisation were asked to try two chairs over the course of two weeks – ie one chair a week. At the start of each week the volunteers were told which of the chairs they needed to use for the week. Once they had taken their chair back to their workstation, they were given a briefing on its use. All other features at their workstation were changed if not set up properly, such as screen viewing height or distance, so that these features did not bias their view of the chair in any way. The volunteer was also given a number of scoring sheets which allowed them to rate the chair at the end of each day and make comments. At the end of the week they were asked to summarise their views on the chair and to compare both chairs at the end of the second week. The responses on the feedback forms allowed the most comfortable, most usable and most popular chair to be identified. This trial enabled the employer to purchase the chair that was most suited to their workforce.

Once users were moved to their new building, they were provided with a new chair, a new desk, a new screen on a height-adjustable bracket and a new keyboard and mouse. Immediately after the move all users had one-to-one coaching on how to set up their workstation to suit their stature and a DSE assessment was completed. Users who needed additional equipment such as footrests and copy stands were identified during the assessment process and these items were provided quickly.

Express checkout

A large homeware firm had installed a number of express checkouts at one of its branches on a trial basis. The intention when installing the checkouts was that they would be used for brief periods to cut queuing time for customers if they had small numbers of items to purchase. However, after the checkouts were installed, it was evident that they were open for longer than was originally envisaged and some operators were complaining about backache.

The checkouts were used from the standing position. Observation of the operators using the checkouts revealed there were several design issues which were likely to be creating problems for the workforce, and these were more likely to result in operators experiencing discomfort when they spent longer periods of time working at the checkouts.

It was clear that customers used the express checkouts whether carrying one or two items to the till or whether they had filled a basket with products. The products ranged in size from very small items about the size of a pencil to larger items about the size of a briefcase.

The surface of the checkout was measured at 920 mm, which would generally be considered to fall within a comfortable range for most operators. However, when operators handled and scanned the bulkier items, they had to work with their hands and arms raised to a point above elbow height, which is fatiguing for the upper limbs.

Customers who used baskets when choosing their items placed their basket in a well located on the far side of the checkout from the operator. Although the reaching distance across the top of the checkout to the closest point of the basket fell within acceptable limits, the checkout did not incorporate undersurface foot clearance, meaning that operators were held back from the leading edge of the checkout by the length of their feet. This caused them to reach to the baskets when removing products for scanning. If operators had to reach to the far side of the basket to grip a product, the distance was such that they had to reach and lean forward at the waist. Given the depth of the basket, operators were also removing products, especially smaller items, from a point that was below the checkout work surface. This increased the need for them to reach and lean forward.

The bags used for customer purchases were stored to the right of the operator but under the surface of the checkout, and were presented perpendicular to the operator. The bags were set at a height such that their highest point was below the knuckle height of the taller operators. This resulted in most operators leaning and reaching to the side. The situation was compounded by the operators' practice of reaching to the centre of the bag, and not the nearest handle, so that as the bag was pulled free from the batch it partially opened the bag and avoided ripping the handle.

The till drawer was partially sunk into the surface of the checkout, effectively splitting the worksurface into two distinct areas with different levels. This made it more difficult to pack customers' purchases into the bags.

The scanner was located to one side of the checkout surface but the scanning face was presented so that it faced left to right across the checkout rather than towards the operator. Every product had to be positioned so that it was read by the scanner and this caused the operator to twist to the side.

Following a redesign of the checkout, the operators were presented with a completely different layout. Under-surface clearance was built into the checkout, allowing the operator to step close to the work surface. The customer's basket was placed to the side of the checkout, closer to the operator, rather than on the far side, eliminating the need for the operator to reach and lean forward. If necessary, they could step towards the basket. The height of the basket was such that operators would not need to lean forward when removing products from its base. The shelving previously under the worksurface was removed so that operators could sit on sit/stand seats, which made their work less fatiguing. The bags were presented in a more accessible area to eliminate the leaning and reaching previously observed. The scanner was rotated so that it faced the operator and a handheld scanner was provided for large and bulky products. The till drawer was repositioned so that, when closed, it was flush with the main checkout work surface.

Index

abduction 182–183
access 12, 32–33, 49, 54, 73, 76
adduction 182–183
adjustability 35, 48, 57, 145
age 14, 43, 50, 132–133, 172, 232
air hoses 68–69, 75
anthropometric data 13–14, 74, 233, 235–236, 238
anthropometric tables 11, 13, 15–27
anthropometrics 9–28, 31–32, 54, 64, 192
assessments 71, 101, 103–105, 115, 127, 130, 141, 167, 194, 200–201, 203–232, 245
automation 91–92, 96
autonomous working groups 84

backache 6, 12, 29–30, 37, 49, 106, 145, 153, 156, 170, 174–175, 177, 242, 245
back belts 140–142, 227, 231
back injuries 53, 110
BlackBerry 161, 213
body size 9, 11–14, 27, 31, 54, 115
bonus systems 87, 95, 232
breaks 6, 79, 85–87, 95, 104, 110, 142, 167, 173–177, 190–191, 196, 205, 223, 227, 231, 232–234, 236, 241

cable management 151
carpal tunnel syndrome 69, 185, 188
cervical spondylosis 188
chairs 6, 30–31, 49, 57, 122, 145–149, 152, 156–157, 175–177, 214–215, 234–236, 244–245
  armrests 18, 39, 49, 57, 147–148, 151, 176, 215

backless 149
backrests 6, 49, 57, 145–149, 153, 158, 169, 176, 236
  five-star base 145
  lumbar support 49, 57, 146, 158, 236
checklist 40, 80, 104, 200, 205, 208–209, 213–219, 224–227, 228–231
clearance 11–12, 28, 32–33, 38–39, 55, 66, 69, 114, 129, 141, 232, 238, 244, 246
coding 44–46, 56, 102, 125, 143
colour 42, 45–46, 102, 125, 143
constraints 6, 10–11, 28, 82, 105, 129
controls 37–39, 43–46, 56, 82, 148, 232
  compatibility 45, 56
  functions 44–45, 47, 56

design 5–6, 9, 11, 13, 29–60, 61, 73–75, 115–116, 124, 129, 142, 149, 161, 163–164, 170, 192, 200, 232, 234–237, 238–246
desks 38, 145, 147, 149–154, 171, 176–177, 214, 235, 241–242, 244–245
  drawers 151
  layout 152, 160
  surface area 150–152, 154–156
  under-surface 38, 151
disabilities 36–38, 55, 115, 133–134
discs: see intervertebral discs
discomfort questionnaire 209, 211–212
displays 30, 37, 42, 46, 56–57, 241–242
display screen equipment 86, 145–180, 213–219

document holders 154–155
DSE assessment 213–219, 245
Dupuytren's contracture 185–186
dynamic muscle work 67–68, 110, 232

environmental conditions 52, 58, 196, 200, 222
epicondylitis 187
epilepsy 89
exercise 110, 196
expectations 5, 44–45, 79

feedback 5, 44, 50–52, 69, 79–80, 94, 135, 139, 153, 160, 240–241, 243, 245
fitness 29, 43, 90, 132, 138, 143
 task 85, 95, 197–198
footrests 31, 49, 57, 149–150, 153–154, 157–158, 177, 245
force 12, 37, 41, 43–44, 48, 56, 62–64, 66–68, 73–74, 111, 121, 130, 159–60, 176, 189, 192–193, 195–196, 201, 231
frozen shoulder 188

ganglion 187
glare 39, 53, 170–171, 177

handedness 36, 55, 65–66, 74
handle design and construction 6, 63–67, 73–74, 114, 195
handling aids 106, 115–117, 119, 125, 133
hazard 49, 111, 120, 130, 142, 203–204
hearing impairment 37, 52
hernia 110–111, 132
housekeeping 52, 58, 111, 129, 135
humidity 53, 129, 131, 143, 172, 177

illuminance 53

input devices 158–164, 177, 216–217
intervertebral discs 109

job design 79–97, 136
job enlargement 84, 94, 205
job enrichment 84, 94

keyboard work – style of operation 156–160, 176, 191

labels 45–47, 57, 119, 125
laptop 154–155, 159, 162–169, 177
layout 6, 11, 36, 38, 44, 46, 50–51, 56, 58, 120, 152, 192, 206, 246
ligaments 110–111, 132, 183–186
lighting 7, 52–53, 58, 81, 111, 131–132, 143, 156, 170–172, 177, 217, 226, 230
limiting user 11–12, 28
lumbar region 107–109
lumbar support 49, 57, 146, 158, 169, 236
luminance 53
lux 170

maintenance 11, 32, 40, 52, 54, 58, 104, 112, 193
manual dexterity 53, 69
manual handling 6, 99–144, 166–167, 175, 204, 219
manual handling checklist 224–227
maximum reaching distance 23–24, 26, 34
mock-ups 50, 58, 238
motivation 81, 87, 94–95
mice 161–162, 164, 166, 177, 241
mini-mice 162, 177
mousemats 161, 217
multiskilling 84, 94

NIOSH lifting equation 127–128
noise 7, 52, 58, 218, 222, 232
normal distribution 10
normal working area 34–35, 191

optimum reaching distance 35, 51, 55
osteoarthritis 188–189
overtime 87, 95, 100, 197, 201

pedals 27, 33, 35, 43, 49, 55, 58, 234–236, 243
percentiles 14
personal space 36, 55
piece-rate systems 87, 190
popliteal 19–20
posture 7, 11–12, 29–32, 41–42, 46, 48, 54, 62–63, 72–73, 109–110, 117–118, 120, 129, 135, 145, 147, 149, 155, 157–159, 165–167, 176, 181–182, 189, 191–192, 198, 221
power grasp 61, 192
precision grip 61–62
pregnancy 132–133, 143, 185, 198–199
primary work envelope 35, 44, 152
prolapsed disc 108–109
pronation 159, 182–183
pulling 103, 111, 121, 128, 141–142, 225, 228–231
pushing 103, 111, 115, 121, 128, 130, 137, 141–142, 228–231

questionnaire 208–209, 211–212, 234, 237
Quick Exposure Checklist 208

radial deviation 182–183, 192
ratings scale 208–209
reaching 23–26, 32, 34–35, 49, 51, 55, 58, 118–119, 162–163, 176, 192, 238–239, 246–247

reading slopes 156, 177
Rapid Entire Body Assessment 208
repetition 82–85, 87, 94, 122, 189–191
risk assessment 115, 167, 200, 203–232
rotation 6, 21, 72, 83–84, 94, 122, 142, 182, 187, 190–191, 196, 205
Rapid Upper Limb Assessment 208

safety 12, 48–50, 58, 81, 88–90, 135, 203–204, 236
schedules 81, 87, 95, 189, 191, 194
screen riser arms 155
screen risers 155, 177
seating 49, 57, 145–149, 234
secondary work envelope 34, 152
sex 14, 31, 43, 132–133, 172, 232
sharp edges 48, 57, 63–64, 67, 74–75, 102, 185, 215
shift work 88–90, 95
sitting 17–18, 25, 30–31, 54, 110, 145–149, 155–156, 168, 171, 173, 177, 219
slope 113, 115, 122, 129–130, 141, 143, 156, 177, 226, 230
split-level surfaces 151, 246
standing 15–16, 24, 28, 30–31, 33, 42–43, 54, 110, 137, 163, 166, 245
static effort 30, 54, 221
static muscle work 30, 67–68, 75, 87, 110–111, 147, 156, 189, 194, 201
stature 9–10, 14–15, 32–33, 41–42, 114, 223, 245
stereotypes 44–45, 46
stress 44–45, 72, 84, 86, 91, 108, 110, 112, 114–115, 118–120, 128, 141–142, 188, 191–192
supervision 6, 51–52, 58, 82, 140, 144, 197

supination 182–183
symbols 47, 57, 125, 143

task analysis 40, 43, 55, 191, 205–208, 233
telephone headsets 155–156
temperatures 7, 48, 53, 63, 69, 74, 87, 105, 129–131, 171–173, 177, 194–196, 201
tendinitis 187–188
tendons 110–111, 182–185, 187–188
tenosynovitis 182–185
thermal environment 52–53, 131, 172–173
thoracic outlet syndrome 188
tools, hand 61–77, 161
   domestic 72–73, 76
   multifunctional 72, 76
   off-the-shelf 72–73, 76
torque response 72, 76
touchscreen 163, 168–170
training 6, 38, 51, 58, 81–82, 89, 92, 104–105, 116, 133, 140, 143–144, 166, 169, 175, 196–197, 204, 206
trials 13, 28, 38, 50–51, 58, 146, 152–153, 162, 177, 236–237, 239–240, 243–245
triggers 12, 67, 75, 185, 193
trolleys 102, 110, 112–115, 121, 137, 141, 206, 231, 236–240, 242–243

ULD risk assessment 200–201, 220–223
ulnar deviation 159, 165, 182–183, 192

upper limb disorders (ULDs) 7, 29, 48, 53, 63–64, 67, 69, 83, 85, 106, 132, 173–176, 181–201, 208, 220–223, 233–234, 237

ventilation 81, 131, 143, 172
vertebrae 108–109
vibration 7, 52–54, 58, 68–72, 75, 185, 195–196, 201
viewing distance 39, 42, 154, 169, 175
visual acuity 41
visual fatigue 175, 177
voice recognition software 164

wheelchair users 12, 32, 37–39
wheels 112–114, 141, 231, 240
working height 13, 32, 40–42, 50, 56, 119–120, 192, 238–239
workload 31, 85–86, 95, 114, 140–141, 154, 162, 164–165, 173–174, 176, 197, 207
work organisation 79–98, 122–123, 232–233
work rate 84–85, 94–95, 187, 197, 233
wrist extension 182–183
wrist flexion 182–183
wrist rests 177
writing slopes 156, 177

zone of convenient reach 34–35

Printed in Great Britain
by Amazon